Sweet Honey, Bitter Lemons

Travels in Sicily on a Vespa

Matthew Fort

D0514753

EBURY
PRESS

1 3 5 7 9 10 8 6 4 2

Published in 2008 by Ebury Press, an imprint of Ebury Publishing
A Random House Group Company

The Random House Group Limited Reg. No. 954009

Addresses for companies within the Random House Group can be found at
www.randomhouse.co.uk

A CIP catalogue record for this book is available from the British Library

The Random House Group Limited supports The Forest Stewardship
Council (FSC), the leading international forest certification organisation.
All our titles that are printed on Greenpeace approved FSC certified paper
carry the FSC logo. Our paper procurement policy can be found at
www.rbooks.co.uk/environment

Mixed Sources
Product group from well-managed
forests and other controlled sources
www.fsc.org Cert no. TT-COC-2139
© 1996 Forest Stewardship Council

FSC

Printed in the UK by CPI Mackays, Chatham, ME5 8TD

ISBN 9780091910808

To buy books by your favourite authors and register for offers visit
www.rbooks.co.uk

For Mary

Contents

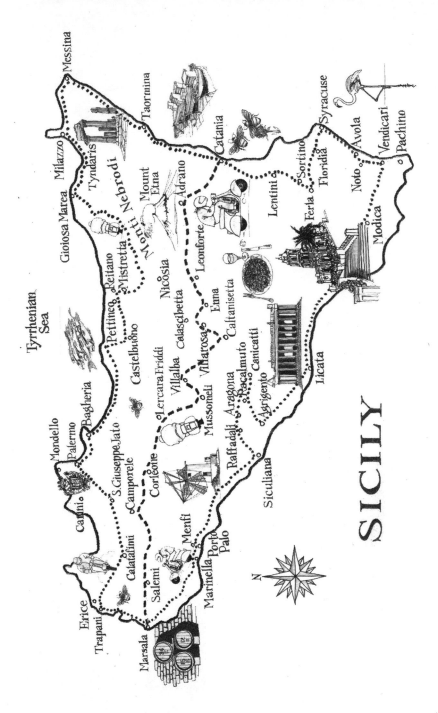

Messina
Milazzo
Gioiosa Marea
Taormina
Tyndaris
Catania
Syracuse
Vendicari
Avola
Pachino
Monti Nebrodi
Mount Etna
Adrano
Noto
Sortino
Floridia
Ferla
Reitano
Pettineo
Mistretta
Nicosia
Leonforte
Lentini
Modica
Tyrrhenian Sea
Castelbuono
Villalba
Calascibetta
Enna
Caltanisetta
Villarosa
Lercara Friddi
Mondello
Palermo
Bagheria
S. Giuseppe Jato
Camporele
Corleone
Mussomeli
Racalmuto
Aragona
Canicatti
Agrigento
Licata
Raffadali
Cammarata
Erice
Trapani
Calatafimi
Salemi
Menfi
Marinella
Porto Palo
Siculiana
Marsala

SICILY

N

IX

Acknowledgments

I owe a huge debt of gratitude to many people in Sicily, some mentioned in the following pages, and some, perforce, not. These acknowledgements would begin to read like the Sicilian version of an Oscar winner's speech of thanks if I noted them all, so I will simply express my thanks to them collectively. But for their generosity, kindness and openness with me there would have been no book at all.

Many of them also very kindly provided some of the recipes that round off each chapter. Some I have given in Italian and some in Sicilian, according to their source. I should point out that Sicilian recipes lack the precision which we take for granted. The treatment of exact measurements is distinctly variable. Recipes are filled with such helpful instructions as '*alcuni*' (a few), '*un tocco di*' (a touch of) and '*cuocere la carne in brodo*' ('For how long?' I would have liked to ask), so a good deal is left up to the experience and instincts of the individual cook. In keeping with the spirit of Sicilian cooking, I have included measurements where I have been given them or have worked them out for myself. And in other cases I leave it to the discretion of the reader and cook. After all, cooking is a moveable feast.

Such book as there is would be far more flawed had it not been for John Irving and John Dickie, both of whom know more about Sicily and its surrounding mysteries and delights than I will ever. First of all, I cannot express how much the encouragement and enthusiasm of two such eminent figures meant to me. The amount of time and effort they put into correcting my Italian (fluent in the mouth; pretty dodgy on the page), challenging my assumptions and sifting out my inaccuracies is beyond counting. And if there are still mistakes, questionable conclusions and the odd inaccuracy, they are not to be blamed. They are entirely of my own making.

I am also deeply grateful to Hannah Macdonald at Ebury Press for having the wisdom to commission this book and the patience to wait for it, and to Charlotte Cole and her team at Ebury for wrestling so heroically with the ms. I bend my knee to my agent, Caroline Dawnay, whose powers of negotiation kept Cary Street waiting a little while longer at least.

Eland Press, Canongate and Carcanet have been generous in allowing me to quote from *Sicily: Through Writer's Eyes* by Horatio Clare, *Conversations in Sicily* by Elio Vittorini translated by Alane Salierno Mason and *The Idylls of Theocritus* translated by Robert Wells respectively.

I have dedicated this book to my late sister-in-law, Mary Fort. From her eyrie in Rome, she was the project manager for these journeys, just as she had for my earlier ones up through Italy. Even though suffering with the cancer that killed her before I finished, and from the consequent treatments, she continued to find hotels and *agriturismi* for me to stay in, restaurants to eat in, suggest places to visit and people to seek out. 'There's this really interesting sounding *agriturismo* ... Oh, how I wish I could see it too ... That sounds so delicious ...Where to next?'

At all times she was curious, enthusiastic, completely involved. Her support and guidance, not to mention humour and powers of organisation, were absolutely invaluable. She kept up a constant stream of advice and encouragement. Her courage and determination did not simply inspire awe, but also a determination to do the best I could by her.

Shortly before she died, I was able to read to her early drafts of the first chapters. She lay in her bed in the flat in which she and my brother lived. At one point her eyes where closed and her breathing so rhythmical, I assumed that she had fallen asleep, lulled by the mellifluous sound of my voice – or bored by it. I stopped reading for a moment. In a weak, but imperious, voice she said 'I want to know what happens next. I'm enjoying it so much. Oh, do go on.' Thanks to Mary, I did.

*Domenico Buffa, marsala maker, La Casa
Vinicola, Buffa, Marsala*

Taking a Deep Breath

☯

I stood in darkness. I sensed rather than saw vast, somnolent presences. The warm air was suffused with the sweetness of caramel shaded with apricot, cardamom and cloves. Slowly lights overhead came on, glimmered softly, throwing a gentle amber glow over the *botti*, giant barrels twice my height, and round in proportion and black with age, ranged round the walls of the room. The space in the middle was filled with smaller barrels, blonde *barriques* of French and Slavonian oak that smelt of vanilla. Inside the large and smaller barrels the great alchemical change was taking place as grape juice ripened into marsala over the years.

Domenico Buffa drew the cork on a bottle of his family's Vergine marsala, ten years old, made only with *grillo* grapes, and poured a generous measure into a wine glass the size of a goldfish bowl. The colour shimmered in the gloom – buttercup yellow, rich and textured. I sniffed it. Layers of scents drifted in on the 18 per cent alcohol, heady and rich. I picked out sweet pea, broom, peach, toffee, primrose, and a trace of pipe tobacco. It seemed hardly necessary to drink the liquor at all. A pity not to, though. Domenico Buffa took his nose out of his glass and looked at me.

'Oh, very fine. Complex,' I said. I sipped. The marsala slid over my tongue as elegant and captivating as a silk scarf, restrained and rich, releasing an astonishing range of flavours with an airy sweetness, unlocking honeyed memories of my first visit to Sicily.

'Tip top,' I said.

⚭

I first came to Sicily in 1973 with my youngest brother, Tom. I was 26 and he was 22. We had decided to spend part of the summer driving round the coastline of the island. Sun, seafood and swimming, we thought, would be the order of the day, with a bit of temple gazing and light culture thrown in here and there. You felt you could just do these things at that age. It was all so easy.

There had been an outbreak of cholera in Naples earlier in the year, and we were advised to avoid salads and shellfish at all costs. Further, we were told that the weather – we were travelling in September – was likely to be unsettled. Undaunted, we took the ferry to Messina, hired a car and set out.

We spent several nights in Taormina, at the Villa San Pancrazio. We shared a room, and on that first morning I threw back the shutters and was dazzled by the sun scintillating on a brilliant blue sea. On the far distant horizon, a single cloud rested, like one of those fluffy things women used to use to powder their faces. Tom peered at it.

'The weather's breaking,' he said in a voice of unalloyed gloom. Glorious day succeeded glorious day. The temperature never dropped below 28°C all the time we were there. And so we chatted and ate and argued and laughed, and ate and chatted some more, our way around the island. Tom had a habit of never being satisfied with where we were, of always wanting to peer round the next corner, explore the next bay, wander to the next café, just in case we should miss something. It irritated me to begin with, but after a while I came to appreciate this irrepressible inquisitiveness. He was the best of companions: curious, conversational and, like all my family, immensely greedy.

Our resolve to avoid salads and seafood lasted barely through the first lunch. It was just as well. As we skimmed around the coast from Taormina to Catania, Siracusa, Gela, Agrigento, Marsala, Erice, Palermo and back to Messina, there was little else on the menu. Anyway, it was so good, the stuff of dreams: prawns and octopus and fish, straight from the sea, seared on the grill – that intoxicating combination of acrid charcoal and marine sweetness sharpened by lemon juice, unobtainable in England at that time. I had a sausage epiphany in Erice; just two sausages on the plate, plump, glossy, naked. They tasted more of sausage than any sausage I had ever eaten, firm, juicy, salty and sweet. There were resonant vegetables: scarlet tomatoes of exhilarating intensity; and salady stuff that crunched; and leaves with unfamiliar, refreshing bitterness; and fruit – peaches, nectarines, melon and figs, figs above all, fleshy, indiscreet, juicy; and ice creams and *sorbetti* and *granite*, cleansing and refreshing in the heat.

We did culture, too: temples, churches, Greek theatres and Roman villas. The cholera in Naples had scared off all but the most determined of tourists, and so we had the island pretty much to ourselves. We were impressed by the savage splendour of the Peloritani mountains, and struck by the small, depressing, run-down villages and precarious hill-top towns tumbling down vertical hillsides. We remarked on the 'depressing black lava walls & buildings of the area around Etna' and the 'curious, luxuriant fertility of the pumice vineyards', as I wrote in my notebook at the time. We almost gatecrashed a Mafia wedding by mistake. We fled from a village square lined with old men sitting on chairs, their faces pared away by sun and life, and young men standing beside them, round-faced and olive-skinned, because, old and young, they all had the same eyes, black and shiny as wet jet.

As we travelled, I became fascinated by the endless disjunctions of the island, between the wealth of its cultural heritage and its impoverished present, between the magnificence of its monuments and the meanness of its villages, between the tumult of the towns along its shore and the savage, impassive beauty of the interior, between the generosity of the food and the obliqueness of the people. It was different from Britain, from France or America or anywhere else I had visited. It wasn't just a superficial difference, of customs, language, manners or food. Sicily seemed different in some profound, subtle way that I couldn't put my finger on. It was complex, convoluted, weird. I couldn't make sense of it.

As I read around the subject, I discovered that I was not alone in my addiction or my puzzlement. Sicily has exerted a hold over the imagination of foreigners that is quite out of keeping with its size or political importance or obvious cultural influence. Great and not-so-great writers – Guy de Maupassant, D.H. Lawrence, Gavin Maxwell, Lawrence Durrell, Norman Lewis, Peter Robb – had come, stayed, pondered, and retreated baffled by its complexity, enigmatic qualities and paradoxes. Even Sicilian writers, too, seemed to struggle to break out of the hermetic nature, a kind of intellectual *omerta*, of Sicilian culture and society.

After visiting the island in 1786, Goethe wrote: 'To have seen Italy without having seen Sicily is not to have seen Italy at all, for Sicily is the clue to everything.' 'Sicily is the schoolroom model of Italy for beginners, with every Italian quality and defect magnified, exaggerated and brightly coloured,' wrote Luigi Barzini in *The Italians*. Were either of these observations true? There was something about the certitude of the writers that seemed rather suspect to me. But if Sicily is not the clue to understanding Italy, the schoolroom model, what is it?

I meant to go back. I always meant to go back. No matter where I travelled, Sicily haunted me. It was unfinished business. Time and again I made plans. Time and again my plans turned to gravy. Several times I despaired of ever exploring this island that so fascinated me. But finally, I managed to organise my life so that I could immerse myself in Sicily once more.

I was now 59, with rather more tummy and rather less hair than the sprauncy young fellow of 33 years before, beaten around the head a bit by life, older certainly, but not necessarily wiser; a bit antique to decide to become an explorer, some might think. But I didn't see why curiosity about the world should shut down just because I had passed through some of life's notional watersheds. I wasn't proposing to track across the Gobi Desert or swim down the Amazon. All I wanted to do was pass a reasonable length of time in a place that had played across my imagination and memory for three decades. It's not that I thought I could crack the Sicily code where other rather more talented figures had been left scratching their heads. I simply wanted to know more than I had known before, and to know it better.

If there was a key to the riddle of Sicily food would be it, it seemed to me. Cooking and eating are central to Sicilian life. The Sicilians I had met were passionate about what they ate to a degree that made even Italians on the mainland seem positively diffident. If I could understand just some of the food, some of the dishes, I thought, discover where they came from, find out why they were the way they were, then perhaps I would appreciate better why Sicily continued to mesmerise me. If I could look at the dishes I came across with enough understanding, so my theory went, I could learn much about a village, town or region as I went. For food is history on a plate. No ingredient or combination of ingredients arrives by accident. There's always a reason for them being there. They tell of trade, conquest, migration, social change. Any people's fundamental identity is lodged in their food. Anyway, it would be more fun than reading parish records or local archives.

So that's what I would do: come to understand Sicily by eating it. I planned to divide my explorations into two parts. For the first leg, in spring, I would travel from west coast to east, straight across the middle of the island from Marsala to Catania, when the weather would be balmy, warm, so I reasoned, but not locked into the burning heat of summer. This would be the season of the first figs, and cherries and early peaches, zucchini flowers and wild flowers. Then I planned to return in late September, when the summer heat had died down, and ride around the circumference, starting and finishing in Catania, sampling, what? Late figs? Late peaches? Grapes? I wasn't quite sure.

And I wasn't going to rush it. It was going to take seven weeks or so in all – say three weeks across the middle, and a month round the edge. I wanted to take my time, to meander, to pause when I felt like it and move when I felt like it, potter off along byways, explore at will. I was only going to be able to make these journeys once. It wasn't practical to walk. Bicycle? I think not. Too many very steep ups and precipitous downs. Car? There's no romance about a car. It would make the journey simply a data-collecting exercise. No. A scooter, a Vespa, stylish, iconic, practical, and, in my hands, slow. And, I hoped, safe.

Fish Market, Porta Garibaldi, Marsala

CHAPTER ONE

Time Present and Time Past

◎◎

Marsala

In 1973 Tom and I had travelled in breezy innocence, with easy optimism and careless curiosity, stopping where we felt inclined. The one introduction we had been given was addressed to Manfred Whitaker, who lived in the Villa Ingham just outside Marsala. Instructions as to how we could find him were hazy in the extreme. Indeed, there was something slightly makeshift about the introduction itself, but we felt that we had better call in out of courtesy, if nothing else, and so we did.

Manfred turned out to be a stocky, energetic figure, and vigorously, if not rampantly, homosexual. When he saw two strapping lads getting out of their hire car he evidently thought that Christmas had come, a point on which we had to disabuse him rapidly. With the foreplay out of the way, he became the most delightful, charming and obliging of hosts, learned, funny, acerbic and individual. Sadly, I kept no record of his views or our conversations, but I can still sense the mercurial force of his personality, his endless kindness and high good humour.

I remember being told, probably by Manfred himself, that the Villa Ingham had been built, and its extensive gardens laid out, by a member of the wealthy Ingham family for the delight of his mistress. It didn't look like my idea of a love nest. It remained in my memory as a large, sober-looking building with an apparently endless sequence of crepuscular rooms, full of shadows and cool air and an accumulation of heavy-gravity, dark-shaded, plumply stuffed Victorian furniture, books, portraits of distinguished ancestors and a random and eccentric cluster of objects, which included a standard lamp made from a stuffed anaconda rearing to its full height. There was Manfred's throne-like lavatory and the plumbing that had a will of its own. It didn't strike me as being a grand house, but it did have a certain seriousness about it, a seriousness which Manfred belied.

He died in 1977 and the house passed to his nephew, William Richards, and his wife Val, who greeted me as I buzzed up the drive in time for lunch. William was a lawyer, successful, jovial, kindly and generous. The Villa Ingham was now a family holiday home, he said. They had thought of selling it at first; it needed so much attention, and Marsala wasn't exactly convenient. And then they decided they couldn't. The family loved it too much. Their children came and went, and other family members, too. And yes, they had done a good deal to the house, attended to the plumbing for one thing, and sorted out the kitchen, and turned the water tank above the house into a swimming pool.

I wandered around the rooms and couldn't tell what had changed over the intervening years. The furniture seemed the same, the books, the steadfast pictures, the clutter of knick-knacks, and, oh yes, there was the anaconda standard lamp. More than that, the spirit of the place was still the same, that curious combination of the serious and the fantastical, of Victorian worthiness and pagan hedonism, one room leading to the next and to the next and to the next – like some Borgesian metaphysical structure, the crepuscular cool made more crepuscular and cooler in contrast to the brilliantly lit landscape below, where olive and orange trees had been planted in neat rectangular plantations. I didn't remember the paintings in the manner of Rex Whistler on the high ceiling in the sitting room, and, indeed, it turned out they had been painted by a young friend of the family only a few years earlier, but even they had been absorbed into the patina of the house so that they looked as if they had always been there.

The garden, too, retained its rambling charm. It had seemed deliciously dilapidated to me 33 years earlier. It did so now. Paths, strewn with withered leaves that crackled explosively underfoot, wove their way between trees and shrubs of luxurious splendour, to crumbling flights of steps leading to another sun and shadow dappled level. Scents rose up where the hot sun struck the shrubs, peppery, pungent, spicy, herbal; thyme, rosemary, clove, aniseed.

Here was a statue of some antique dryad lurking at the end of a gravel cul-de-sac, peering from a bower of acanthus leaves. Here was a stone trough with lily pads and reflections. Here was a water tank without any water, a line of curious majolica miniature obelisks the colour of the sky ranged along the top of one side. A scuttling in the bushes reminded me of the peacocks that had nested in the trees all those years ago.

'The peacocks are still here,' said William. 'There are only two left now, both males. We introduced a couple of females a few years ago in the hope they might breed, but we found them dead a few days later. It seems that the males didn't appreciate them very much.' I wondered what might have happened if Adam had taken a similar attitude to Eve in the Garden of Eden.

The sense of timelessness, of social continuum, carried over into lunch. There were other friends and members of the family staying, too, just as there had been in Manfred's time, and we sat outside at a table big enough to seat 20 under an awning, shaded from the hot sun. There were only nine of us, but conversation, erudite, funny, discursive, generous, never flagged for a moment. We talked about food and TV chefs in disrespectful terms that Manfred would have approved of, and George Borrow, and the problems of photographing food, and the group of Surrey pensioners who came to pick the olives every year, and Manfred's idiosyncrasies, and the changes at the Villa Ingham. If I wasn't quite same figure who had sat in this same place all those years ago, nevertheless there was enough of my young self left to catch the sweet echo of the past.

We ate *panelle*, Sicilian fritters made from chickpea flour, bought in the market that morning, and olives from the Richards' olive trees, and then salami and prosciutto and salad and bread and cheese and fruit, and finished with a granita made from oranges that grew on the estate. There was nothing fancy about any of it, except its quality, the exactness and clarity of flavours. 'What else did you want?' I thought, as I sank another glass of chilled *rosato*, crisp and fresh as ice melt. Not much. Nothing in fact.

Revisiting the past can be a tricky business. Too often it seems shrunken or down at heel or at odds with the mellowness of memory, but in this case I could feel no difference between past and present. Even Manfred seemed to be about the place, even if I couldn't quite see him.

@@

I woke to the smell of the sea, a soup of sharp iodine, seaweed, salt, marine life, sunlight, wind. Marsala is defined by the sea. The sea sits on three sides of it. From the sea came the Greeks, Romans, Arabs, Spaniards, British, Americans, each of the peoples that made and marked it, the fish and trade that fed it. Across the sea went the wine that gave Marsala its last great, rich incarnation a hundred and fifty years ago.

In 1773 John Woodhouse came to Marsala from Liverpool looking for ingredients for soap. He found the fortified local hooch instead, and decided marsala was the very thing to become smart society's tipple of choice. The business was given a shot in the arm when Admiral Horatio Nelson ordered several pipes of the stuff for his sailors after the Battle of the Nile in 1798. Over the following century colossal fortunes were made out of the wine. The English connection flourished as the Woodhouse family embraced the Inghams and the Whitakers, the 'Princes under the Volcano' as the marsala families were known. Sicilian families, too, joined in the fun, one family in particular, the Florios, becoming the richest and grandest of them all. Each went on to make marked contributions to the cultural life of the island and to the gaiety of nations in general (during Prohibition in America, marsala was classified as a medicinal tonic, and sold as such).

And then the eminence of marsala began to decline as the founding families sold out to the big commercial battalions; the wine became debased as corners were cut, quality sacrificed to price, and industrial production methods took their toll. As Harry Morley, a determined traveller and devoted classicist, had written as early as 1926: 'The only good thing you can say about Marsala is that it goes well with gorgonzola. At best it is a poor substitute for sherry or madeira, without any real character of its own.' The consequences were inevitable. People stopped drinking marsala. Ah, marsala, they said, fine for cooking, but for sipping? And they reached for their glasses of chardonnay.

The long seafront of the town was lined with the husks of the great *bagli*, walled, fortified compounds, where the marsala had once been made and stored, and from which it had been shipped across the globe – monuments now to the fall of the great marsala families. Most were derelict, dumping grounds or storage depots for building materials and the like. Dust and plastic bags and bits of paper and dead leaves blew about the courtyards. The three-storey Whitaker *baglio* had been one of the greatest, with its shaded, arcaded ground floor, Corinthian pillars above, and elegant, shuttered windows on the top floor. Now the golden stucco was fading, stonework crumbling. The shutters sagged on their hinges and the Corinthian pillars held up – what? A vanished history? Not quite.

Life was beginning to stir in the some of the *bagli* once more. Marsala was staging a comeback. Its renaissance had begun when a talented winemaker, Marco de Bortoli, decided that redemption lay in quality not quantity, and set about re-creating the wine to new standards. The Buffa family, with one or two others, had joined him, and, little by little, marsala's reputation was improving. What was it Edward Lear had written?

> *He sits in a beautiful parlour*
> *With hundreds of books on the wall;*
> *He drinks a great deal of Marsala,*
> *But never gets tipsy at all.*

Lear can never have come across the Buffa marsala, that's all I can say.

As I said goodbye to Domenico Buffa, a stiff wind stirred up the dust in the courtyard of the *baglio*. Sharp waves flicked the scrubby coastline on to which the building faced, and against the hulls of leisure craft in the marina, against the jetties, against the hulls of the fishing boats – smaller, multicoloured inshore boats; larger, grubbier, more purposeful deep-water boats with names like *Turridu*, *Carmelo* and *Pinturicchio* – moored within the long sheltering arm of the mole that formed the harbour wall.

I found their harvest in the compact, cruciform fish market just by the Porta Garibaldi, the gate through which Garibaldi entered the town in May 1860 to begin his conquest of the island and start the process that led, with extraordinary rapidity, to the unification of Italy within two years. The Porta Garibaldi was not always the Porta Garibaldi. It had formerly been the Porta di Mare, but history has always marched through and over Marsala. It had been Lilybeaum to the Carthaginians and Marsa Ali, the Port of Allah, to the Saracens. The gate had been built to mimic a Roman triumphal arch. The eagle on it was the emblem of Spanish royalty, from the time when Sicily was part of the Spanish Empire. But the fish and the fishermen have always been there.

The market may not have been as vigorous as it was once, to judge by the areas not occupied by stalls, but it still supported 15 or so fishmongers, three greengrocers and a *salumeria* where I could have bought *bottarga* and *strattu*, ultra concentrated tomato paste, pecorino and salted anchovies in great round tins. There were a couple of butchers, too, decked out with skinned sheep's heads that peered with bloody melancholy from the display cabinets.

It was spring – this was May – and the sloping display counters were crowded with cephalopods: octopuses in four sizes;

tiny *moscardini* like dominoes; squid, flaccid and startlingly white; plump, speckled cuttlefish; and fish – whiting, hake, bream, anchovies, dogfish, gurnard, sea bass in all their shimmering, glittering, scaly glory. Above all, this was the season for *pesce spada* – swordfish – with the world's smallest specimen on display, its bill pointing skywards; and for tuna. Each stall had its display, gunmetal skin, round surprised eye in head shaped like a howitzer shell, barrel torso slashed in half presenting a lambent, burgundy surface to the world. And in front six, seven, eight different cuts, ranging in colour from coral pink to a deep, purplish damask.

According to Alan Davidson in his encyclopaedic classic *Mediterranean Seafood*, there are several members of the tuna family: bluefin – *tonno*; albacore –*alalonga*; little tuna– *tonnetto*; skipjack – *tonnetto listato*; and frigate mackerel – *tombarello*. Of these, the bluefin tuna, the largest, is the most highly prized.

Traditionally these were taken at the *mattanza*, the annual ritual in which migrating tuna were herded into nets and then gaffed and slaughtered in a bloody frenzy, just off Favignana, one of the Egadi islands visible from Marsala. The ritual is as old as history. Aeschylus likened the slaughter of the Persians at the Battle of Salamis to the *mattanza*. Modern historians gave the same name to the ferocious Mafia war that raged between 1970 and 1983, which saw the Corleonesi families rise to control the island's criminal activities.

The old *mattanza* still went on, said Salvatore, a large, genial fishmonger with a shaven head and unshaven chin, but it was not what it once was. For all its picturesque brutality, it was, in fact, an environmentally sustainable way to catch fish. More tuna escaped than were taken, and, before more functional modern methods came along, the *mattanza* ensured a healthy supply of fish for each season. These days the future of the Mediterranean tuna is debated in the same lugubrious tones we use when considering North Sea cod. It is the appetite for this splendid fish in the rest of the world that is threatening its future. Not that there seemed to be any shortage in the market in Marsala.

'This is good for *ragù*,' explained Salvatore. 'This for *brasato, con cipolle e aceto*. This you cook *ai ferri*, grilled. And this in *padella al limone*.'

They all looked much the same to me.

'And this?' I asked, pointing at a piece of tuna the size and thickness of a steak, with thick, creamy seams of fat running between the stratas of purple flesh.

'*Ventresca*,' he said, and pointed to his ribs. I understood. It's the tuna equivalent of belly of pork, the richest part of the fish. Later I ate a thick steak of *ventresca a padella*, roasted in a pan, in the Trattoria da Pippo; in a stubby backstreet, it was as functional an eatery as I have come across in some time. But the fish was immaculately cooked, crusted outside, its oily richness spreading over my mouth, its roof, sides, nooks, crannies, coating my tongue and throat – a fatness more extreme than mutton, pig or beef fat, but with a bit of beef and lamb about it. This was the true fatness of the sea, the fatness all the sea creatures on which the tuna had been feeding.

☙☙

The Via dei Mille runs from the Porta Garibaldi and the market down to the Piazza della Repubblica, the hub of the town. It was down this road that Garibaldi led his ragtag and bobtail thousand in 1860 at the beginning of the campaign that resulted in the unification of Italy.

'*Ma per me, Garibaldi non era un eroe* – Garibaldi wasn't a hero as far as I'm concerned,' said my guide and mentor Nanni Cucchiara, a civilised and cultured man, lawyer and gourmet, with a round face shaded by a three-day stubble, wary, clever, dark eyes and unruly black hair. He was, by turns, perceptive, subtle, expressive and generous with his knowledge, but guarded with himself. It was as if he was always gauging what I had meant by what I said, or whether I had really meant what I said, or if there was some other layer of meaning to my words. Or it may have been he just had trouble understanding my Italian.

'Garibaldi had always been a republican, but he sold out to the king and the interests of the north,' Nanni said. He went on: 'When he came to Sicily, Garibaldi acted like a dictator. He removed the old structures but did not replace them with anything better. Sicily became a lawless place as a result. It is interesting that the banditry and the Mafia, that have been so difficult for Sicily, only developed after the unification of Italy. Since then we have added Piedmontese exploitation and corruption to the exploitation and corruption of our own.'

We were standing in the Piazza della Repubblica. The old centre of Marsala had a curious air to it, antique and pristine at the same time, having been scrupulously rebuilt after the Second World War. I was particularly taken with the ingenious system for keeping the main streets clean. Sunken culverts ran down the edge of the streets, tucked beneath an overhanging lip of pavement. Any rubbish at street level was brushed into these, hidden from sight and then flushed away at regular intervals.

One side of the piazza was dominated by a handsome cathedral dedicated to St Thomas à Becket. Thomas à Becket? Not the English archbishop murdered by the thanes of Henry II? The very same. Marsala seemed an odd place for him to crop up, for I had always thought of him as a very British figure. On the opposite side of the piazza was the Caffetteria Grand' Italia, a handsome place run with the cheery professionalism that seems commonplace in Italy. Service was sharp, leavened by free and easy banter with the regulars, and the flow of coffees, made to a uniform excellence that would be remarkable in Britain, crisp. The coffees were buttressed by *cornetti con crema*, gloriously crunchy-squidgy croissants stuffed with crème patissiere that would deposit a light fall of icing sugar down my front if I wasn't careful. I was rarely careful enough. During the early morning, a steady stream of men and women on their way to work stopped in for a cup of dark espresso, a glass of water, a *cornetto*. One minute, two minutes, three minutes maximum, and they'd drunk, eaten, chatted and gone. But briskness and efficiency didn't preclude civility.

'But the relationship between the Mafia and Sicilians is very ambiguous, The Mafia is still "respected" in Sicily,' said Nanni, as he sipped an espresso, picking up the thread of our earlier conversation.

'Respect? What do you mean?'

'It's difficult to explain to anyone who isn't Sicilian,' he said. 'It's a kind of understanding, esteem.'

'So will the Mafia ever disappear?' I asked.

'Everything disappears eventually,' Nanni said. 'The Greeks, the Romans, the Arabs, the Spanish. They all went. In the end.' Bearing in mind the way the Mafia had assassinated Borsellino, 'his sangfroid seemed remarkable.

Out in the piazza groups of men moved in a stately quadrille, talking. It seemed curious that in a town so richly endowed with *orologerie*, watch and clock shops, time was treated as an illimitable resource. No one hurried. Everyone always seemed to have time for a coffee, a pastry, a chat, to exchange pleasantries, discuss politics, haggle over food. Time was spent with a lavishness that contrasted sharply with the way we treat it in Britain. We are, we claim, time poor. Asset rich, but time poor. We never have time to cook, to eat, for our children, for each other, for ourselves. Sicilians might not be asset rich, but they have all these other things.

@@

That evening Nanni took me to Il Gallo e l'Innamorata, a small restaurant with the lively informality of a bar and some very serious food.

We started with antipasto: a little stack of *neonati* – tiny fish, fried crisp like tiny wisps of straws; an octopus salad, muscular and sweet; *bruschetta* of salty *bottarga*, dried tuna roe, a concentrate of marine life lightened and made fresh with bouncy tomatoes 'from Pacchino'; fried fillets of sardine, the flesh firm and flaky, dusted with oregano; and *moscardini* – diminutive squid. Each dish was characterised by the luminous freshness of the ingredients, by the limpid quality of each flavour. I wiped up the smears of sauce with bread scattered with sesame seeds.

'And now we must have tuna,' said Nanni. 'The tuna season starts in May and ends in June. You won't find any fresh tuna after that. It'll be frozen. It's only worth eating when it's fresh.'

So we had *busiati con ragù di tonno*. The tuna in the sauce had melted into a rollicking tomato sauce. This was stiffened with a compound of *pan grattato* (dried breadcrumbs), olive oil and basil added in place of grated cheese. The precise use of the *pan grattato*, basil and oil was exactly the kind of small detail that makes a dish sing.

The *busiati* – 'This is the right pasta to have with tuna,' said Nanni emphatically. 'You might try a broad, flat pasta, like pappardelle, but this is better' – looked very like the *fileji* I had come across in Calabria a few years before: slender coils made by twisting the soft dough around a metal core not unlike a knitting needle, which had been used for the same kinds of fish-based sauce. The *busiati* were longer than *fileji*, but the principle was exactly the same. Goethe recorded watching a family making pasta in exactly the same way during his trip to Sicily in 1786.

'We get olive oil from the Greeks,' explained Nanni, 'bread from the Romans, sesame seeds, sorbets, rice and pastries from the Arabs, tomatoes and chocolate and our sweet tooth from the Spaniards.

'We may take their food,' he went on, ' but all the foreigners who come to govern Sicily end up by becoming Sicilians – Greeks, Romans, Arabs, French, Germans, Spanish. Even you English. There is something about this island.'

In view of what we had already eaten, we decided to pass on the *secondo piatto*, and go straight to pudding. I was grateful for this consideration. I was beginning to learn that a Sicilian's notion of portion control makes the average helping in Yorkshire seem like an offering from WeightWatchers.

Pudding was *cappidduzzu*. 'Or *cassatedda* as it is known in Trapani. Or *raviola* in Mazara del Vallo,' explained Nanni. I said that didn't explain anything, and just made matters very diffi-cult for us foreigners. *Cappidduzzu* or *cassatedda* or *raviola* turned out to be golden-brown crunchy *raviolo* stuffed with sweetened sheep's ricotta. It came with a white mound of almond ice cream complete with shards of almond.

Replete and cheerful, we made our way back through the darkened, deserted streets. We paused at the top of the lane leading to my hotel. A stiff wind blew, sending the odd scrap of paper scurrying down the street. I would be leaving the next day. I thanked Nanni for his time and generosity. It had been his pleasure, he said.

There was an affinity between Sicilians and the English, he went on. 'We are both eccentric people,' he said. 'Eccentric in the original meaning of the word. We live away from the centre – *ex centro* to give the Latin origin. We are island peoples. We resist any centralising process that tries to make us all behave in the same way.'

We shook hands and parted. I pondered on his observation. I wasn't so sure I could see the similarities. Sicilians had murderous vendettas spanning decades. We had *leylandii* hedge feuds.

∾ Panelle ∾

You find *panelle* all over Sicily, although it's claimed that they are native to Palermo. That might have been true once upon a time. Unquestionably they are a Moorish nibble, not unlike *fatayer bi hummus* from the Lebanon. There's not really a secret authentic recipe. To be honest, this is an amalgam of several I was given.

Makes about 20 *panelle*
Salt • 500g chickpea flour • 2 tbsp chopped broad-leafed parsley • Freshly ground black pepper • Vegetable oil

Bring 2l water to a gentle boil and lightly salt. Add the chickpea flour a little at a time, stirring to make sure the mixture is smooth. Always stir in the same direction. Add the chopped parsley and season with black pepper. Go on cooking until you have a smooth paste that begins to pull away from the sides of the pan. Turn out onto an oiled surface and smooth out until it's about 0.5cm thick. Allow to cool. Cut into little rectangles. Heat vegetable oil in a pan and fry a few of the rectangles at a time until pale golden brown. Drain on a kitchen towel and eat while still warm.

∞ Granita d'arancia di Racalia ∞

A delightful refresher from that memorable lunch at the Villa Ingham, a.k.a. Racalia.

Serves 6
150g granulated sugar • Juice of 8 freshly squeezed Tarocco oranges • Juice of 1 lemon

Put 250ml water and the granulated sugar into a saucepan. Heat until the sugar has dissolved and then boil for at least a minute. Allow it to cool completely. Add the orange and lemon juices. Transfer the mixture into a plastic container and pop the container into a freezer. Leave for 2 hours, stirring with fork every 10–15 minutes. The granules should be fine, almost mushy by the end.

∞ Tonno con cipolle e aceto ∞

Serves 4
600g tuna • Olive oil • Flour seasoned with salt • 2 large onions • 1 tbsp sugar • 50ml red wine vinegar • 25g chopped mint

Wash the tuna and cut into thickish slices, maybe 1cm thick. Pat dry. Heat the oil in a frying pan. Dip each tuna slice in the seasoned flour and fry quickly for 1–2 minutes on each side until they are golden-brown. Leave to drain on kitchen towel.

Peel and slice the onions very finely. Fry in the same oil used to cook the tuna. Add a tablespoonful or so of water and cook over a very low heat for about an hour. Add the sugar and sprinkle the red wine vinegar and the mint. Leave to cook for a further couple of minutes. Place the tuna on a plate, pour the sweet and sour onion mixture over them and leave to cool for a few hours.

∞ Busiati con ragù di tonno ∞

Serves 4

1kg tuna • 1–2 garlic cloves • Dried oregano • Extra virgin olive oil • 1 onion • 3–4 very ripe tomatoes • 2 dsp strattu *(very concentrated tomato purée) • 3 tbsp red wine • 1 dsp red wine vinegar • 1 clove • Salt and pepper • 600g* busiati *or pasta of a similar class (eg* bucatini *or* maccheroncini*)*

Wash and dry the tuna and cut into chunks. Peel and cut the garlic into slivers. Stick a sliver of garlic into each tuna chunk, along with a pinch of dried oregano. Put a dash of oil into a frying pan and fry the tuna until golden-brown all over. Drain on kitchen towel. Slice the onion thinly and peel, seed and chop the tomatoes. In another pan fry the onion in a little more oil until golden. Add *strattu* plus the wine and vinegar. Cook over a low heat for a minute or two. Add the tomatoes. Cook for 20 minutes over a low heat. Add the tuna chunks and the clove. Cook over a very low heat for an hour or so, until the sauce has become quite concentrated. Add salt and pepper according to your taste. Meanwhile, cook the pasta in boiling salted water until al dente. Serve it with the sauce.

∽ Cappidduzzu ∽

Makes about 25 *cappidduzzu*
Olive oil • *Ground cinnamon* • *Caster sugar*
Pastry: *750g flour* • *30g caster sugar* • *250ml white wine* • *70g*
sugna *(pig fat)*
Filling: *750g ricotta* • *300g caster sugar* • *Grated rind of a lemon*

Sift the flour and sugar together. Make a well in the middle. Add enough of the wine to make a stiffish dough. Add the fat in small pieces, kneading it well into the dough. Knead for 15–20 minutes until you have a smooth, silky dough, stretching it out and folding it over to incorporate as much air as possible. Place the dough in a bowl, cover with a kitchen towel and let it rest in a cool place for an hour or two.

Pass the ricotta through a sieve. Beat in the sugar. Pass it through a sieve again. Stir in the lemon peel.

Roll out the dough into a very thin sheet. Cut out circles approximately 8cm across. Plop a 1½ dsp of the ricotta mixture on one side of each circle, and fold the dough over into half-moons, wetting the edges and pressing them together to get a complete seal.

Heat the olive oil until very hot. Fry each *cappidduzzu* until golden-brown. Drain on kitchen towel. Sprinkle with a little ground cinnamon and caster sugar. Serve warm.

Carmelo & Giovanni Pomella, Macelleria degli
Fratelli Pomella, Corleone

CHAPTER TWO

Rollin', Rollin', Rollin'

@@

Marsala – Corleone – Ficuzza

The next day dawned bright and blowy. It was time to be on the move. I was ready for the road. Bold adventure stirred in my veins. Bold adventure mixed with a good deal of apprehension, to be exact. It had been five years since I had last spent serious time in the saddle or on a Vespa and I wasn't exactly sure what to expect. But the open road beckoned. The interior stretched before me. On, on, to Salemi, Corleone, Mussomeli, Caltanissetta, Enna, Adrano, Catania. The names rang like – well, like points on a map, to be truthful. Tom and I had not really explored the interior, and while I had read as extensively about Sicily as I could, I had only the vaguest of ideas as to what it would be like away from the coast. Perhaps I lack imagination, but in truth, I didn't want to imagine too much. I wanted the shock of discovery. And there would be remarkable discoveries, wouldn't there? There would be serious research, too, earnest fieldwork, mysteries to unravel. Oh, and the chance to eat a good deal of tip-top tucker as well.

Beside him golden pots of myrrh are placed
And fruit fresh from the tree, the season's best;
Mouth-watering dishes; every kind of meat,
Elaborate cakes and puddings, moist and sweet;
The world of fancies pastry-cooks devise
From honey and oil and coloured essences.

That's what Theocritus wrote about Sicily a couple of thousand years before, and what had been good enough for Theocritus, I thought, would be good enough for me.

⊚⊚

My new Vespa, 125cc of racing power, scarlet as a tart's fingernails, gleaming and glossy. She had a throaty roar, a bit like a singer who has overdone the whisky and cigarettes. She was my vessel on my voyage of discovery, my companion in the adventures ahead. I had been getting into intellectual training for the trip by trying to read the *Odyssey*, much of which, according to most authorities, is set in or around Sicily. I identified with the great voyager, particularly as he was setting out: 'Odysseus ... sat with his hands on the steering oar, and in expert fashion began to shape his course.' I mounted Monica, sat for a moment with my hands on her handlebars, and in expert fashion shaped my course.

Twenty minutes later I was drawn up on the side of the road, puzzling over the map. A car drew up alongside me. The window went down.

Did I need help? the old man driving asked courteously. His wife, sitting beside him, smiled encouragingly.

Was this the road to Salemi? I asked.

No, he said. This was the road to Mazara del Vallo.

'Follow me,' he said. 'I'll show you the right one.'

I followed him back into Marsala, and then out on another road. Finally, he stopped and leant out of the window.

'Just keep going straight on,' said the old man. 'You can't go wrong.' With that he turned his car round and went back into Marsala, and I went on towards Salemi and Corleone beyond, marvelling at the gracious kindness of people. A surge of sunny optimism flooded through me. Eastward ho, the land was bright.

It was grand being back in the saddle, if a touch nerve-racking. I hadn't actually ridden a scooter since I finished an epic journey on mainland Italy, from Melito di Porto Salvo on the ball of the toe, to Turin, in 2002, so my Vespacraft was a touch rusty. I was grateful that the traffic to Salemi was light. I wasn't quite ready to have my inadequacies as a knight of the road exposed to the wondering eyes of real Vespistas, or car drivers, for that matter.

Monica behaved impeccably, in spite of being heavily and unconventionally loaded. As well as one portly, balding Englishman, she was required to carry a large bag-cum-rucksack, which contained most of my travelling gear. This was wedged between the steering column and the rounded point of the saddle and was kept in place by my knees. A smaller ruck-sack, containing maps, notebooks, pens, books, camera and other assorted impedimenta with which I contrived to look like a serious researcher, rested on top.

Now that I had found it, the road unravelled before me, a grey ribbon rising and falling over land that rolled and swelled like a great sea. It stretched away to a low horizon, broken into rectangles, squares, hexagons and other straight-sided shapes stitched together, most of them a brilliant, fresh, frothy green with new vine growth. The green foam was broken here and there by the odd golden, sandy-brown carpet of wheat field and silvery-grey plantation of olives. But it was the vines that dominated this landscape between Marsala and Salemi – ranks of them, platoons of them, brigades of them, marching in blocks of dead straight lines to an arbitrary edge, with another block set at a slight angle marching in a slightly different direction. They were neat, flat blocks from far off, leaves frilly and ruffled closer to.

In 1926 Harry Morley wrote of the area around Marsala: 'One enters a country that might seem to be all vineyard.' Not much had changed. 'But these vineyards are comparatively modern and bear witness not even to Sicilian but to foreign enterprise. Here is grown the Marsala wine which Messers Ingham-Whitaker, Florio and Woodhouse manufacture.'

The landscape stretched away, colossal, impersonal, abstract. I didn't see another human being in all its mass. There was a complete absence of anything that gave a sense of human scale at all, person, building or machine. In spite of the evidence of intensive cultivation an air of isolation, and of desolation, cloaked it all. There were none of those aesthetically pleasing villas, farmhouses or picturesque villages crowning the tops of hills that illuminated the countryside of mainland Italy.

Then, little by little, I adjusted to the emptiness, and became absorbed by its own particular beauty. The sheer scale was breathtaking. There was an illimitable sense of space and light, and the neat shapes of the fields were as orderly as a Mondrian painting. The exterior landscape seemed to open up interior ones, much as abstract paintings probe us in a way that figurative art does not. It was a strange mix of the primitive and the contemporary, of the highly worked and the impersonal. It was open and impenetrable at the same time. As I puttered on, first one hour and then the next, I began to feel as an ant might crossing a desert.

I was puttering rather slowly too, not just because I was only gradually recovering my scootering skills and the *élan* of old, but also because there was a bloody, biffing and buffeting wind. Oh, where were the warm sun and gentle zephyrs of which I had dreamed when planning all of this? Instead of the rush of air over tanned arms and face, the built-in air-conditioning system cooling body and soul, I was grateful for the layers of T-shirt, shirt and lightweight motorcycle jacket that protected the upper part of my body, and wished that I was wearing something heavier than jeans to cut the chill to my lower half. I was grateful, too, that my head was completely encased in a helmet.

In theory, all Italians had been required by law to wear protective headgear for some years, but Sicilians at any rate did not seem to have the nice regard for the letter of the law that is the hallmark of the British. Helmet-wearers were in a distinct minority. When I had waxed over-lyrical on the joys of the scooter to my brother Tom – the ease of travel, sweetness of country smells, sunlight on brow, refreshing breezes, etc. etc. – and floated the idea that I might go helmetless from time to time, he had hooted with laughter, and commented with earthbound practicality that should I fall off my scooter, which in all probability I would, and damaged or even broke my jaw, my primary research tool would be rendered useless. I saw his point. So helmeted, booted and spurred I was.

In my efforts to find shelter from the hideous inconvenience of the wind, and to see if I could find any evidence of human occupation, I turned on to one of the minor lanes that formed a loose netting between the main roads on the map. This was easier. I bowled along on Monica, as merry as a grig, not too many cares in the world, curious about what lay before me. I began to feel a real sense of exhilaration and wonder at the land through which I was passing. Tom and I hadn't penetrated far inland on our trip, so what I was seeing was unfamiliar and fresh. Insignificant I might be in the vastness, but it was a new vastness, prompting new responses and questions.

And then, as I went past one of the very few inhabited buildings in the area, two dogs of uncertain pedigree came ripping out, barking and snapping at Monica's wheels in a manner that I hadn't come across since the days when I used to drive around the remoter parts of the Irish countryside looking for places to fish.

I was all right for about 50 metres. I held my nerve and the road. Then I hit one of those rogue patches of road surface with which I was to become increasingly familiar in the weeks ahead. A wobble became a slew as I overbraked on the front wheel. One bag fell off one way. The other bag fell off the other. I fell off a third just as Monica came to a halt at the side of the road. She slowly slid on to her side with an air of injured dignity. One of the dogs came up and sniffed my feet, and then trotted off with the unmistakable air of a job well done.

Luckily, no damage was done to person or scooter, although my self-esteem took a bit of a bruising. I was able to get back in the saddle and continue on my way, glad that my humiliation had not happened in front of an audience.

On, on, cleaving a path through the ocean of vines. Who was going to drink all this liquid? I like the odd glass myself, and the reputation of Sicilian wines might be going up in the world, but these hectares after hectares after hectares looked as if they were intended to satisfy the thirst of the entire world.

Presently I came to and passed Salemi. It was quiet and a bit battered now, but it had known days of glory. It had been one of the few Sicilian towns that offered shelter to the Moors and Jews after Ferdinand of Spain banished them from Spanish territories in 1492; and in 1860, early in his campaign to liberate the island from the Bourbons of Naples, Garibaldi had declared it the capital of Sicily. This heady period lasted three days. It was a long time between excitements, but Salemi seemed to reflect a thread of nonconformity running through Sicilian culture. Occupied, dominated, exploited, coerced, superficially compliant they may have been; biddable Sicilians were not.

The road ran up into some broken hills that formed one side of the lovely Valle del Belice, the beauty of which was interrupted by an example of the surreality that already struck me as an integral part of Sicilian life. A great section of hillside was covered by a duvet of concrete; just there, suddenly, in the middle of nowhere. This was an extraordinary monument to what had once been the town of Gibellina, destroyed by an earthquake in 1968. The idea to cover the remains with cement to create a vast open-air memorial had been the brainchild of Alberto Burri, an Umbrian sculptor and founder of the influential Gruppo Origine, about which, I admit, I knew very little. In spite of the hideous brutality of the visual effect, it was, in an odd way, a curiously effective memorial. There was something so mad and peculiar about it. And you couldn't miss it.

As I approached Corleone, the wind grew less and the sun

grew stronger. An agreeable warmth spread through me. The verge beside the road and the fields beyond were studded with wild flowers – poppies the red of fresh blood, vetches a bruised purple-blue, brilliant yellow thistles, wild cress, valerian and a creeping plant with minute, star-shaped flowers on pinkish stems that I couldn't identify. The great blocks of vines gave way to groves of tufted olive trees, pruned into the shapes of Afro haircuts. There were more rectangles of wheat, too, biscuity gold, and swathes of *sulla* – clover – purple as a cardinal's cassock. The sweeping hills looked smooth and glossy in the sunlight, except where stark masses of rock, stubbled with dark green ilex and sessile oak, suddenly erupted through the skin of the well-tended, fertile fields.

◎◎

Corleone has a peculiar place in modern iconography as the archetypal Mafia town. Not only did it give its name to the most famous of all the cinematic Mafia families in the *Godfather* films, but it produced two of the most remarkable recent *capi di tutti capi*, Toto Riina, the man who declared war on the Italian state, and Bernardo 'the tractor' Provenzano, recently arrested after 45 years on the run.

It was a curious sensation coming from the open country-side flooded with light into the old section of the town. The houses on either side of the narrow, vertiginous, winding streets seemed to close in around me. The sense of claustrophobia was increased by a heavy religious presence. Then the old, medieval core of Corleone gave way to the untidy, open, more recent accretion with taller modern buildings. There were a couple of smart bars, too, but the apparent wealth of the surrounding countryside (or the phenomenal amounts of money generated by the primary local businesses) was not reflected in the status of the town as a whole. (This scruffiness may have been deliberately illusory. According to a lawyer I met later, while the outsides of the buildings may have been shabby, the insides were not. The Mafia bosses of Corleone didn't believe in external displays of wealth. They kept their luxury well hidden, 'rather like Arabs', said the lawyer.)

But in the town's dark streets shone an astonishing delight.

The shop on the small square looked nothing special. There was no name above the door, simply the word *Dolceria* in Gothic lettering with *Droghe – Liquori – Gelati* as a subscript, like an afterthought. I wondered at the inclusion of *droghe*, which according to my dictionary could mean either drugs or spices. It had nothing of disposable contemporary retail design about it. Indeed, it was gloomy, almost fusty, like an old-fashioned sweet shop, with glass-fronted wooden cabinets stacked with pastries, sweets and, very oddly, an astonishing array of whiskies, brands I had never heard of. And *cannoli*.

Cannoli are *the* classic Sicilian pastry – '*Su biniditti spisi li dinari, ogni canola e scettru di re* (Blessed is the money spent to buy them, every *cannolo*'s the sceptre of the king)' quotes Mary Taylor Simeti in *Sicilian Food*. They come in various sizes, but they all consist of a round pastry casing, like a section of edible piping, that has been deep-fried and stuffed with ricotta sweetened with sugar and honey, and dotted with chocolate nibs and nuggets of candied fruit.

That cosmopolitan, jolly and scholarly writer Waverly Root reckoned the origins of *cannoli* were phallic rather than monarchical, although, come to think of it, a sceptre has something of the phallus about it. The semiotic references may have been phallic, but the finished article was a compendium of references to Sicily's textured history. The frying of the pastry casing is distinctly North African. The Romans used honey as a sweetener. The origins of ricotta are far older, classical, pre-classical even. It's probably been made as long as shepherds have been making cheese. It's a kind of second-growth cheese, made by reheating the whey after cheese-making proper, and scooping off the resulting light nimbus of curd that rises to the surface. The chocolate introduced the Spanish element – the successors to Columbus brought it to Europe from Central America when Sicily was part of the Spanish Empire. And so each moment anyone closed their eyes in pleasure at that hedonistic explosion of sensations was registering 2000 years of history or more.

Vincenzo and Sanchez Iannazzo made *cannoli* at the back of the shop, as the Iannazzo families had been making *cannoli* '*dall'antichita*, from antiquity' said Sanchez. She had the dark hair and pale, alabaster skin of an eighteenth-century Madonna, a gentle manner and a splendidly toothy smile.

When I had first gone into the shop, she had given me a *cannolo*. The biscuity *scorza* – pastry case – sloped to a point at either end like a very large brandy snap, its surface pitted, dark brown, and was stuffed with pure, snowy-white, sweetened ricotta. The *scorza* crunched, snapped into crisp shards resting on the pillowy softness of the filling. The first impression was of an extraordinary smoothness, of velvet creaminess. And then the sweetness came, explosive, overwhelming, a tsunami of sweetness, sweetness piled on sweetness, sweetness of another dimension, hallucinatory, luxurious and heady. The filling coated the mouth in a molten, ambrosial, honeyed fur. Then, as my taste genes, taste buds, mind adjusted, I picked out the tiny details: the dark bitterness of chocolate and the delicate subtleties of candied *zucca* – pumpkin.

'Come back tomorrow,' she had said when I asked if I could see how she and her husband made their *cannoli*.

It was 7.15 p.m. on a Saturday when I arrived, and a large part of the Iannazzo family were engaged in the production process. They made the pastries every Saturday because Sunday was the big *cannoli* day in Corleone. Yes, they were eaten through the week, said Sanchez, but traditionally Sunday was the day for *cannoli*, along with big religious festivals. This went back to the days when most people in and around Corleone, and the rest of Sicily, come to that, were poorer, when these potent pastries were foods of luxury and so of celebration, an occasional indulgence not an everyday commonplace.

The bakery had the well-ordered, well-used look of practical usage. The space wasn't large, but it was enough. There was machinery, but no gadgetry. This was here because it worked, and that was there because it worked. The family went about their jobs at an easy, steady pace in companionable silence. There was no sense of hurry. It was a calm, orderly process, in which each participant knew their role from long practice.

Salvatore, the eldest Iannazzo son, was rolling out the raw creamy *cannoli* dough on a semi-automated roller. He moved the long sheet on to a stainless-steel table dusted with flour. Rapidly he stamped out the *scorze* shapes, flat, oval and white at this stage. He whipped away the unused dough to re-roll it. Niccolo, the second son, retrieved the cut shapes and neatly stacked them on another part of the table. He handed them on to his mother who deftly wrapped them round short wooden pegs blackened with use, squeezing the curved edges together just at the centre so that they formed a tube, and placed the *scorze* on a metal tray. The neat rows of white dough curved around the blackened pegs looked like a heraldic device. 'No, it's not hard work,' Sanchez said, 'being a baker. You just work with your hands, that's all. But it's not easy making a living. People don't want to pay the prices for products made by hand, that take time and care and the best ingredients. They seem to be happy with industrial products that cost less.' This modern habit left her disappointed and at a loss.

'You see,' she said, 'you have to look after the quality. And that takes time and care. There's the flour and honey and sugar and *sugna* –'

'*Sugna*?'

She searched for a word I might understand. '*Strutto*,' she said. Pig fat. 'For the *scorze*.' Sicilians aren't afraid of sugar, or pig fat come to that. When diet specialists and food writers extol the virtues of the Mediterranean diet so readily, they tend to forget to mention that the shortening for all pastries and other baked foods is pig fat, or mutton fat in North Africa. The idea of using olive oil is anathema. The taste would be all wrong. Anyway, olive oil would have been too expensive for such prodigal use during the times when these delicacies were being created. 'And there's the ricotta, the best ricotta, *ricotta di pecora di questa zona* – sheep ricotta from around here.' The ricotta is mixed with tiny nibs of dark chocolate and best quality candied peel of *zucca*. But this being Sicily, it has to be a very particular pumpkin, a pumpkin that is only suitable for candying. Finally the sugar. That has to have the right texture and quality, too.

'You have to make sure every detail is right', said Sanchez. She didn't pause from wrapping the uncooked *scorza* shapes around the wooden pegs and putting them on the tray. When the tray was full, she carried it through to a further room at the back, where Vincenzo fried them in a great vat of roiling vegetable oil.

'There's no secret to *cannoli*,' he said, echoing his wife's explanation. 'You just have to make sure that everything is the best.' He was a neat, trim man, with a long, handsome face, naturally graceful in his movements.

He lifted out a handful of raw *scorze* and dropped them, still wrapped around the pegs, into the quietly seething oil. A couple more handfuls and the tray was empty. Almost immediately the *scorze* began to colour. He stirred them with a wire ladle, turning them over and over to make sure they cooked evenly. The air was rich with oil vapour braided with the sweetness of butterscotch and honey. The *scorze* quickly went a deeper cream, and then a golden, sandy brown. At this stage, when the shapes were just set, Vincenzo whipped out the wooden pegs with a pair of tongs. The *scorze* went on cooking – amber, leather brown, bark brown.

Then he scooped them out into a large wire drainer. The surface of each *scorza* was pitted and cratered like the moon's surface in photos. The whole frying process took three minutes at most.

'How many are you making?'

'Enough.'

'How often do you make them?'

'When we run out.'

'How long do they last?'

'Two days maybe.'

I ate an unfilled *scorza*. It was crunchy, flaky – *croccante*

39

was the word – slightly sweet. I could pick out the honey and the pig fat made my lips glossy. Sanchez stacked the cool, dry *scorze* neatly on a wooden box on rollers lined with brown paper. It was eight o'clock, and there were only a couple of trays left to fry. The boys were already cleaning up the preparation area.

Tomorrow, Sunday, they would make the ricotta filling, beating in the honey and sugar, working the mixture again and again to lighten it before mixing in the chocolate nips and candied *zucca*, ready to smear it into either end of the *scorza* as the customers filed in. 'The filling must be fresh,' said Sanchez. I marvelled at their dedication, their matter-of-fact practicality, their willingness to show and share their skill and expertise, their innate modesty.

It was that gradual accumulation of details, attention to the smallest element, doing the same things in the same way with the same pride and faith in quality, that made the Iannazzo *cannoli* so addictive. The *cannoli* of the Piano degli Albanesi, a few kilometres from Corleoni, are the most famous in Sicily, but I couldn't believe they could be things of such thrilling beauty as these of Corleone. I begged another and had a second heady sugar rush and felt a little sick.

◎◎

Sausages have run like a juicy seam through my life since I first ate peerless bangers of Vic Franklin of Twyford, Berks when I was growing up. I have been on the look-out for sausages of quality ever since. While pork plays an important part in the Sicilian diet, it didn't strike me as having been raised to the specialised heights it has on mainland Italy, where every community had its *capocollo, salciccie, salame, sopressata, lardo*, prosciutto, *culatello*, etc. etc. Even though I had that sausage epiphany in Erice on the earlier trip with Tom, the range and variety of Sicilian pork products were limited by comparison.

The *salsiccia di Corleone* was another matter, even if what made the *salsiccie di Corleone* the *salsiccie di Corleone* was a matter of controversy. I had been told, on the highest authority, that it consisted of pork, veal and the seeds of the wild fennel that grows on the mountains round about, and that it was quite different say, from the *salsiccia di Marineo*, just down the road, which consisted only of pork and fennel seeds, although there was a version that contained orange peel as well.

Not so, said Carmelo Pomella, inside the Macelleria degli Fratelli Pomella. In keeping with the almost wilfully anti-commercial traditions of Sicilian small towns, all that marked the brother's butchery was a battered sign with the single word *Carne* on it. As the building in which the shop was housed was covered in scaffolding, it would have been easy to miss even this modest advertisement. The inside was utterly without pretension or glamour. It felt as if it had been this way since the Pomellas' father first opened the doors of the butchery. With pride, the brothers showed me old black-and-white photos of the shop, with the outside festooned with cuts of meat and sausages, like large, odd Christmas decorations.

Carmelo was a great advertisement for the brothers' products, large, thickset, solid and rounded. His head was round. His face was round. His body was round; but it was a muscular roundness, a formidable roundness. Giovanni was smaller, thinner, slighter. He didn't have his brother's imposing presence, but he had a wiry strength and a quickness about him.

They were both more than cheerfully voluble. They gushed words. They talked torrentially. They said the same things. They backed each other up. They filled out what each other said.

'The sausage of Corleone –'

'Our sausages –'

'We only put pork and seasonings into them –'

'Salt, black pepper, red pepper –'

'Just a little red pepper –'

'And *semi di finocchietta*, wild fennel seeds –'

'They come from wild fennel around here –'

'It's the *finocchietta* that is the special ingredient –'

'It's different from the *finocchio* from anywhere else –'

'And we use the whole pig –'

'Five parts –'

'Shoulder, belly, leg, cheek and back fat –

'That's what makes it special.'

'What about rusk or bread?' I said. 'That's what we put in British sausages.'

They looked at each other. They had no idea what I was talking about. Sausages just consisted of meat, fat and seasonings. Rusk smacked of sharp practice to them.

Carmelo cut me off a piece of raw sausage from a single long, thin link, and handed it down to me. The brothers dispensed their wares from on high, quite literally, the counter being a half a metre or so above the floor on which the customers stood.

The link was as thick as a finger, fresh pink and mottled with fat.

'Eat it,' Carmelo commanded. 'It's good like that. That's how you tell the quality of a sausage.'

The filling was sweet in a fine, meaty way, the seasoning perfectly balanced, with just a touch of chilli – ah ah, the red pepper – to lift it. If it was this good raw, cooked it must be a masterpiece of the sausage-maker's art. That's what I told them. They agreed as if this was a self-evident truth.

I mentioned that someone had told me that the classic Corleone sausage was made of veal and pork. The brothers were incredulous, faintly scandalised –

'Pork AND veal –!?'

'No. Absolutely –'

'Not.'

There had been Pomellas the butchers for a hundred years, they said, so they should know.

'What about the *salsiccia di Marineo*?'

'What about it?'

'Is it any good?'

'Boh.' The brothers shrugged.

'How is it different from the *salsiccia di Corleone*?'

'It's completely different.'

'Not the same at all.'

Well, that sorted that, then.

Out of curiosity I rode over to Marineo, about 20 kilometres away, to see if I could find a butcher there to interrogate about the differences between the sausages of Corleone and Marineo. It was an attractive town in the shadow of a hill the shape of a shark's dorsal fin, drawn up around a picturesque Aragonese castle. In a street leading to the castle there were 20 or so old men sitting on benches in the sun, like so many resting rooks.

'Where can I find a butcher to tell me about the *salsiccia di Marineo*?' I addressed the question to three of the rooks perched on one bench.

'Just over there. He's very good,' said one, pointing to a butcher's shop at the end of the street. His friends nodded.

'Do you eat his sausages?'

'Oh, yes. When I can afford to.' His friends nodded.

'What do you eat when you can't afford them?'

'Pasta.' His friends nodded.

'What? Every day?'

'Certainly. It's different every day. You change the pasta like you change your shirt,' said one of the friends.

'What do you mean?'

'Well, there's *pasta con ragù, pasta con sugo, pasta con melanzane, pasta con funghi, pasta con pomodori,*' said the second friend.

'And meat? Do you eat meat?'

'Oh yes. But not every day.'

'And wine?'

'What would food be without wine?' He laughed.

They looked pretty hale and sprightly, these old men, although few had a full head of teeth. Perhaps that accounted for their pasta diet.

The butcher they had pointed out was Franco Muratori in a blood-smeared pinny and a smart white peaked cap with *Il Re della Salsiccia* stitched on it. There was nothing he did not know about sausages.

And, no, there was no *salsiccia di Marineo* that included orange peel or lemon peel or peel of any kind, he said. Except there was a butcher in town who did include such ingredients, but only to disguise the fact that he used such inferior meat.

He, himself, the King of Sausages, made his with the five parts of the pig, shoulder, belly, leg, cheek and back fat. Twenty per cent of each sausage was back fat. Fat was essential because it carried so much flavour. He used only local pigs. No, not free-range. Free-range weren't good for his sausages. They tasted too strongly. And he seasoned only with salt, pepper and fennel seeds and tied the finished sausage into links with lengths of raffia. In other words, but for the absence of a small amount of chilli, and the raffia links, his sausages were identical to those of Corleone.

No, not identical, he said. Absolutely not. They were quite different.

❦

I headed for the Antica Stazione di Ficuzza, some 15 or so kilometres the far side of Corleone, and on my way I passed three men bent double, plucking something from among the silvery grasses at the side of the road. They were wearing almost identical blue shirts with identical blue jeans. Their average age must have been in the mid-seventies, but they looked fit and weather-beaten.

You might think it would have seemed odd when a complete stranger in a motorcycle helmet wheeled round in mid-road, stopped his scarlet scooter and came and asked you, in not very good Italian, what were you doing. The chap I spoke to behaved as if this happened every day, not pausing in his steady harvesting.

'What are you picking?'

'*Babbaluci*.'

And he went on picking.

'*Babbaluci*?'

He held out his creased, brown hand. It was full of tiny creamy/grey snails.

'Ah ah. *Lumache*.'

'*Babbaluci* in Sicilian.'

'And this is the season for them?'

'This is the best time. Before it gets too hot and dry and the *babbaluci* become too tough. They are good now.' And he went on picking. I noticed that his mate had a big bag fixed to the belt at the back of his trousers. It was bulging with snails.

'You need a lot of them.'

He agreed.

'And how do you cook them?'

'You boil them first, and then fry them with garlic and oil. Salt and pepper. That's it.'

'No wine?'

He paused for a moment then looked up at me and smiled. 'We drink the wine with them. But not cook with it.' And he went back to picking the *babbaluci*.

'*Buona giornata,*' I said.

'*Buona giornata,*' he said.

It reminded me of a scene I had read in *Conversations in Sicily* by Elio Vittorini, published in 1930. Later I looked it up. The unnamed narrator is talking to his mother about what they used to eat.

And my mother: 'Yes, poor people ate only snails, most of the time. And we were poor the last twenty days of every month.'

And I: 'We ate snails for twenty days?'

And my mother: 'Snails and wild chicory.'

I thought about it, smiled and said: 'But I bet they were pretty good, anyway.'

And my mother: 'Delicious. You can cook them so many different ways.'

And I: 'What do you mean, so many ways?'

And my mother: 'Just boiled, for example. Or with garlic and tomato. Or breaded and fried.'

And I: 'What a thought. Breaded and fried? In the shell?'

And my mother: 'Of course! You eat them by sucking them out of the shell … Don't you remember?'

And I: 'I remember, I remember … Seems to me that sucking the shell was the best part.'

And my mother: 'Hours can go by just sucking.'

(Translated by Alane Salierno Mason)

It is a long time since we knew such poverty in Britain. In fact, the whole tradition of foraging for food in our countryside to supplement a meagre diet has disappeared. Hardly anyone bothers to pick blackberries any more. I don't suppose that the *babbaluci* hunters needed the snails any more, either. It was just what they did at this time of year. I could see them sucking at their snail shells, as they had always done, and their parents before them. There was a sense of a seamless continuum between past and present in Sicily. Indeed, the past always seemed to be present in the present, which was very confusing. Where did one end and the other begin? In an age when history comes neatly packaged, into decades or eras or specified periods, the fluidity of the island's own history, and how and where it suddenly popped up, was beginning to make my head spin.

∞ Cannoli alla famiglia Iannazzo ∞

Naturally, Vincenzo and Sanchez don't make *cannoli* in the small quantities suggested by the recipe below, but the result should be very close to their ambrosial, hallucinatory sweet creations. I have suggested candied lemon and orange peel in place of the candied pumpkin as they may be a little easier to get hold of.

Makes about 20 small *cannoli*

Scorze: *300g sifted flour* • *10g granulated sugar* • *1 pinch salt* • *1 tbsp honey* • *30g* sugna *(pig fat) or dripping, plus extra for frying* • *White wine*
Filling: *500g sheep's milk ricotta* • *200g caster sugar* • *2 tbsp honey* • *100g candied pumpkin or lemon and orange peel cut into very small bits* • *75g dark chocolate nibs*

Combine the flour, sugar, salt, honey and pig fat and enough wine to make a dough. Cover and rest in a cool place for an hour. Divide dough into four. Roll out each piece until very thin. Cut out ovals about 10cm across (or circles if you can't manage the ovals). Wrap each oval around a mould (a wooden dowel about 3cm round should be fine).

Heat pig fat or dripping until 190°C/375°F/Gas 5. Drop in the *scorze* a few at a time, and fry until the pastry is set and begins to turn creamy-gold. Whip out the dowels using tongs. When the *scorze* are deep brown, lift out and put onto a rack to drain.

Mix the ricotta and sugar and beat very thoroughly. Pass through a sieve. Stir in the honey and beat thoroughly again. Stir in the candied fruit and the chocolate nibs.

Fill the *scorze* generously just before serving them.

∾ Lingua di bue con patate degli Fratelli Pomella ∾

The Brothers Pomella weren't exactly precise in their cooking instructions, and didn't get any more so when I pressed them, so this is my interpretation of their dish.

Serves 6–8

1 calf's tongue • 1 kg onions • 1kg potatoes • Olive oil •
Peperoncino *chilli flakes • Vegetable stock • Salt and pepper*

Boil and peel tongue and cut up into small pieces. Peel and slice
onions. Peel and cube potatoes. Put the tongue, onions and
potatoes in a casserole with a little oil. Stir them round to cover
them with the oil. Season and sprinkle a little *peperoncino* over
them. Pour in enough vegetable stock to cover them, and braise
gently until the potatoes and the onions are cooked.

∞ Farsumagru ∞

This is one of Sicily's universal dishes, except, of course, no two
versions are the same. *Farsumagru* is usually made with beef or
veal, but the Pomella brothers insisted on the heretical view
that it can also been made with pork.

Serves 6–8

*A large piece of veal or pork (about 1 kg) • 2 garlic cloves •
Olive oil • 2 tbsp fresh breadcrumbs •* Peperoncino *chilli flakes
• 2 tbsp pine nuts • 55g pork fat • 115g ground veal or pork •
Salt • 'And whatever else you please' – Carmelo Pomella (eg*
caciocavallo *cheese, ham, etc) • 4 hard-boiled eggs • 400ml
stock • 200ml white wine • 100g fresh peas • 100g chopped
blanched carrots • 100g diced potatoes*

Flatten out meat into one thinnish piece about 2cm thick and
20cm x 30cm. Be careful not to tear the meat. Crush the garlic
to a paste and fry in a little olive oil. Add the breadcrumbs,
enough of the chilli flakes to give the *farsumagru* enough pep

for your taste and season with salt. Fry until the breadcrumbs are golden. Decant into a bowl and add the pine nuts. Cut the pork fat into small bits and fry with the ground veal or pork. Add 'whatever else you please'. Mix well and season. Peel the eggs and slice the end off just exposing the yokes. Lay the beaten veal or pork flat and spread half the stuffing mixture over its surface. Lay the eggs in a line down the middle, then spread the rest of the mixture over the top. Roll the meat over the stuffing so that it is neatly wrapped up. Tie at strategic points to keep in place and tuck in the ends so the whole package in sealed.

In a pan, heat some oil and brown the outside of the meat all over. Add the stock and wine. Poach gently for an hour, turning regularly. Take out the *farsumagru*. Add the vegetables to the poaching liquid and turn up the heat to reduce. Slice the *farsumagru* and serve with the vegetables and reduced juices.

∞ Babbaluci a picchipacchi ∞

The dish of snails suggested by the *babbaluci* hunter of Corleone seemed just a bit minimalist, so here is a slightly more sophisticated classic.

Serves 6
200g bran • Several handfuls of little grey snails • Vinegar •
Olive oil • 1 onion • 1 stick of celery • 500g very ripe tomatoes
• Salt and pepper

Put the bran into a bucket and leave the snails in it for six to seven days to purge themselves. Wash the snails thoroughly in water and vinegar. Put the snails into a saucepan, cover with water, bring to the boil and simmer gently for about 20 minutes. Put some oil in a terracotta dish and heat gently. Chop the onion and celery finely and add. Cook until soft. Peel, deseed and chop the tomatoes. Add them. Season and cook for 15 minutes. Add the snails and cook for a further 5–6 minutes.

Signor Siracusa the Elder, by his vats of wine, Villalba

CHAPTER THREE

Grace and Flavour

❧

Ficuzza – Villalba

The Antica Stazione stood in the middle of the great Bosco di Ficuzza, a forest of oak, chestnut and ilex, much reduced in size according to the guidebooks, but still large enough to be remarkable in Sicily, which had been thickly forested a thousand years ago. The trees had been gradually stripped away by the island's succession of invaders and conquerors to provide the raw materials for their navies. Somehow the Bosco di Ficuzza survived.

The Antica Stazione, as its name suggests, had been a railway station in its glory days. It's hard to see why there should have been a station there at all, had it not been for the passion of the Bourbon royal family for hunting in the Bosco di Ficuzza. In 1803, Venanzio Marvuglia had built a splendid neo-classical hunting lodge for his royal patrons nearby. As a result of royal patronage, the station, while not on the same grand scale as the hunting lodge – the Bourbons must have taken their hunting very seriously indeed – had a certain four-square magnificence to it. But the last train pulled out of Ficuzza in

1954 and the station stood neglected, slowly becaming derelict, ruined and roofless, trees and vegetation growing up through its finely proportioned rooms.

In 2001 its cause was taken up by Nino Barcea, a young man of extraordinary energy and determination. With the help of his family and a motley collection of friends, this railway palace was brought back to life. Little by little the fabric of the building was reclaimed, the trees evicted, the roof replaced, the outside repointed and painted a rich cream, the land around landscaped, the dining room and kitchen equipped – and the station was reinvented as a restaurant with rooms and regular jazz concerts. In front was a delicious garden on which a hoopoe hopped and dug for its dinner as I arrived to get ready for mine.

᠙᠙

Dinner. Normally I am all for conviviality at the table. Food and drink and conversation, amity, affection, laughter, are all of a piece. Eating together has always seemed to me to be an essential human activity, if not *the* essential human activity (all right, eating and sex are the *two* activities without which the human race cannot continue, as Carlo Petrini, the saintly founder of Slow Food, is fond of pointing out; the rest is shadow play). Many of my happiest moments have been spent at one table or another. But food can't make a memorable occasion on its own. You can eat the finest food in the world, and if the company is dross it will be ashes in the mouth. You can have shepherd's pie or corned beef hash with a bottle or two of Bulgarian merlot in the privacy of your own home, in the company of friends and family, and remember it for ever. In the end, food is not simply about the immediate sensation. It's really about memory. It's about those divine moments you can call to mind 20, 30, 40 years on. And, of course, best of all are those times when food, drink, company all fuse into a perfect crescendo of pleasure.

Having said all that, there are times when I like eating on my own, undistracted by the need to make intelligent conversation with someone else, simply watching the dramas unfold at other tables or drawn into a process of profound contemplation on some matter or other on a tidal rip of wine.

That was how I became thoughtful about *caponata* in a way that only the best part of a bottle of burly, ink-black Nero d'Avola can make you thoughtful. The wine reminded me of a gloriously ridiculous scene in a ludicrous film called *The Adventurers* starring the late, great Alan Badel playing a rampaging South American dictator in a very dressy uniform. At one point he hurls away a flagon of wine with the words, 'Take away this cat's piss and give it to the women. Bring me the strong red wine of Corteguay,' or some tosh very like that. It's been a family saying ever since. This Nero d'Avola put me in mind of the strong red wine of Corteguay. Briefly I missed my brothers and my sister. Given their greed, they would have enjoyed the Antica Stazione and its *caponata*.

This was dark-hued, glossy and sumptuous. It came as part of the antipasto package, alongside slices of *melanzane*, the variety of aubergine known as *violetta*, cut as thin as a page of this book, grilled and dusted with slivers of raw garlic and chopped parsley; slices of mild mannered pecorino; thick, soft, amiable slices of unaged salami; and cheerful, slippery pickled mushrooms and artichoke hearts. These had long since vanished. Only the *caponata* remained. I turned it over with my fork. I prodded it and pondered on its origins.

Essentially *caponata* is just a vegetable stew, based on *melanzane*, onions, celery and tomato. Its defining characteristic is that it is sweet and sour. That's the easy part. Dig around a bit, and things start getting complicated. To begin with, no two *caponata*s are the same. This was a great, dark, sticky, long-braised version, with the texture of celestial mulch and a deep, rich, booming flavour. I ate other versions that danced and tripped over the taste buds, as dainty as fairies. On my Sicilian journey I ate *caponata* studded with olives, and *caponata* with capers. I was told of *caponata*s adorned with squid and octopus tentacles, and others with almond slivers and chocolate shavings. It all depended on the personal or local loyalties of the cook. I might have got fed up with its appearance on each and every menu, had it not been like eating a different dish every time. Like pasta, *caponata* may be generic in its title but it is most particular in its reality.

The secret lies in how much vinegar you use, says one cook. No, you can only use this particular *melanzana*, says another. The point is the celery, says a third. It can be made with artichoke hearts, says a fourth. That's heresy, says a fifth. It's only a vegetable stew, says a sixth, so you can use whatever vegetables are in season. It was created by fishermen as a way of preserving vegetables when they went to sea, a seventh offers, and they would have added the tentacles of squid or octopus. So there is no single, authentic recipe for *caponata*. There are as many versions as there are cooks, and each cook holds to their own, passionately and unswervingly.

The truth is that *caponata* is a concept. It has a general structure and a few loose rules, and away you, the cook, can go. *Melanzana* has to be the base. That is a strict rule. But how much? And which type of *melanzana*? The long, black ones, the fat black ones or the round pale purple ones? And how large or how small should the pieces of *melanzana* be when you cut it up? That is as much a matter of debate as rival interpretations of certain biblical or Koranic texts.

☙❧

Vinegar. You have to have vinegar, because vinegar gives the *agro* part of the *agrodolce* effect that is one of *caponata*'s distinguishing characteristics. But how *agra* should your *caponata* be? Barely perceptible? Mild and gentle? Or firm and assertive? Or somewhere in between?

Vinegar is an ancient condiment. That's not surprising. Wine has been going off since man first started making it. It happens when certain naturally occurring bacteria drop in uninvited, and set off a chain reaction that turns alcohol into acetic acid. Vinegar's gifts as a preservative and flavouring agent have made it a store-cupboard essential since before records began. It seems that the Babylonians were making vinegar from date wine, raisin wine and beer in 4000 BC.

These days we don't like leaving things to nature. Nature can be a bit arbitrary in her results. There are three methods by which most vinegars are produced: the Orleans method, which has been on the go since the Middle Ages; the trickling method, which we owe to the eighteenth-century Dutch scientist Herman Boerhaave; and the submerged culture method, which is thoroughly modern. You can make vinegar out of practically any liquid as long as it contains alcohol, because you need the sugars in alcohol to turn to acid. Vinegars vary in acidity from 7 per cent at the high end, which is pretty enamel-stripping, to as low as 2 per cent in black Chinese vinegar. Aside from balsamic vinegar, the instant miracle condiment of the contemporary kitchen, which is made by none of the above methods, Sicilians don't seem too fussy about their vinegars. Any old vinegar will do. *Caponata* has to have a sweetness, too. Although the Arabs introduced sugar cane to Sicily, and Sicily exported sugar to Italy and elsewhere during the Middle Ages, earlier honey would often have been the more widely used sweetener (and still is in some areas) – sugar was a prohibitively expensive luxury until well into the nineteenth century, when a method for extracting it from beet was perfected by Franz Karl Archard in Germany.

❧

However you adorn and decorate it, the body of *caponata* still has to be made of *melanzane*, onion, celery and tomato, although I did come across a celery-less one in Catania. So we know that *caponata* in its present form is a relatively recent dish. By relatively recent, I mean it can't be older than five hundred years, because tomatoes, like the chocolate favoured by some Sicilian *caponata* cooks, didn't get to Europe from Mexico and Peru until the Spanish brought them back around 1543. At that time Sicily was part of the Spanish Empire, and ruled by Spanish viceroys, so it would have been a natural progression for these exotic fruits to have made their way from central court to satellite colony.

Melanzane are not indigenous to the island, either, although they have been around rather longer. The eggplant, as we used to call the vegetable in our homely way, has made a long journey from the shores of India, where small versions grew wild, via the eastern Mediterranean and Turkey. Neither the Romans nor the Greeks seem to have known anything about it, and it would appear that it is yet another vegetable that the Sicilians owe to their cultured Moorish occupiers. It has been cultivated since the fifteenth century. (It had reached England by the late sixteenth century, where John Gerard sounded a familiar grumpy note in his *Herball* of 1597, advising his readers 'to content themselves with the meate and sauce of our own country than with fruit and sauce eaten with such peril; for doubtless these apples have a mischievous quality.'

Celery, on the other hand, is made in the Mediterranean where it grew, and still grows, wild. The wild variety has to be cooked to be edible, and has a much more penetrating flavour than the civilised, crisp and crunchy versions we are familiar with today. The Romans used it as seasoning, a quality it brings to *caponata*. They also believed that wreaths of celery leaves could ward off hangovers. It seems that they were as self-delusory about hangover deterrents as we are.

But where did the taste for sweet and sour originate, and why has it survived? Chinese cooks have been whipping up sweet and sour combinations for several millennia. The Romans had a penchant for sweet and sour food: Apicius lists various *agrodolce* dishes – *porcellum coriandratum* (pork in coriander) in *piscibus elixis* (sauce for poaching fish) – in his compendium of recipes, *De Re Coquinaria*, which appeared in the late fourth or early fifth century AD. The combination was not unknown in the Arab world either, where fruit – apricots and pomegranates – is used to achieve this result.

Or could the taste for a mixture of sweet and sour be a survival of the dietary theories of the second-century Greek physician Galen, which held sway over European tastes until medical advances in the seventeenth century? Galen came up with the higher theory of humours (humours being black bile,

bile, phlegm and blood) first propounded by Theophrastus, a follower of Aristotle and, incidentally, a vegetarian. According to Galen humours were formed in the body, rather than ingested. He believed that different foods could produce different humours, and that humours could be regulated through correct diet. Hence sweetness balancing sourness. It seems curious that the heavy artillery of modern science seems to be moving towards a modified version of Galen's dietary theories.

And so on. Each ingredient has its history, which it brings to the history of the dish, and that history, too, will vary, according to the ingredients used in a particular place because that place has its own history, and food is a record of that history. Even if the history was sometimes confused and confusing. But no more confused and confusing than so much else.

As I attacked the rest of the Nero d'Avola, a plate of tagliatelle streaked with a sauce of tomato and pork arrived and was demolished. Then a veal chop arrived, and such a veal chop, too. It was massive. It looked as if it had been cut from a brontosaurus. But no, Nino Barcea assured me, it came, like all the other ingredients, from around Ficuzza; in this case an organic farm near Godrano. It certainly was not from one of those soft, pappy, milk-fed calves that had never seen the light of day. This veal had seen the sun and moved about those clover-rich fields. It had a bit of muscle to it, and so texture and so flavour, and so satisfaction – and so to bed, head singing slightly, more questions than answers.

ℰℰ

I left the station at Ficuzza after a short, sharp coffee and a *bocconcino*, a kind of pyramidal scone made of flour and *sugno*, split in half and spread with ricotta. The crumbly, wheaty and slightly malty *bocconcino* made just the kind of frugal breakfast needed to speed me on my way in the highest of spirits. It was a grand day, hot by 8 a.m., hotter by 9, and the temperature still climbing. The sky was the purest eggshell blue, profound, limitless.

I took the road to Godrano which led through the Bosco di Ficuzza, populated with docile cattle. The brilliant sunshine through the leaves caused the floor of the forest to ripple as if under water. The verge was brilliant with wild euphorbia and delicate thistles the nacreous pink of mother-of-pearl. Not only had the forest once been a favoured hunting ground for the Bourbon kings, but in recent years it had been a convenient dumping ground for dead bodies by various Mafia dons. It was difficult to think of either. The shade and flow of air over arms and legs was deliciously cool.

The forest ended at Godrano and I came out into the full blaze of the sun. I stopped to buy lunch at a *salumeria* in Lercara Friddi.

In 1952 Lercara Friddi had been at the centre of the first-ever strike by sulphur miners, about which Carlo Levi had written at the time, and which I had found in a collection of his perceptive journalism about Sicily, *Words are Stones*. He told how the strike had been set in motion by the death of a 17-year-old miner, crushed by a fall of rock. 'A deduction was made to the dead boy's final pay packet,' wrote Levi, 'because, by dying, he had failed to complete his working day; and the five hundred miners each had an hour's pay deducted too – the hour in which work had been halted to remove the boulder from the boy's body and carry it up, from the bottom of the mineshaft, into daylight.'

Levi's lucid prose explores the political, social and criminal issues surrounding this event, always putting them in their human context. He described a pattern of subjugation and exploitation that was essentially feudal – and yet this had happened, I realised, within my own lifetime. Even by the time of the strike, the local sulphur industry was in terminal decline brought about by the production of much cheaper sulphur in America. Lercara Friddi did not seem to have recovered its nerve since. It had a quiet, dusty air to it, as if the life had passed out of it. I went into the *salumeria* in the piazza in front of the cathedral, and asked for bread and sausage and cheese for my lunch.

The proprietor chose a salami. 'This is the best local salami,' he said, and cut a slice. 'Here. Try it.' He said it with a casual, almost throwaway pride.

It had a beautiful, clean flavour, big-hearted and salty. He cut me a slab of salted ricotta – 'our own. And this is the bread you need. The best. Fresh this morning.' Like all the bread I had eaten, it was of exceptional quality, yellow as primroses, firm and springy, with a thick, chewy crust covered in sesame seeds. Was this another reminder of the pervasive influence of Arab tastes? Or could it be a leftover from an earlier period, when Sicily was part of Magna Graecia? The Greeks were also partial to sesame seeds. Did it matter? Did I care? Each item was carefully wrapped. I bought some green and red tomatoes and a bag of cherries at a down-at-heel greengrocery on another part of the square.

I ate my lunch sitting under a bridge over a nameless river that had shrunk to a clear-watered brook in the heat. I squeezed the cherry stones between forefinger and thumb, sending them shooting out into the pool at my feet where a shoal of small, silvery dace darted at them, eagerly stripping the last of the cherry flesh from them. A brilliant red dragonfly hovered and zagged its way over the surface of the water. It was cool under the bridge, where the breeze blew into the shade.

A past, which seemed irretrievably distant in Britain, still framed a whole set of attitudes and behaviour in Sicily. The constant need to adjust to changing perspectives of time and history was perplexing and stimulating in equal measure. The more I got to know the island, the blanker my mind became.

෯෯

The Agriturismo Mappa, just beyond Mussomeli, was literally at the end of the road, and felt like the end of the world – or rather, the whole world seemed to be spread out below the escarpment on which it stood, an undulating, pitching, yawing, hypnotic ocean.

The whole system of *agriturismo* seems admirably rational and intelligent to me. It certainly makes travelling throughout Italy a delight. Certain agricultural establishments – farms of various kinds – are licensed to take in paying guests and run what amounts to a restaurant service. They get financial incentives and tax breaks. In return, they have to serve traditional local dishes based on produce from the farm or the immediate surrounding area. In this way, the farmer gets another source of income, the local cooking traditions are observed, local artisanal produce is preserved and the passing stranger gets a damn good feed. I can't quite see the flaw in that, so perhaps there isn't one.

As I drew up in the area outside the gates of the Agriturismo Mappa, which led on to a fine courtyard, the road was beginning to crowd with smartly dressed men and women standing around with their smartly dressed kids. Suddenly I overheard someone speaking English. After several days of wrestling with Sicilian and Italian, I fell on the speaker with the relief of a thirsty walker who spots a pub. Yes, he said, he lived in Yorkshire, Scunthorpe, to be precise. He had been born at Villalba, just ten minutes away. He had meant to go to America, got as far as Scunthorpe 'and that's where I've been for 20 years'.

His name was Giovanni – or Giova' to his friends – and he ran a successful pizzeria in Scunthorpe. He was here to celebrate the first communion of Salvatore Siracusa, the son of his oldest friend, Loreto, who still lived in Villalba. Giova' introduced me to Loreto, a small, handsome, smiling man with a mobile face and dancing eyes, dapper in a dark suit and white shirt.

'You must join us,' he said, with an expansive, graceful gesture.

'Er. Ahh. Well, no. I'm not sure,' I said with typical British elegance and forthrightness. I wanted to, naturally. It was the kind of chance opportunity of which I had been dreaming since I set out, but I felt I would be taking advantage of his kindness.

'But you must,' said Loreto.

'No. no. It's a family party,' I said.

'It would be an honour for us,' he said.

An honour? I couldn't quite see how, but could I refuse such an open-hearted invitation? So I joined the throng going up the steps to the dining room of the *azienda*, a long vaulted room with a beamed roof supported on stone arches and a terracotta-tiled floor.

There must have been close on a hundred people: parents, grandparents, uncles, aunts, children, grandchildren, nephews, nieces, friends, friends of friends, and me. The dress code ranged from considerable formality to careful informality, from dark suit and tie to carefully pressed jeans and fabulously decorative shirt, from matronly matching skirt and top to figure-caressing white trousers and dashing blouse. If dress expressed different views of self and life, there was nevertheless a deep sense of harmony, of community, about the gathering. There was none of the social awkwardness or painful exploration of social niceties you get in Britain. People talked to one another with absolute familiarity and confidence. It was easy to settle into it.

People were curious about me, but politely, carefully, warmly. I explained my mission, and because it revolved around food this was something with which they could identify. Food was a passport, a lingua franca we could all speak.

The guests eased themselves into dinner in stages. There was a lot of kissing, embracing, rapid exchanges, wandering round, coming, going, coming back again, admiring a baby, kissing a baby, chucking a baby under the chin, talking all the time. And then, quite suddenly, like a flock of starlings coming in to roost, they settled and began to eat, steadily, rhythmically, talking, talking, talking. According to Leonard Sciascia, the great Roman orator Cicero said that 'rhetoric had its origins in Sicily'. It was easy to believe. God knows, Italians are fluent conversationalists but these Sicilians made them seem positively Trappist. The level of conversation was pitched at *allegro vivace*, and it remained that way for the next four hours, fuelled by not inconsiderable amounts of food.

Aperitivo analcolico, tartine, sfogliatine, olive ascolane, mozzarelinne, vedurine panate, read the printed menu. *Insalata di mare; risotto con asparagi e funghi; gnocchetti alla norma; agnello al forno; nodo di salsiccia alla griglia; cosciotto di maiale perigordina; patate mascotte; melanzane alla sarde; macedonia di frutta al maraschino; torta.*

It very nearly did for me, As course succeeded course, and the strain on the top of my trousers grew exponentially, my system groaned under the onslaught, but, spurred on by cries of *'Mangia come un Siciliano* – Eat like a Sicilian' I tore through it all. Around me the other guests ate with the same exuberance with which they talked, the women on equal terms with the men, quite as opinionated, formidable and expressive; qualities shared, it seemed, by all generations. Conversation flowed inexorably and vigorously, taking in the price of *motorinos*; the slavish attitude of the young to brand names; *consumerismo* generally; the differences between the age at which children left home in Sicily – when they get married – to that in Britain – the sooner you can get the little blighters out the door the better; the virtues of eating together; and food. First, foremost, above all, they talked about food.

'No, we don't eat a full four courses at each meal, probably only two, *primo* – pasta – and *secondo* – meat,' said one of the ladies at my table.

'Yes, we still cook every day,' said another.

'Of course our children eat with us. That's normal, isn't it?'

'Not in England?'

'Why not?'

It was a question that I didn't particularly want to go into. The conversation moved from the social to the practical.

'We made our own passata in summer to keep over winter. Don't you have some things you make in summer to remind you of summer in winter?'

'Oh, yes, we make chutney.'

'Chutney? What's that?'

'It's a kind of jam made with apples and raisins or big zucchini and sugar and vinegar and spices.'

'A kind of *mostarda*. It sounds very good. Will you send us a recipe?' And they all laughed.

And yes, they still made the traditional pastries, *mustazzoli*, *biscotti al fico*, *rametti di miele*, *biscotti al lievito*, by hand, at Easter and Christmas and feast days. And yes, the hills produced wild fennel and *origano* and chicory, which they just went out and picked when they needed them. The best of all dishes at this time of year was *spaghetti con le fave*, spaghetti with broad beans, cooked with wild fennel and olive oil.

And there was a whole lot more which, frankly, I didn't quite manage to catch as they slipped into Sicilian and out of it again. The surfeit of food seemed to impair my hearing. The evening was taking on a certain dreamlike quality. I had a heady sense of well-being, of excitement, of pleasure in companionship for the first time for several days. How agreeable it was to abandon myself to pure fun.

The first communicant, aged nine, was presented with a mini-motorcycle which he rode round the courtyard to wild applause, an expression of focused terror on his face. A first communion cake appeared, a crest of cream, coloured a strange, hallucinatory shade of irridescent blue, running round it. Social niceties became increasingly fluid. How often in England, I wondered, would you see a waiter slumped in a chair beside one of the people he was supposed to be waiting on, chatting away as if they were in a bar together? Perhaps it wasn't so surprising. They had all grown up together.

There was champagne to finish. I went over to Loreto Siracusa to give my thanks.

'You must come for lunch with us tomorrow,' he said.

'But I –'

'Please. You must come. Now you are a friend.' And he

placed a hand upon my arm with such grace that I couldn't refuse.

〇〇

Villalba is one of those villages that it's easy to pass through or round, without really giving it a second thought. It has no baroque cathedral to lure the culture hound, no classical remains of note for the antique-bibber. It is much like a thousand other villages all over Sicily: a scramble of streets, some which are cobbled and others a crazy paving of tarmac, three- or four-storey houses, and nondescript shops; quiet, ordinary, apparently orderly. But the appearance of order can have many shades.

Villalba had been the home village of Don Calogero Vizzini, the man responsible more than any other for the re-establishment of the Mafia in Sicily after the Second World War. In John Dickie's masterful and deliciously readable history of the Mafia, *Cosa Nostra,* he tells how the advancing Americans threw out the sitting Fascist mayors and replaced them with other local notables with anti-Fascist credentials, recommended by the Catholic Church or other august bodies.

A key local personality during the years when Mussolini's chief of police, Cesare Siepi, had largely suppressed the Mafia through draconian powers, Don Calo had a de facto record as an anti-Fascist. This made him an ideal figure to be appointed mayor of Villalba by the victorious Americans. From this base he set about rebuilding Mafia power, and became the first true *capo dei tutti capi.* The story is a long and complex one, and anyone even marginally interested could do no better than get hold of Dickie's book.

Don Calo died in 1954, but his legend lived on it seemed. 'He was a man of honour,' Giova' said. 'If you had dispute with a neighbour, you took it to Don Calo and he would decide. You have to remember things were very different in those days. People were very poor then.'

'And if you needed money, he would give to you out of his own pocket,' Loreto assured me. He pointed out his house to me, on the other side of the same street, but further up.

I thought of trying to put a counterview of Don Calo, but decided that it would be discourteous. I wasn't here on a mission of justice, but to listen and learn. It was another of the curious obliquities of the Sicilian relationship with the world.

In Don Calo's time Villalba had been a thriving place of 9000 people or so. Now the population stood at about 1200. The mechanisation of agriculture, and emigration, had thinned the numbers in every town and village in this part of Sicily. There was little industry inland to provide employment.

However, Villalba still managed to keep many of those services that have long since disappeared from British villages of the same size, and which gave it layers of a rich community life. There were at least two butchers, a bakery, a couple of greengrocers', and several bars. And Loreto's – well, what was it? Emporium? General store? Ironmongers? Treasure house? Stacked around the walls and on every conceivable surface were walking boots, kitchen accessories, garden tools, seeds, plumbing equipment, rolls of wire, lengths of plastic piping, hammers, screwdrivers, things to be hammered and screwed, boxes of this, boxes of that, cages for birds, bowls for goldfish, all piled up in an intoxicating jumble. Whatever it was, it kept him and his family, and me, well fed.

Three generations of the Siracusa family lived in a modest

three-storey house a few streets away. The shaded terrace at the top of the building looked out over the rooftops of the village and formations of swifts scything through the warm air, towards the celebrated vineyards of Regaleali. The entire terrace had been rearranged in my honour, so that 11 people could sit down for lunch. There were Loreto and his wife, son, daughter, a brace of formidable grannies, one grandfather, a cousin who lived in Switzerland with his rather sumptuous Brazilian girlfriend, and Giovanni, the pizza king of Scunthorpe, who was stocking up with food and gossip before setting off for England in a van loaded with olive oil and other mementos of home.

I can eat the lunch again in my memory: *ditalini con fave e piselli finocchietti*; *costoletta di maiale alla griglia*; *melanzane alla parmegiana*; *insalata di fagioli*; *frutta*; *tiramisu di fragole*, Sicily's answer to Eton Mess.

The *ditalini* came first, small, cream-coloured tubes with a beige-green vegetable stew in which I could see limp feathers of fennel. It wasn't a dish which advertised its beauties extravagantly, but when I slipped a spoonful of it into my mouth – it was more of a thick soup than a conventional pasta dish – the earthy sweetness of the vegetables sharpened by the intensity of the wild fennel lifted it to a level of celebration. It was pleasing in its soothing slipperiness, in the exquisite harmony of its flavours, in the way it filled out to envelop my senses, in the degree to which it spoke of the people and the place and the seasons. Next week the Siracusa family would not be making this dish, explained one granny, because the broad beans would be finished, and they would be moving on to lentils and tomatoes.

'You see,' said the granny, 'until the last war most people might only eat meat once a week. They ate vegetables, But lentils were a very good source of protein, like chickpeas. Not too many people grow them these days. People can afford meat now, and like to eat it to show that they can. And growing lentils is a lot of work. By hand. Planting them, keeping them free of weeds, digging up the plants when they're ready. That'll be in a week or so's time. And drying them and then shucking the tiny lentils from their pods. It's so time-consuming, and who has the time any more? And who wants to pay the price for the time that it takes? Still, we grew them because the lentils of Villalba are like no other.'

(Later, when I asked other people about the lentils of Villalba, they were gently dismissive in that uniquely subtle way all Sicilians seem to have. Ah, yes, one would say, the lentils of Villalba, very good. But have you tried the lentils of Leonforte? And they would say this in a tone of voice that suggested – no more – that the lentils of Villalba weren't quite so good as those of Leonforte. Sicilians are just as unimpressed by other villages' or regions' produce as other Italians; but they are more subtle in the way they express their discrimination.)

The pork chops arrived.

'Matteo, you're the guest. You must help yourself first.'

The chops were gilded in parts, thinner than those you would find in Britain, which meant they could be grilled through without taking on the texture of old rope. The delicacy of knives and forks was dispensed with, the grannies leading the way. We all ate with our fingers.

The green bean salad was good, but it was the Siracusa version of *melanzane alla parmegiana* that pointed to the beauty and brilliance of Sicilian home cooking. In this case the *melanzane* had been sliced very thin, almost paper-thin, cooked *a padella* – fried very quickly in very little oil – and then spread lightly with tomato passata and sprinkled with grated *ricotta salata* (salted ricotta). This treatment turned a dish that can be something of a stomach stopper into a light and elegant delight.

What was remarkable about any of the food? Nothing, in truth. It wasn't flashy or extravagant. It was everyday food, plain, straightforward. There was no pretence about it or the way it was produced. But it was a joy to eat. It wasn't simply the occasion or the company. Each dish had a particular beauty, made a point with a direct simplicity that disguised immaculate craft. The two grannies and Signora Siracusa went about their business in the kitchen with that unfussy, unhurried, confident manner that comes from long, long practice. This was the way they had cooked every day of their lives. They were intelligent, independent-minded women, but they stayed at home, ran their households and cooked the meals for their families. That was how life was. But it is difficult to see this rigorous, prescriptive pattern lasting much longer. Even in Sicily women are beginning to assume the right to go out to work, to escape for a time from the tyranny of domestic servitude, or from some of it anyway.

I felt ambivalent about this. On the one hand, I could see just how limited, stifling even, this pattern of life would be for anyone with ambition or curiosity. On the other hand, it created such a sense of family, of community and security. And, of course, it preserved the food culture. What would be lost if, like the rest of Europe, the family unit dissolved in Sicily? What would happen to Sicily if it did? It provided a measure of stability and protection in a chaotic and brutal world, just as mine had done for me throughout my life. At the same time, family loyalties and connections created the nexus through which the Mafia exerted its influence.

Suddenly I realised with some alarm that I was sloshing back the family red wine in a very un-Sicilian manner, putting away two glasses to each one of theirs. The family drank very frugally, like all Sicilians I had come across, and only when food was on the table. I throttled back on my consumption.

By various degrees, we got around to discussing the difficulties I had had finding somewhere to have a siesta after lunch. As pants the hart for cooling stream when heated in the chase, so I panted for a bit of shade and some ground on which to lie in it after another oversubstantial tuck-in. When I made a similar trip up Italy a few years before, it was easy to pick some likely olive grove or shady spot tucked away, park the Vespa, lay down my bleary head and snooze away until refreshed. The trouble was Sicilians seemed to have a great respect for private property, and when I spotted shade and ground they were invariably surrounded by a fence or barbed wire, or entry was prevented by a length of chain, and I was forced to ride on unrefreshed. It was a problem, they all agreed.

Lunch finally came quietly to a close at about 4 p.m. after the luscious strawberry tiramisu and coffee. No, they didn't eat like this every day, they assured me. The pattern now was to eat *il primo piatto*, the pasta course, at lunch, and then the *secondo piatto*, meat, in the evening. They had made this lunch for me, to make me feel welcome in Sicily. I wanted to embrace them all. I felt overwhelmed by such kindness, and rather ashamed that I hadn't any way of returning it.

At this point Old Man Siracusa, the grandfather, who bore an uncanny resemblance to Malcolm Muggeridge, a waspish, Jeremiah-like pundit of my youth, spoke to me for the first time. He had had an operation on his throat some years ago, reducing his voice to a whispery rasp, which rendered his Sicilian even more difficult to decode. After much patient repetition, and gracefully eloquent gestures of his hands and arms, he got me to understand that big meals were very much a family habit. Why, down on the smallholding where they grew the vines and made the wine we were drinking, they had lunches for 50 or more, underneath the white mulberry tree – children, grandchildren, nephews, nieces, friends. Would I like to go and see it? Feeling both full and sleepy, rather grumpily I went with him.

We rattled out of town in his incredibly dilapidated Fiat 850, turned off the road on to a bumpy track and finally stopped by a large shed. This was where he spent most of his days now, from about seven in the morning until six in the evening, he explained, as we drew up, He was very happy here after a lifetime on the road selling electrical goods all over Italy. No, he had never been abroad, had never felt any need to travel that far.

And here were the Guasco vines from which the wine was made, and here the press where the grape juice was extracted, and the plastic drums where it gradually turned into the eminently drinkable stuff I had been downing with such enthusiasm at lunch. He grew olives as well. There was a medlar, a lemon tree, apricots and peaches. There was the considerable vegetable garden, with the last of the broad beans and peas looking brown and wilted. But artichokes, zucchini and *melanzane* were well on their way, and tomatoes and basil. He showed me the chickens in their run, and the long trestle table underneath the white mulberry tree where the great family picnic barbecues were held. I tried to show the appropriate interest and enthusiasm, but I was feeling sleepier and sleepier, wondering when I could decently escape and resume my search for a quiet patch of shaded land and a nap.

'And now you must have a sleep,' he said. I gawped at him. 'Here,' he said. He opened the door of the shed. 'See, there's a bed.'

It suddenly dawned on me that he had picked up on my plaintive remarks over lunch and, with such grace and tact, had brought me here. I nearly burst into tears. Instead, I lay down and slept while he sat on a chair under the mulberry tree outside in the heat of the afternoon.

∾ Caponata del Antica Stazione di Ficuzza ∾

I could have filled the whole book with recipes for *caponata*. It crops up as part of every selection of antipasti in every trattoria, restaurant or home. And no two versions are the same. Anyway, here's one of the best.

Serves 8

10 medium melanzane (aubergines) • *250ml extra virgin olive oil* • *1 celery stalk* • *500g green olives (stoned)* • *1kg onions* • *250ml red wine vinegar* • *5 tbsp caster sugar* • *1l sugo (tomato sauce)* • *200g strattu (very concentrated tomato purée)* • *50g capers*

Wash the *melanzane* and cut into 1cm cubes. Do not peel. Heat some olive oil in a frying pan. Fry the cubes of *melanzane* until lightly browned. Drain on kitchen towel.

Slice the celery stalk and blanch the celery and the olives briefly in boiling water. Refresh in cold water.

Heat more oil in the frying pan. Slice the onions very thinly and fry until soft. Add the vinegar and the sugar. Cook until you have a sweet-sour mixture. In a saucepan heat the *sugo* and

SWEET HONEY, BITTER LEMONS

the *strattu*. Add the sweet-and-sour onions and the olives, celery, capers and, finally, the *melanzane*. Take off the heat and mix thoroughly. Cool for at least 24 hours.

∾ Ditalini con fave e piselli finocchiati ∾

This recipe, and the two following, have been provided by the wonderfully hospitable Siracusa family.

Serves 6

1 small onion • 1 bunch wild fennel • 150ml extra virgin olive oil • 1kg podded broad beans • 300g podded fresh peas • Salt and pepper • 500g ditalini *pasta • Mature ricotta*

Chop the onion finely and chop the wild fennel into small bits. Put them into a pan along with the olive oil, broad beans and peas. Cook very gently for 20 minutes stirring frequently. Season.

Cook the *ditalini* in boiling water. Drain, keeping a little of the water. Add to the vegetables along with enough water to make a slightly sloppy mixture. Serve with mature ricotta to grate over each plate.

∾ Melanzane alla Parmegiana versione la famiglia Siracusa ∾

Serves 4

2 round violet melanzane *(aubergines) • Salt and pepper • Extra virgin olive oil • 1 garlic clove • 500g tomato passata • 1 bunch basil • 100g grated Parmesan*

Cut the *melanzane* into slices about 5cm thick. Sprinkle salt over each slice of *melanzane* and leave them under a weight for 2 hours. Wash and dry them thoroughly. Heat some olive oil in a frying pan and when smoking, fry the slices until lightly browned on each side. Drain on kitchen towel.

Pour some olive oil into a saucepan. Fry a garlic clove in it until it begins to colour. Add the tomato passata. Simmer gently for 45 minutes. Season and allow to cool completely.

Arrange the slices of *melanzane* in a serving dish, spreading each with some of the tomato salsa, basil leaves and grated Parmesan as you go.

∽ Tiramisu alle fragole ∽

Serves 6
300g ripe strawberries • 7 dsp caster sugar • 3 egg yolks • 500g mascarpone • 1 box of pavesini *biscuits*

Hull the strawberries and sprinkle with 3 dsp of sugar. Beat the remaining sugar into the egg yolks. Add the mascarpone and most of the strawberries. Mix well. Arrange the *pavesini* in a layer in a dish. Spread half of the mascarpone/strawberry mixture over it. Another layer of *pavesini* and the rest of the mixture. Chop up the remaining strawberries and dot the bits all over the surface of the tiramisu. Chill in the fridge for at least 2 hours.

*Market day at the Scuola Elementare Statale
Don Milani, Caltanissetta*

CHAPTER FOUR

'E Novi Canzuni
Putiri Cantari'

('And new songs to sing')

☯☯

Villalba – Caltanissetta –Villarosa

The countryside beyond Villalba was soundless under the brilliant sun. This was the region of wheat, the *grano duro* or *frumento duro*, hard durum wheat for which Sicily had been famous since the Greeks. Cato the Wise had called the island 'the nation's store house, the nurse at whose breast the Roman people is fed'. It seemed to me that the interior of Sicily wouldn't have changed much since Cato's day. There would have been more people to work it and more trees to give them shade. But the wheat stood as it must have stood then, in various stages of ripeness.

From far off it had a soft, downy quality, where the sun caught the long thread-like extensions of the husk round each ear. In some of the fields the harvest had already been taken in, the straw lying in long, snaking, golden necklaces or baled into neat blocks like some abstract art installation in a monumental setting. Beyond these, other fields fell away to yet others, one growing beans for silage to judge by its dark brown colour and rough texture, and in a fold there was a river of fluid, green grass set with umbellifers of mustard-yellow fennel. And then more wheat, still green and ripening, and further irregular-shaped sections mounting up the hills on the far side. There were rocky outcrops, and a dusty white road winding over the brow of a lower hill and disappearing behind it, and a small village on the crest of the further hill that defined the view. And above it all was the unbroken blue of the sky, shading from pale, hydrangea blue in the far distance to a cobalt of infinite depth overhead.

For someone brought up among the rich water meadows of the Thames valley, where intimate panoramas were bounded by green woods and polite rounded hills, and the sound of traffic moving along roads was ever present, there was something inexpressibly exotic and thrilling about the openness, brilliance and silence of this landscape. I felt as if it really lay the other side of a window against which I was pressing my face.

A small blue butterfly jigged beside the road. A pigeon winged its way downhill. Then everything was still. While the land further west had been an ocean of green vines, here it was spread out like a great, undulating display of carpets, each slightly different in shape, colour and texture from the next: sandy yellow, sandy brown, coir brown, tan brown, milk chocolate brown, brown tinged with green, brown dotted with dark holly tufts, brown stitched with red of poppies round the edge, and then green, sea green, spring green. But it had the same roll and a sweep to it, a leisurely, unpredictable, asymmetrical ebb and flow from horizon to horizon.

It was too hot to stay still. I climbed aboard Monica and set a course for Caltanissetta, suddenly cooled by the rush of wind caused by being on the move. It was a delicious moment.

◎◎

In one of the side chapels of the cathedral in Caltanissetta is the bust of Johannis Jacomo, once bishop of Caltanissetta and Ragusa, frozen in full oratorical flow, mitred head thrown back, arm flung out. The sculptor had clearly done nothing to diminish the bishop's passion for the good things in life. Hs chins lap down over the collar of his surplice. His lips are full and fleshy and the lids of his eyes heavy. There's something repellent about the man, but there was something deeply humorous in the way the sculptor had passed judgement on him.

Normally I am not one for baroque ecclesiastical architecture. I was schooled in the graceful modesty of Norman churches and the soaring purity of Gothic cathedrals. The combination of the spiritual and worldly theatricality in Baroque was too extrovert, too indulgent, too fanciful for me. Nevertheless, I fell in love with the duomo in Caltanissetta, with its unintimidating scale, with the plants sprouting from various corners and cornices outside, with its cool, rippling interior and delicious riot of ornamentation. There wasn't a surface that wasn't covered with paintings, mouldings, trompe l'oeil, decorative folderol of some kind. The elegant, fluid lines of the pictures were contained within formal frames of confident flamboyance, and the colours were the pastel shades of the ice creams I had seen in the tubs at the Gran' Caffe up the road – pistachio green, raspberry red, strawberry pink, cherry purple, almond white, custard cream.

Caltanissetta marks the centre of Sicily, but guidebooks do not treat the town kindly. They lavish their encomiums on the more celebrated and better preserved beauties of Enna not far away. They tend to be dismissive of Caltanissetta's qualities, seeing little of interest in its undulating, serpentine streets.

It was true that it seemed to be a town still struggling to come to terms with the loss of its once prosperous past. Until its collapse in the 1950s, Caltanissetta had been the hub of Sicily's sulphur production. However hellish working conditions had been, and however appalling had been the exploitation of the miners, the industry had still brought some kind of well-being to the town to judge by once handsome terraces of miners' houses and some of the more substantial buildings. But that was all long gone. The last sulphur mine had closed decades ago. Severe bombing during the Second World War had damaged the fabric of Caltanissetta further, but even that did not account for the air of having been passed over that hung about parts of the town. Its most recent brush with celebrity, when the trial of the then *capo di tutti capi*, Toto Riina, had been held there 15 years ago, seemed to have left little of lasting consequence, aside from the brutalistic high-security courthouse.

But Caltanissetta's slightly hangdog manner appealed to me. Even in its down-at-heel state, it was so much more vital and attractive than the dreary sameness of so many pros- perous and bustling British towns, with their identical identikit town centres, their high streets a corridor of the same chain stores with the same fascia selling the same cloned products, so that it is difficult to tell whether you are in Cheltenham or Ipswich, Taunton or Aberdeen. The acme of civic achievement in the UK is the presence of M&S, Boots, Waitrose, Tesco and Sainsbury's, Costa Coffee and Starbucks, McDonald's and Pizza Express, Monsoon and Fat Face, and no town council can rest until it has a full house. Homogeneity, similarity, imitation, replication are seen as the criteria for success – not difference, variety and diversity. It is one of the abiding ironies of an unregulated capitalist commercial sector that it produces a uniformity almost as drab, tedious and limited as the state control of communism.

This is not an accusation that could be made about Caltanissetta, with its *gelateria* and cafés, wine bars and restaurants, butchers and bakers. Almost every street away from the centre had a greengrocery stall parked in it. It might lack Max Mara and Armani, McDonald's and Auchan, but it had Giuseppe Castiglia, a butcher shop specialising in meat from local, rare breeds of cattle, sheep and pigs; Il Geraci, makers of *torrone* (nougat). Above all there was a rich daily market in Via Benintendi, snaking between the old Piazza Mercato (now a municipal car park, itself a comment on changing urban values) and the Corso Vittorio Emmanuele, Caltanissetta's main street.

Here were cascades of peas and broad beans, cataracts of cherries, glowing mounds of apricots. Here was a universe of tomatoes – small tomatoes, large tomatoes, tomatoes the size of cherries, tomatoes like plums, tomatoes as squat as toads; lambent, fully ripe tomatoes, tomatoes streaked with gold and tomatoes as green as apples. There were capers in salt, capers in vinegar, fresh capers in a plastic bowl, caper leaves for a salad. There was a profusion of chicories and lettuces, with deckled-edged leaves, smooth-edged leaves, leaves curved gracefully to a point, leaves tinged with purple, shaggy leaves, shiny leaves, shades of infinitely varied green, glistening, pearls of water hanging to them.

There was something so voluptuous about the sheer abundance, something seductive and playful. It made me feel slightly drunk. It reminded me why I fell in love with food in the first place. Why is it that you can spend 20 minutes and £75 in a supermarket and come out feeling depressed? Why is it you can spend twice that in a market, feel your arms being pulled out of their sockets and your fingers cut from your hands by the weight of the bags you are carrying, and still come out sunny and exalted? Well, I do, anyway.

There was real competition between the stalls, unlike the artificial, carefully graded, highly organised competition among the cartel of supermarkets in the UK. In the market in the Via Benintendi I could have shopped at a dozen fruit and vegetable stalls that differed in the price, quality and frequently provenance (Ribera, Gierra, San Marzanno – *feschissimi*, Romana – Sexy, Dolce, Dolcissimi, Teneri) of their melons or apricots or peas or borlotti beans or broccoli or onions in less time than it would have taken me to wheel my trolley from one end of the fruit and vegetable section of a Tesco's to the other – let alone get in my car and drive to another supermarket to compare prices and quality.

There were the small, incidental scenes, too, like details in a painting by Renato Gattuso – the man with no teeth selling bunches of pungent dried oregano on the bonnet of his car; the saucy banter between a busty young blonde woman handing over melons to a middle-aged man in a blue cap; a wrestling match between a couple of white-haired ladies whose baskets on wheels had become interlocked; a small boy hawking shiny, purple-black *melanzane* from a blue plastic tray balanced between the palm of his hand and his shoulder who made his way carefully up and down between the stalls. He had a shy, serious look. He couldn't have been more than eight.

As the day advanced and the air became hot, the smells in the market grew sharper, stronger, more insistent, more tempting – the keen tang of olives (black olives, green olives, stoned olives stuffed with peppers, small wrinkled olives and olives as big as strawberries, olives sprinkled with rosemary and garlic and lemon peel and oregano); oregano itself, wild and heady, in bunches resting on the back of a *motorino*; basil; wild fennel; garlic hanging in tangled tresses; pungent salted anchovies; peaches; perfumed strawberries; rank fish and fruity cheeses; smells tangling round each other, fusing then separating, always intoxicating.

And here was something I'd never seen before: fresh chickpeas, like marrowfat peas, in their short, fat pods still attached to the plants on which they grew.

And here was something I'd never seen before: long, dusty green, ridged cucumbers, coiled like snakes in a tray. These would never get a showing in a British supermarket. Far too odd and not encased in plastic.

And here was something I'd never seen before: what appeared to be small, dry artichoke heads the size of large thistles, neatly bagged up in brown paper bags.

'What do you do with those?' I asked the man selling them. He had a face like a punctured football. He said something in dialect I couldn't understand. I told him I hadn't understood. He tried again. I still couldn't understand. A friend came to his aid. My confusion was doubled. Embarrassment piled on top of incomprehension. I pretended that enlightenment had suddenly dawned on me. I explained that I was a tourist and so, sadly, had nowhere to cook these exquisite delicacies. They waved me goodbye in high good humour.

All around the voices of the stallholders ululated like muezzins calling the faithful to prayer, words slurring together until they became a single sound, rising and falling, rising and falling. Perhaps this echo of the Muslim world was not accidental. Arab culture runs through Sicilian life like so many threads: through the names – Caltanissetta, itself, is the Italianisation of Kal'at el nissat, the castle of young women – through the language, through the relationship to time, and through the food. So many of the fruits and vegetables on display in the market owed their place to the influence of agricultural techniques introduced by the Moors – oranges, lemons, aubergines, rice. The influence extended beyond growing to the cooking as well. Spices and their uses, sorbets and granitas, sweet pastries, spit roasting, deep frying and stuffing vegetables, are all markers of the Arab kitchen.

'How is the market?' I asked one fruit seller, as I bought a kilo of fuzzy yellow peaches from Ribera. Each proclamation of geographical provenance had a particular significance. The peaches of Ribera are famous for their quality, and these were the first of the season.

'It's OK,' he said. 'It's true that more people use the supermarkets these days. But I still make a decent living. Mind you, I won't get rich. But I won't starve, either.'

I wandered off, the sharp-sweet juice of a peach running down my chin, my only regret that I wasn't walking home with my arms being dragged from their sockets by the weight of the foods I had bought, my fingers being cut off by the thin, stretched handles of the bags I carried, my heart singing with the prospect of the food I was going to cook.

❦

'Ah, but the market isn't what it used to be,' said Pasquale Tornatore, marketing man, food lover, music lover and an evangelist for Caltanissetta. He was concerned about the market's future. 'Young people don't shop there any more. How many young people did you see?'

We were having lunch in the airy flat where he lived with his wife. They both led busy professional lives, but they had made lunch that day as they did most days, quickly and without fuss. It was frugal – a plate of local salamis; pasta with zucchini and garlic; cheese and fruit; one glass of wine each – but the quality of the ingredients radiated good cheer and it was a proper meal, prepared from scratch, eaten at a table, decked out with conversation; not a snack and a smoothie grazed in silence at the desk between meetings.

Actually, I told him, there seemed to be a fair mix of ages among the shoppers, and the majority of the stallholders seemed young. Well, younger than me, anyway.

But Pasquale was not to be comforted. The market was in decline, he declared, the food traditions of Sicily were not what they were. How often had I heard the same lament on the Italian mainland?

There were the supermarkets, of course, he said, although I had yet to see serious one, and it was difficult to find parking in the centre of town so that people could shop at their ease. But the main problem, as he saw it, was that the council had been far too free with the licences they issued to mobile food stalls, to fruit and vegetable sellers in particular, whose produce I had admired. It allowed them to set up their stalls in particular neighbourhoods, taking the market to the customer as it were. This might make life easier for the customer, but it reduced the critical mass of the market, which would go on diminishing as a result.

Pasquale combined an exuberant pleasure in people, food and his other passion, music, with a profound pessimism about the nature of life and the future of the country. He seemed to agree with the great man of Sicilian letters. Leonard Sciascia had said that decadence wasn't a temporary state in Sicily, but a permanent one. It was as if repeated invasions, occupation and exploitation had left Sicilians with a pessimism so deep and so ineradicable that it had turned a kind of defining nihilism into a vital energy.

It led to a disorienting bipolar response to the world. On the one hand, Pasquale saw food as the key to encouraging tourism as a means of regenerating Caltanissetta. He outlined plans for food festivals. He talked enthusiastically about local delicacies such as the *cuddrireddri di Delia*, a kind of biscuit recently rescued from near extinction. At the same time, he was distressed by the lack of food knowledge among the town's children that, together with Slow Food, he had helped to create a vegetable garden at one of the large primary schools. To both responses he brought a burning enthusiasm, profound engagement and an unquenchable energy. I was very happy to be swept along by his enthusiasms, particularly when he told me that the school would soon be selling some of the produce from its garden.

ॐ

Market day at the Scuola Elementare Statale Don Milani. The school was a large, utilitarian building of raw red brick and raw grey cement, surrounded by apartment blocks. It had an unlovely awkwardness about it, even in the bright sunshine. But at the back was the blossoming Progetto Orto Scolastico, tufty rows of sprouting vegetables each authoritatively labelled: *Cavolo, Cipolla Rossa di Tropea, Fragola, Zucchine, Sedano, Ceci*. There must have been half a hectare of them, each row sown with obvious care and marked by black drip-watering hoses. Some vegetables had done rather better than others. The chickpea plants looked robust and healthy, the lettuces sparkled and the cabbages, too, but the onions seemed a bit lost, and the celery definitely needed attention.

On the wide stretch of concrete between the school buildings and the kitchen garden, there must have been over 150 children milling about. Some were helping to cover tables with crêpe paper in eye-wateringly vibrant yellow, green, pink, orange, each decorated with cut-out and coloured-in carrots, *melanzane*, onions and peppers. Behind the tables, posters made by the children, illustrating the key stages of the Progetto Orto Scolastico and strung on cords, drooped in long curves between the cement pillars. As I arrived, a small boy in jeans with massive turn-ups and a white jacket with blue stripes down the sleeves stood in front of them, studying them intently. He remained there for several minutes, quite still, his hands clasped in front of him. Behind him a small, seething scrum of boys and girls surrounded a teacher.

'*Quanti pennarelli, Giuseppe?* How many pens, Giuseppe?'

'*Trenta sette.* 37, miss.'

'*Non si preoccupa.* Don't worry.'

'*Primo scriviamo* – First we write –'

'*Io, signora, io. Sono* – Me, miss, me. I –'

'*Calma te, Salva.* Calm down, Salva.'

Other children with smart greeny-blue peaked caps were busy picking the lettuces that were the mainstay of the day's market. The produce was carefully packed into boxes, roots downwards. Once full, a box was put on one of the tables, with more full boxes stacking up in the shade behind. There were about a hundred and fifty children between eight and ten years old hurtling about. I wondered how their English counterparts would respond to a similar initiative. Probably no differently. It was more interesting than sitting in class. Why had my schooldays never involved selling vegetables we had grown to our parents? It seemed a whole lot more pleasurable and ingenious than the regular crude demands for money for a new gym, swimming pool or school hall.

'How much does each lettuce cost?' I asked one fellow.

'*Boh. Non lo so.*' He had no idea, so he said.

A small girl in pink and grey trainers, pink and white T-shirt and with a pink band in her black hair sat on the kerb running round the edge of the garden, resting her chin in her hands.

The parents started to arrive just after 9 a.m., socially mixed but smartly dressed. Women were in the majority, but there were plenty of dads who had turned out to support their darlings' commercial initiative. The atmosphere was sociable and chatty. No one seemed to mind standing around interminably. From time to time the varied music of mobiles chimed like triangles through the burble of chat.

'Yes, the market is a good idea, very good for the kids,' said one mum in jeans, shirt and trainers.

'They need to know where their food is coming from,' her friend chipped in.

'We're becoming cut off from the past, from our traditions,' said a third woman.

'And they really love it,' said the lady in jeans. 'They take a real pride in it, too.'

Finally everything was ready, the headmistress and dignitaries assembled and the speeches began. No ceremony in Italy is complete without a fairly lengthy demonstration of oratory. The words flowed on and on. Everybody was thanked and clapped. Exhortations were made. The hundred or so parents stood and listened with admirable good humour and patience. There was a low level countercommentary from some of the more restless kids drawn up in massed ranks, the blocks of green-blue caps arranged behind each of the tables.

And then, just before 10 a.m. the market was finally, at long last, declared open, and there was a mad dash to the stalls and bedlam ensued. It made the cut and thrust of the market in the Via Benintendi look as orderly as a village fête. Eager parents pushed to the front waving notes. The kids held the lettuces and cabbages like bridal bouquets. The teachers struggled to control the vigorous engagement of the parents as well as the commercial enthusiasm of their charges. Gradually the mass of parents rotated, those at the back working their way to the front in waves. Further supplies of produce were called for, and picking parties move back on to the garden. Everyone was milling round. Everyone was involved. Everyone was enjoying the occasion hugely.

'How much is a lettuce?' I asked the boy who had previously declared he had no idea how much they were.

'*Due euro, signor.*' However ignorant he might have been about the pricing of the wares earlier, the instincts of street traders obviously lurked just beneath the surface. The official price of each lettuce was one euro.

The market had been a huge success. Everyone said so.

Even Pasquale was delighted, cheerful, energised as I said goodbye to him with much regret. His fervent advocacy of the charms of his native town, the succession of edible delights he had put my way, his intelligent despondency, had cast Caltanissetta in another, gentler, heartening light to the one I had found when I first arrived. It was tempting to linger, but there was more to explore, just over the horizon. There was always somewhere else, there was always the next place.

There were times when the imperative to move felt like a form of tyranny. How often was I tempted to stay where I was, linger a little longer, explore a place more, enjoy the company of its inhabitants a day or two longer? It was a curious relationship, meeting people, becoming friends with them, entering their lives for a few days, becoming involved in their affairs, understanding just a little more about the forces that directed their lives, just beginning to develop the roots of true friendship – and then deliberately breaking all this apart, tearing up the roots and moving on. I never got used to this abrupt separation.

ⓐⓞ

The buzz phrase 'alternative land use' being touted around British agriculture came to mind as I looked out over the demesne of the Azienda Agricola San Giovanello between Caltanissetta and Enna, placid and well tended in the golden evening light. I suspected the story of the place was a familiar one in Sicily; the story of the past coming into bruising collision with the present.

The farm was owned and run by Pietro la Placa and his wife. It had been part of the *tenuto* – feudal estate – of the Barone Bartocelli d'Altamira, Spanish grandees. Pietro, whose nut-brown face peered out at the world from under an unruly mass of grey hair like a shy but inquisitive animal emerging into daylight, was descended from the Bartocelli d'Altamiras through his mother. This vast hereditary estate was preserved intact until the Salic law, which perpetuated the principle of primogeniture, was abolished by the British during the Napoleonic Wars. Since then the estate had been endlessly subdivided between children, which had a marked effect on its economic viability. This was further diminished by the collapse of the sulphur industry – there had been a mine on the estate into the 1950s since the beginning of the twentieth century.

Pietro's share of the great d'Altamira estate had shrunk to 75 hectares, not really workable in economic terms, even when devoted to the organic production of traditional varieties of wheat, olives for oil, almonds and grapes. So he and Signora la Placa took in paying guests like me, with the promise of walking and pony trekking, spa treatment and all the rest; everything, in short, to try and keep the place going. I got the feeling that this was something of a strain on Pietro and his wife, who had the languid style and abrupt manner of Happy Valley habitués in Kenya in the old days. Still, there was no doubting their passion for food.

I was the only guest eating that night in the comfortable, rustic dining room, which made me feel like the only person in a theatre for the performance of a play. If it wasn't for me, the la Placas could have had a night off. But the show had to go on, even if it was only for one. Dinner, which Signora la Placa cooked, began with an *arancini* about the size of a floating mine with a crunchy crust holding together soft rice and a rich centre of minced pork and peas. It was solid, filling, well flavoured and generally rather good.

I had planned another assault on the *Odyssey*, but this virtuous intention was discreetly put aside as Pietro fixed on me in the manner of the Ancient Mariner, clearly determined that my meal should not be a sad, solitary affair. While I dealt with the *arancini*, Pietro introduced the subject of potatoes.

'Potatoes,' he said, 'are curious. They don't play much of a part in Sicilian cooking. Aside from *patate fritti*, that is. Do you know that the only proper Sicilian potatoes come from near Ragusa?'

'Oh,' I said. 'No, I didn't know that.'

'Generally Sicilians', he said, 'aren't so concerned with the minutiae of cooking as Italians.'

That hadn't been my impression ... I just grunted.

'Why, we can only cook *arancini* because the Mori introduced rice growing to the island. That was between 878 and 1060 AD.' He then proceeded to rattle on in an immensely learned and opinionated fashion about Sicilian cooking, about Byzantine influences, Roman remains, Arab elements, Spanish traces. All Sicilians had an astonishing awareness of their own past, it seemed. I supplied grunts and other noises of interest which kept his discourse flowing on.

Spaghetti with tomato sauce arrived. The boiled-milk-and-wheat flavour of the pasta held its own with the fresh, light and fruity sauce.

'And what do you British think of *Principe Carlo* and *la Regina Elizabetta*?' he asked in an abrupt change of direction.

'Eh?' I said.

It was a moment before I worked out he was talking about Prince Charles and the Queen.

'Ah, well. Yes,' I said. ' You see. It's complicated –'

Pietro needed no more from me. He proceeded to have an

intricate, one-man discussion about the advantages and otherwise of a monarchical system over a presidential one.

He didn't even pause when what I had come to realise was the inevitable *secondo piatto* in central Sicily – grilled meat, sausage in this case – arrived. I lost myself in silent contemplation of the virtues of the sausage. It was terrific: dense, salty, meaty. If you have to have grilled sausage, and it seemed I did, then let it be this sausage. But the salad – well, I thought, whatever happens to that delicious variety of leaves you see in the markets? Why were the salads served up in restaurants so anodyne, so boring. It wasn't as bad as in France, where you scarcely ever see a vegetable in a restaurant, but I thought that in Sicily they could do better. Briefly I thought of asking Pietro about this, but decided against it in the interests of harmony and a reasonably early night.

Finally, I said goodnight. So much for my attempt to spend quality time in the company of Odysseus. Given the uneasy nature of my relationship with Homer thus far, perhaps it was just as well. Was I the only person who wished Homer had a bit more narrative drive? Who just wants him to get a move on?

'I have enjoyed our little talk so much,' Pietro said as he showed me out of the dining room. 'Intelligent conversation, discussion, give and take; it's such a pleasure.'

❧

As I swept into Enna, I hit a haze of warm toasting wheat, warm sugar, spice and chocolate. It came from the Caffe Italia in the Piazza Garibaldi.

As a boy, the great Victorian traveller and linguist Sir Richard Burton used to test his will power by placing his favourite dish, strawberries and cream, in front of himself until he had conquered his desire to eat it. And then he would reward himself by scoffing the lot. I took a leaf out of Sir Richard's book. For the moment I resisted temptation for the rewards of high culture, traipsing up to the Castello di Lombardia and stopping off at the duomo on the way, wondering at the hanging garden of weeds sprouting from high on the outside wall and noting the wheat motif at the top of the pillars inside, delighting in exquisite Moorish decorations around the windows of an unnamed, ramshackle building in an unmarked courtyard. Oh yes, Enna has history by the bucket load: Sicel history, Greek history, Roman, Moorish and Norman history, and more besides. It has character, and from the vantage point of the Rocca Cerere above the town you can see all Sicily, or feel as if you can. At 931 metres, it is comfortably the highest town in central Sicily.

But Enna's cultural wonders have been described by far more eloquent and learned minds than mine, and once I had fed my aesthetic spirit I felt it was time to reward my baser, physical nature on the Burtonian principle. I hurried back to the Caffe Italia.

It was an exemplary establishment in every way. It was smooth. It was smart. It gleamed and glinted. The service was crisp and civilised. And then there was the most mind-expanding, drool-inducing display of pastries I had yet seen, *cannoli* in various sizes, *musticioli, cornetti, tartufino, tartalette di frutta, barchette frutte, barchette crema, limoncini, sospirini, mimosini, buschet, babaini, bigne*. It was a treaure chest of goodies, winking and sparkling. I chose a *sfogliatello all' pistaccio*, its glossy, amber-gold corrugated shell, almost as big as a scallop, filled with sweet ricotta pebble-dashed with emerald-green chopped pistachios, and took my place among the coveys of German and French tourists sitting in the sun outside.

It was curious how Sicily's former conquerors and occupiers returned to recolonise it. I remembered Nanni Cucchiara's remark that all Sicily's invaders became Sicilian in the end. Would these ones gradually cease to pour earnestly over their guidebooks, planning their next assault on the next citadel of history or art? Would they be drawn in to the habit of fluent conversation like the Ennesi around them? See this as a purposeful activity? Would I? In truth, this passion for talk made me uneasy. What was the point of it? Did it have any point? Shouldn't it have a point? Shouldn't the conversationalists have been doing something? Such apparently purposeless proceedings conflicted with my more puritan ethic. That, I thought, is my loss. Conversation is a mark of high social culture.

It was one of the many contradictions with which I was wrestling. Every day Sicily threw up notions and experiences that challenged the orderly orthodoxies framed by growing up in northern Europe. Time seemed more flexible, expansive even. Sicilians embraced vitality and what I took to be inherent pessimism with equal vigour. They spoke more and told you less than any other people I had ever come across. Actually, it wasn't so much that they told you less but that what they told you was set out with such obliquity, hidden references and layered significance it might as well have been in code. In fact, it was in code of a kind, and every time I thought I might have cracked part of it something happened that caused me to question my understanding.

The coffee was rich and intense, just as Sicily was turning out to be.

෧෧

I have eaten the Menu aux Truffes in Jamin in Paris when Joel Robuchon was in his pomp. I have lingered over the table at Georges Blanc in Vonnas, and smacked my lips at the cooking of Bernard Loiseau when he was still aspiring to three Michelin stars. I have discussed the fine points of finer dishes with Raymond Blanc and Heston Blumenthal while eating with them. I can still taste the *zuppa di virtu* and frittata of herbs and black truffle that I ate at La Bandiera at Civitella Casanova in the Abruzzo; and the *gnocchi al ragù di capriolo* at La Taverna de li Caldora at Pacentro not far from Sulmona. But I think I can safely say that I did not enjoy the fabulous dishes at these fabulous places any more than I enjoyed four courses at the station café at Villarosa. Great meals are about memory even more than they are about sensory pleasure. This lunch was about both.

It was the sheer improbability of it all that made it such a delight. I had noticed a reference to the Treno Museo at the station in Villarosa, a small town not far from Enna, and with it the briefest of mentions of a café that served traditional Sicilian dishes. It didn't seem a lot to go on, but I saw it signposted as I was zooming along and, on a whim and a prayer, I decided to drop in and take pot luck.

The station seemed completely deserted. Of the promised museum I could only find a few yellowing brochures pinned up inside a glass-fronted noticeboard, but, exploring further, I came across two men seated at one of three or four plastic tables on the platform of the station, chatting away companionably.

'Any chance of something to eat?' I asked, expecting them to say no.

'Certainly,' said one. 'Where do you want to eat? Inside,' and he gestured vaguely down the platform to somewhere I couldn't identify, 'or here?'

'Well, here, I think,' I said, and sat down at one of the plastic tables on the platform.

In short order the man produced a paper tablecloth, a couple of glasses, a knife, fork and spoon.

'What would you like? Antipasto typical from around here – ham, cheese, olives?'

'Very nice,' I said.

'And then for *primo piatto* there's *spaghetti alla carbonara* or *penne con salsa di pomodoro, salsiccie e ulive.*'

'Oh, that one. The second. More Sicilian,' I said.

He agreed that it was more Sicilian.

'And then some meat?'

'With a salad?' I said.

'With a salad. And to drink, wine and water?'

'A quarter of red,' I said. 'And water.'

He disappeared, and I was left looking out across the track to where the main Catania to Palermo motorway curved across the floor of the valley on stumpy pillars. The steep hillsides beyond were tanned and dull gold where the wheat was ripening, and spotted with clumps of dark trees and rectilinear plantations of new olives. The tops of the hills were sharp, rocky and pointed. Downy white clouds drifted across the deep blue sky, their shadows gliding over the rippling, shifting landscape. The railway line bent away to left and to right. The only sound was that of swallows shrilling and sparrows carrying on a hectic social life around the platform. My nostrils pricked at the rich, sweet savour of onions being fried, and garlic and tomatoes. A small, scrawny cat watched me silently in anticipation.

The man appeared holding a plate with three pieces of bread, which had been lightly toasted before being covered with roughly chopped raw tomato seasoned with raw onion in olive oil, and dusted with oregano. The bread had a slight crunch to it and tasted of malted wheat and nutty boiled milk. The tomato was light and fresh, and reminded me that tomatoes were a fruit. The onion added a punchier seasoning, with a breath of oregano. Golly, it was good. The cat miaowed pitifully.

Then came the antipasto. It was, as the man had promised, just ham, cheese and olives. But such ham, such cheese and olives, with precise, pure flavours. The ham was cured pancetta, with creamy fat and sweet, salty meat the colour of coral. The cheese was *toma primo sale*, a local sheep's cheese studded with black peppercorns. It had the softness of a drop scone, and a mild flavour to set beside the ham and the salty, pungent olives.

The red wine in the little jug had the refreshing sourness of plums. It wasn't fancy or well bred, but it was right for the food on platform number one at the station at Villarosa. The first cat was joined by two others, all howling pitifully.

Halfway through the pasta dish a train pulled in. It was a sleek, modern train. People got out and made their way past me. Signora la Placa from the Aziend Agricola San Giovanello darted past and boarded with a wave to me. It only added to the surreality of the day. The pasta, on the other hand, was anchored firmly in reality. It was deep red, redder than a cardinal's hat, redder than poppies, with orange and gold worked into to. It gave a blast of flavour as potent as the colour, meaty, fruity, broad-shouldered, swaggering. There was nothing subtle about it, but it was mighty satisfying. It was the sort of food that made you happy to be alive, to be in such a place.

I thought of the meagre baguettes with their uniform fill-ings, and sandwiches as thick as the *Da Vinci Code* and with as much substance, and of doughnuts and burgers and all the other stuff you find on British railway stations, and lamented. Or I would have done had I not been so transported.

What makes penne streaked with a sauce of tomato and pork so satisfying? Could there be anything more straightforward? Well, yes, there probably could be, but you could never have said this was a fancy dish. Yet it was fabulously pleasing on so many levels. Much had to do with the texture of pasta, I decided – supple, subtle, sexy, firm and yielding at the same time. There is something oddly submissive about it.

And then there is pasta's relationship with its sauce, closer than that of any other food I can think of. Mild though its flavour is, it always retains its character and integrity in spite of the sauce. Or should do. Too often, non-Italians seem to think that the pasta is simply a vehicle for the sauce, and drown the unfortunate tagliatelle or fusilli – or whichever of the thousands of shapes have been chosen to carry the burden – in an ocean of highly flavoured gunge.

But the flavour, and so the quality, of the pasta is a critical part of the dish. You should be able to taste the sauce and the pasta. Consequently, for Italians there is a precise relationship between the two, with this sauce good for this pasta but not for that, and this pasta a perfect partner for that sauce but not for this. It has something to do with the shape and tensile surface, which affects the way different pastas hold their sauces. There are even mathematical formulae to express these things, but as my relationship with maths has always been the same as that of the Temperance League and alcohol, I have avoided them in favour of pragmatic experience.

In other cooking cultures the relationship between all other foods and their accompanying sauces is unequal. Either ingredient or sauce is in the ascendancy. Rice, corn, potatoes all absorb sauces, and so their flavours become subordinate to them. Meat, fish, vegetables are elevated by sauces (or beaten over the head by them). Sauces, according to la *cuisine francaise*, enhance the food they accompany. Indeed, sauces are the point of French cookery. And what would English cookery be without its gravies, chutneys, mustards and jellies? Only pasta lives on equal terms with its sauce. The sauce and the pasta are coevals, each essential to the other in an equal partnership.

The slender coil of sausage and slice of veal weren't quite so full frontal as the pasta, but they were hefty and serious for all that. The sausage was so coarse that the meat could have been chopped by hand. It was juicy and salty. The veal was coarse-grained and brown. A mouthful of meat, a mouthful of salad – crunchy leaves with a touch of bitterness to them, a flash of sprightly vinegar, an ease of oil – another mouthful of meat.

There was a *granita di limone* to come, and a small cup of coffee. The granita was silky, and almost burning in its intensity and chill. It swept my mouth clean of fats and meats and oils and vinegars and all else, and the coffee was fine and fierce.

The traffic moved inexorably and silently along the highway. The sparrows chittered in the metal beams overhead, on the track, on the platform. The cats wept.

∞ Insalata di manzo con cipolle, capperi e premezzolo ∞

I tasted this while watching Giuseppe Castiglia, a butcher in Caltanissetta who specialised in meat from rare breeds, dissect a rib of veal. It was so delicious, I asked for the recipe. The onions of Tropea (in Calabria, on the Italian mainland) are celebrated for their mildness and deliciousness.

Serves 6

1 piece beef skirt (about 1 kg) • 1 onion • 1 carrot • 1 stick of celery • Bay leaves • 2 dsp capers in salt • 2 mild red onions (from Tropea) or mild white onions • 2 tbsp red wine vinegar • 5 tbsp extra virgin olive oil • Pepper

Braise the beef in water with the onion, carrot, celery and bay leaves until falling apart. Drain, shred the meat and leave it to cool. Rinse the capers thoroughly. Slice the onions very thinly. Add to the beef along with vinegar and olive oil. Mix thoroughly. Allow to mature gently for a day or so.

∽ Pasta o furnu ∽

To give you some idea of just how complicated recipe research in Sicily can be, here are three recipes for *pasta o furnu* from Anna Fava, a friend of Pasquale Tornatore. According to her, there are two primary traditions of Sicilian *pasta al forno*, the Catanese and the Palermitan, and then there is her aunt's more informal arrangement. I leave you to make your own choice.

∽ Pasta o furnu Catanisa ∽

Serves 4–6

3 melanzane (aubergines) • Olive oil • 3 hard-boiled eggs • 700g penne or rigatoni • 80g mature sheep's cheese (pecorino) chopped into small cubes • 250g meatballs (made by braising minced beef with fresh peas down until the mixture can be moulded into little balls and cooked in a little ragù) • 80g finely fresh sausage meat • 150g fresh sheep's cheese (Tuma) • 300ml sugo (tomato sauce) • 60g la mollica (fresh white breadcrumbs)

Preheat the oven to 180°C/360°F/Gas 4. Slice the *melanzane* thinly and fry in olive oil until golden brown. Drain on kitchen towel. Peel and slice eggs. Cook pasta in salted boil water until al dente. Drain thoroughly. Oil a baking dish and put in a layer of the pasta. Cover with some of the *melanzane*, pecorino, the meatballs with the *ragù* and the sausage meat. Add another layer of pasta, and so on, until you have used up all those ingredients. Cover with the layer of fresh cheese in slices. Cover this with *sugo*, then the slices of hard boiled eggs and finally the breadcrumbs. Pop into oven and bake for 20 minutes.

∾ Pasta o furnu Palermitana ∾

Quite a different dish, starting off with the pasta, which is one of the ringed variety. Then there's beef, walnuts, parsley and spices, too. This is altogether more baroque, cosmopolitan and theatrical.

Serves 4

Olive oil • *1* melanzane *(aubergine)* • *1 chopped onion* • *1 bunch parsley* • *350g minced beef* • *300g ripe tomatoes* • *5 chopped walnuts* • *A pinch of powdered cinnamon* • *Salt and pepper* • *500g* anelletti pasta • *100g* caciocavallo • *50g fresh sheep's cheese (*Tuma*)* • *80g* la mollica *(fresh white breadcrumbs)* • *80g butter*

Preheat the oven to 180°C/360°F/Gas 4. Heat the olive oil in a frying pan. Slice and fry the *melanzane*. Drain the slices on kitchen towel. Add more oil to the pan and brown the onion in it. Add the parsley, beef, tomatoes, walnuts, a pinch of cinnamon, salt and pepper. Mix up thoroughly and then chop finely with a knife. Cook the *anelletti* in salted boiling water until al dente. Grate the *cacicovallo* and chop the *Tuma* into cubes. Drain the *anelletti* and stir in with all the beef and vegetable mixture. Oil a baking dish. Put the *anelletti* mixture into it and cover with the cheeses. Push some of the cheese down into it so that it melts down into it as it cooks. Sprinkle with the breadcrumbs and dot with butter. Slide into oven and bake for 15 minutes.

∾ Lasagna o furnu del zia d'Anna Fava ∾

According to Anna Fava's aunt, to make a good dish you have to use up everything you have in the fridge. Oil a baking dish and put down a layer of whatever you like – cooked ham, *ragù* with ground meat, cheese, bechamel sauce. Cover with a layer of pre-cooked lasagna and follow with another layer of the filling and so on. Finish with *ragù* and grated Parmesan. Bake until you can easily push a fork through it.

Alternately, make layers with *ragù*, slices of uncooked *melanzane*, sliced hard-boiled eggs and fresh cheese, finishing with *ragù* and grated Parmesan. Bake in the same way.

Salvatore Manna, assessore all'agricoltura, Leonforte

CHAPTER FIVE

Racing Pulses

๏๏

Villarosa – Catania

The sun was high. The sky was blue. The air was warm. The road to Leonforte was – what shall I say? – demanding.

The quality of Sicilian roads was turning out to be variable in every sense of the word. I've never been much of a one for the highways. Byways, B roads, C roads, and even tracks on occasion draw me on. What's the point of hurrying? The slower you move, the more you see, and there are few forms of transport slower than me on a Vespa. What was it the motorcycle examiner said to me when he failed me on my test?

'Insufficient forward momentum, sir.'

'Sorry. What?'

'You didn't go fast enough.'

But that was the whole point. I like to dawdle, to potter, to mosey along, to drink in my surroundings, and the road between San Giovanello and Leonforte was made for all these things. The landscape was beautiful to look upon. The hills became more conical, sharper in their slopes. The patchwork of olive groves and wheat fields was there as before, but the fields were smaller, more intimate. At one point a thicket of eucalyptus trees, with slender trunks of oxidised green and shaggy tops, formed a corridor down one side of the road, casting a cooling shadow and filling the air with the perfume of aromatic gum.

But the beauties of the wayside tended to take second place to the imperative to survive. The road itself wound, twisted, snaked back and forth, up and down. The temptation to drink in the details of the rustic scene had to be resisted in the interests of self-preservation. I was quite keen not to plunge into some gorge or other as the road took another unexpected dip or pivoted back on itself. And then there was the road surface – always assuming, of course, that there was one.

It occurred to me that the authorities in Britain have got it all wrong, forever putting down and taking up and changing 'traffic calming devices' – sleeping policemen, roundabouts, traffic lights and all the other paraphernalia of the modern bureaucratic state – at vast public expense. They should follow the Sicilian model. Ignore the roads altogether and let nature take its course. In Sicily nature seemed to look on road surfaces as a particular intrusion, on which it had to impose its own will. This it did by washing them away, turning them to rubble, causing the earth underneath to collapse so that it looked as if someone had eaten a great chunk out of them, or compressing the tarmac into a series of bone-jolting ripples. There was a whole road sign lexicon to describe these road upheavals: *strada interotta*, *strada pericolosa*, *strada strangante*, *strada pericolante*, *strada disestata*, and, most hope-withering of all, *strada intransitabile*.

The road to Leonforte was a compendium of all these, with every possible variation thrown in for good measure. I went round one corner in my usual cautious manner, which was as well because, halfway round it, the road simply ceased to exist; its place was taken by a stretch of what appeared to be open ground covered in boulders before it picked up the thread again a hundred or so metres further on as if nothing had happened. There were sudden, almost invisible, differences in the height of the road surface which I would hit with juddering force. Or carefully concealed mini-trenches. Or potholes. Or random lumps of rock. Or something to keep the pulse fluttering and eyes in front.

◎◎

The streets of Leonforte are cobbled, and vertiginous even in an island of vertically challenging towns. I bounced up and then down, nerves keyed to screeching point, jaw clamped in concentration, knuckles white, sinews twanging like the stays on an America's Cup yacht in mid-race with the effort of clutching the brakes, looking for the office of Salvatore Manna. More by luck than good judgement I found it.

Signor Manna was sitting at his desk surrounded by a sea of papers, files, brochures, computer discs and all the other impedimenta of modern management, a serious-looking man, balding, his remaining hair greying slightly around the temples. He was an *assessore d'agrecoltura* for the Ministry of Agriculture. His job was to support local farmers and, as a result, there was nothing that he did not know about what grew, where it grew, how it grew, why it grew. In a diffident, smiling manner he was more passionate about all aspects of Sicilian agriculture, past as well as present, than seemed quite proper in a bureaucrat or technocrat.

'In reality, agriculture is in crisis in Sicily,' he said. 'Prices are too low and our costs of production are too high. Too many of the farms are too small to be economic. It's cheaper to grow things in North Africa than here.'

Like Pasquale Tornatore in Caltanissetta, he was fearful that Sicily was losing touch with its agricultural past, and, as a result, with many of the products that formed its extraordinary legacy of diversity and the history they embodied. 'Our children, they are growing up without knowledge of our foods,' he said. 'They are the hamburger generation.' I wondered what he would make of Britain's crisp-guzzling, chip-grazing kids.

To illustrate his point, Salvatore Manna pulled out a bag of dried broad beans. These were, he said, the celebrated *fava larga di Leonforte*, a broad bean with a difference. Their most obvious distinction was their size, which was prodigious, almost twice the size of any broad bean I had ever seen. In their dried state they looked like nothing so much as murky grey-green bucklers for gnomes. The *fava larga*, he went on, was the product of a long process of Mendelian genetic manipulation and the benefits of the local microclimate. You get only two of these Brobdignagian beans to a pod compared to four or five in a normal broad bean.

'They have grown here for hundreds of years,' he said. 'They were known as *la carne dei poveri* because they are so high in protein – 27 per cent. People would eat these beans at least once or twice a month, right up until the Second World War. But modern agricultural techniques and the aspirations of former *contadini*, peasant farmers, had rendered the *fava larga di Leonforte* obsolete, irrespective of its nutritional or gastronomic qualities.

'The trouble is,' he explained, 'people think of foods like the *fava larga* as poor food, food of the poor. People want to show they aren't poor any more, so they eat meat, to show they can afford it.'

No one wishes to be reminded of a past marked by deprivation, limitation and inferiority. The *fava larga di Leonforte* summed up precisely the world that new, forward-looking, mobile Sicilians have escaped from. So their children grow up in ignorance of their culinary past.

'Now there are only 30 or 40 people who still grow the *fava larga di Leonforte*. It's in danger of extinction. And that would be a tragedy. It's not just that we will lose part of our biodiversity, and a very good, healthy food, but we will lose part of our history, too. You must take some back with you to try. They are *molto saporite*, very tasty.'

And it wasn't just the *fava larga* he was concerned about. There were the *pesche tardive di Leonforte*, too, peaches that were wrapped in bags to protect them from the chill, so that they could be picked in September or even October. Salvatore Manna pressed a pot of *pesca tardiva* jam on me to go with the bag of broad beans, and then a tiny bag of *lenticchie nere di Leonforte*, the black lentils of Leonforte, which, if I understood him correctly, were more rare than hen's teeth. There was only about 1 kilo of the black lentils in the world. I felt much as a man might had he been given an egg of the last dodo with instructions to hatch it out.

Would it be possible to visit a farmer who grew the *fava larga*? I asked.

The growing season was almost at an end, he said, but he believed that a Signor Scavuzzo still had some to harvest. He made a quick phone call. Yes, he did. And yes, he would be delighted to show me around his plot of beans. And yes, he would be expecting me shortly.

Signor Scavuzzo is expecting me still. I left Salvatore Manna's offices with a rudimentary map and a stream of explicit instructions. But something went wrong somewhere along the way. Perhaps I did not leave the town by exactly the right road. Perhaps I mistook a left for a right or a right for a left or misunderstood the description of a large estate with a house like a castle on it, or something. I spent two hours looking for the Azienda Scavuzzo. I went uphill. I went downhill. I zoomed along this road, and then back again. I stopped to ask a *contadino*, but, sadly, his Sicilian proved so unreconstructed that I could no more understand him than he could me. Clouds began to gather overhead. The temperature began to drop. My patience began to wither. I felt hopeless and helpless. I knew I was a failure as an explorer, as a gastro-investigator and as a man with an appointment in the book, but after two hours I decided to call it a day and headed for Adrano. Perched on the flanks of Mount Etna, this was my last staging post before I returned to Catania and thence to England.

◎◎

Adrano seemed to have been largely passed over by history and by modern tourism. There didn't even seem to be much to be said about the town from a gastronomic point of view, aside from a vigorous market where I bought some salted *lupini* – blanched butter beans – which were worthy rather than exciting, and the first figs I had seen, which had an airy sweetness and delicacy that made them more exquisite than any I could remember. But these were not enough on their own to redress the feeling that Adrano wasn't a centre of culinary excitement. I wandered forlornly around the town looking for anywhere that might bring a prickle of excitement among my taste buds. I feared that I was turning into one of those voluptuaries whose appetites have become so jaded that they can only be stimulated by some strange and exotic new experience. And then I came across the Crespelleria Reitano standing in a parcel of open ground in the middle of the town.

Signor Reitano was a middle-aged man with an amused look, a fine moustache and a tummy that filled out his white chef's jacket, with its blue buttons and blue flashes on the cuffs, into a well-defined curve. *Crespelle*, he explained, were a speciality of Catania.

He deftly scooped a lump of dough from the mass in a large stainless-steel bowl in front of him, flattened it slightly in his left hand, laid a salted anchovy fillet on it and shaped it into a sausage before dropping it into a vat of roiling fat, where several more *crespelle* where already frying.

'It's quite simple,' he said as he rolled them with a deft flick of a wire spatula. 'The dough is just flour, water, salt and yeast.'

The *crespelle* turned a golden-brown and he fished them out and passed me one. The outside was delicately crunchy and gave way to a springy, dense interior. There was just enough salt and flavour from the anchovy to hold my attention and make the *crespelle* satisfying.

'We also make them stuffed with ricotta. And sweet *crespelle* of dough with rice and sugar,' he said. That completed Signor Reitano's product range. It was all he needed, it seemed, as a steady stream of customers came and went, clutching their bags of half a dozen or a dozen, enough for all the family.

Crespelle were another survival of the past, and of Sicilian ingenuity in stretching a few cheap, basic ingredients to make a satisfying, well-flavoured mouthful. I ate another and another. 'How much?' I asked, when I had had enough.

'*Niente*,' he said. 'It is my gift to you.'

⊚⊚

Looking back at the notebook I kept 33 years earlier, I can only curse my lack of application. If only I had kept a more detailed account of what Tom and I had seen, eaten and felt. Reading the notes that I did manage to write, I try and make the connection between the fellow I was then and the middle-aged figure I have become. It's curious. At one level, it's as if I were reading the observations and reflections of someone else. At the same time, I wonder how different I am from the callow youth of 1973. The response to situation, people and landscape seems much the same, although the interpretation of its significance has changed.

Then I remarked on the 'precarious hilltop towns tumbling down the vertical face' of the hills, and 'small, depressing run-down villages' and the 'immense, savage, precipitous splendour of inland terrain cf Peloritani mountains'. I can see the romantic gloss that I threw over much of what I saw – the basket weaver, groves of hazelnuts, sheep 'with long horns curling like corkscrews up from their heads', the beauty of place names such as Taormina, Linguaglossa, Castiglione, Milazzo, Randazzo. Somewhere I referred to 'shards of beauty.'

The sweet honey of Sicily's physical beauty, its fecundity and natural opulence, and the richness of its past fused with my own sensory responses.

Now I sat on a bench in the square in Adrano, and watched the customers come and go at the *crespelleria*. I was near the end of the first stage of my Sicilian odyssey, and after riding across the centre of Sicily I realised that it was not the exquisite idyll portrayed by Theocritus. That tradition had been subverted long ago by invasion, occupation and exploitation. Nor did the island conform to an idealised image of the Mediterranean. It was far wilder, harsher, less personal. It was ravishing, nonetheless. It had the brilliance of light and the magnificence of space, the enchantment of paradox and unpre-dictability. As far as I was concerned, the true nature of Sicily was no longer to be found in the classical ruins of Selinunte or Piazza Armerina that had captivated me over 30 years ago, or in the baroque grandiosity of churches and cathedrals.

I suppose the intervening years have given me a series of experiences and understandings through which I was filtering this new set of impressions. Now I found at least part of the essence of the island in the abstract grandeur of the endless, rolling, pitching sweep of the land, in the oceans of wheat, lakes of vines, pools of olive groves, in the outcroppings of small dusty villages and down-at-heel towns because these made up the true record of immediate history, of the awfulness and poverty that had prevailed within living memory.

☙☙

Until the agricultural reforms of the 1940s and 1950s, most farmworkers had been day labourers, forbidden to own land even in the unlikely event that they could afford to buy it, who sold their labour in return for barely subsistence pay or food. Before mechanisation, all the work on the land had been done by hand; daily, back-breaking labour in a heartless landscape under a roasting sun. Most fields were a long way from the nearest town or *masseria*, agglomerations of farm buildings themselves like mini-villages. Any man who was employed would have had to walk to and from work, several kilometres at the start and the end of long days in the fields. Social isolation, economic poverty, political impotence, domination and exploitation by Church and landlord – that was the life of so many Sicilians.

Poverty of every kind encloses the human spirit, turns it inwards. All choices are restricted to the point where there are none. Nothing is left but personal pessimism or fatalism, and acceptance of the will of others. But such is the energy of the human spirit, it seemed to me, that these people without hope, without choices, had found self-expression through personal and family loyalties, through criminality and subtle, almost abstract subversions of the conventional world. I was beginning to think that food was also among these visible signs of collective resistance.

Anyone expecting the precise harmonies of Italian cooking, with its emphasis on the individual flavours of carefully selected ingredients defined by local loyalties, is in for something of a shock when they come across Sicilian food for the first time. Sicilian cooking embraces contrast, discord, counterpoint, counterpunching, variance and the absence of delicacy. The dishes work through contrast – sweet/sour, hard/soft, sweet/salty, hot/cold. They are rich in their effects, as bold and baroque as any flamboyant building. They steamroller the taste buds: dense, tense, piquant, savoury, fruity, rounded and filling in every sense of the word, tummy-stretching, trouser-tightening, foods of the season, foods of the earth. That's not to say that they lack sophistication. In fact, the sophistication of Sicilian cooking lies in its ability to take in extremes and create dishes that assault perceptions of taste with a stupendous vigour built on a sense of culture, a sense of personality and a sense of history.

◎◎

Each ingredient has its history, which it brought to the history of a dish, and that history, too, varied, according to the ingredients used in a particular place because that place has its own history. So the history of Sicily is written on the plate, in the granitas, *cannoli*, bread, pasta; in the vegetables and fruits; in the *crespelle*, *pannelle*, *fave*, *lenticchie*, sesame seeds and *frumento duro*; in the methods of preservation – salted, sun-dried, *sott'olio*, *sott'aceto*; in the chocolate, rice, tomatoes, *melanzane* and peppers; in the spices, cloves, cinnamon, nutmeg; in the stuffed vegetables, fried fish, grilled meats and the fancy French-inspired styles of the aristocracy – even if sometimes the history is confused and confusing.

But no more confused and confusing than so much else. Since I set out I had had the sense of travelling through history. Sicily, it seemed to me, was where you relived the story of Western civilisation each day. It was all here: the Phoenicians, Greeks, Romans, civilised Arabs, disciplined Norman French, buccaneering Germans, Spanish, French again, Germans again, British, Americans. Its culture and food were shot through with references to the past. The island

was a museum of theatre design over the millennia, of fortifi-
cation theory and practice, of town planning, ecclesiastical
architecture, structural engineering and aesthetic vision, religious belief and philosophical discourse. History was here in
the pillars and pilasters, arches, balconies, cornices, archi-
traves, mouldings. You stumbled across it in the names and
the language.

Above all, history was in the people, both in their kindli-
ness and their opacity, in their generosity and obliqueness. If
you have been occupied, dominated and exploited for 3000
years, I suppose you learn to suppress direct expression of your
natural instincts, open discourse and individual behaviour. It
teaches you to be watchful, wary, to be careful, to have regard.
It teaches you to listen, to be aware of the mental, emotional
and social processes of your occupiers. And it teaches you how
to survive them – more, how to work with them, how to
manipulate them, how to coax and cajole, how to insinuate,
how to achieve your ends by other means, without upsetting
your lords and masters along the way. It breeds a subtlety of
intellect and a suppleness of manner, a judicious realism, a
clarity of judgement as to why and how people do things.
Sicilians have few illusions.

⊚⊚

This awareness of the world, and of the way worldly matters
may affect anyone in a sudden and arbitrary fashion, mani-
fests itself as fatalism, pessimism, cynicism or, on rare
occasions, as a kind of utopian vision. But what struck me,
and stuck with me at the end of this stage of my journey, what
I had not foreseen or been prepared for, was the level of kind-

ness, of generous daily decency, of thoughtfulness, of simple grace. Whatever their suspicions of the wider world, and the elliptical way in which they related to it, when dealing with an individual, with a stranger, Sicilians were unfailing in their warm-hearted kindness. Signor Reitano's munificence was the latest example of a recurring theme. I could call to mind the irritations that distract any traveller – occasional incompetence, inadequate signposting, pettifogging bureaucracy, even the occasional duff dish – but I could not recall a single incident where I had been subjected to meanness, incivility or loss of temper, let alone road rage. It seemed extraordinary, when a single day in Britain can bring all these things. I didn't know whether this made Sicilians a good people, but it made them a civil people, instinctively thoughtful and kind, with an inborn generosity that was extraordinary in its spontaneity.

As I took the road down from Adrano to Catania, through the gulags of indiscriminate commercial building and shambling suburbia, there was no disguising the fact that there was another side to Sicily. Hideous unregulated development, broken roads, the government, and headlines such as the one I read in a paper in Caltanissetta reporting the death of three men in a Mafia feud, made that clear. But I had not been the victim of any of these, except the broken roads. As yet, I hadn't experienced a single moment of fear or a second of anxiety.

I thought that maybe Sicilians, by and large, had a more profound understanding of what it means to be human than any other people I had come across, and a sense of community shared through their passion for food. I felt like Howard Carter on opening Tutankhamun's tomb – but where he had said, 'I can see wonderful things,' I could say, 'I have eaten wonderful things.'

Nanni Cucchiara had told me that when you meet a Sicilian you are set a series of exams, which you will not know you are taking. If you pass the exams, he will hand you the keys to his house, and you will be his friend for ever. It was as if I had been handed the keys, but I had still to explore the house.

☙

Coming down from the highlands of central Sicily to the coastal rim was something of a shock. The litter of industrial zones gave way to uniform, systemic, intensively worked plots and plantations. There was nothing, it seemed, that did not grow with extraordinary vigour and abundance. The number of orange, lemon and tangerine trees, their leaves dark and glossy, was uncountable. There were olive groves and groves of peaches, nectarines and apricots, rectangles of onions, lettuces, tomatoes, zucchini, peppers, *melanzane*, cactus, vines, each plot neatly butted up against the next. There were people, too, tending them, moving up and down between the rows. After the depeopled ocean inland, the land seemed positively bustling.

The earth was the colour of milk chocolate or, where it had been recently tilled, cooked mince. But the most insistent colours were the black or charcoal grey of the walls dividing up the properties, even the stones from which the houses were built. This is all basalt, volcanic pumice, the deconstructed magma that has gushed out of Mount Etna for millennia, and flowed down its flanks and cooled. It takes two or three hundred years for the magma to be transformed into one of the most productive growing mediums known to agriculture.

Etna stood at the back of all this lushness as if drawing the world up towards its crater, which was hidden in cloud. In spite of the explosions of green growth, I found there was something faintly sinister and alien about the region. It suggested impermanence, a temporary occupation that may come to an end at any moment should the arbitrary and insentient volcano erupt again.

As I entered Sicily's second city I felt the familiar feelings of terror, inadequacy and anxiety brought on with major traffic hazards. Little by little, quite soon in fact, these feelings gave way to irritation at the inadequacy of the signposting and the incomprehensible nature of Catania's one-way system. Then irritation turned to anger, and finally anger to insensate fury, as I searched for Via Gabriele d'Annunzio (d'Annunzio was always a suspect figure in my book; bombastic man, bombastic poetry) and the Vespa agency on it, where I was required to leave Monica for safe keeping until the second leg of my voyage of exploration in the late summer. I got lost not once or twice or even thrice, but uncountable numbers of times. Having finally located the street, I discovered that it was almost impossible to get to the agency.

On the nth attempt I managed to land, and my mood was instantly transformed by the cool efficiency of Silvia la Vecchia, who was to take charge of Monica. She showed no surprise at my lateness, or apprehension at my distinctly sweaty and dishevelled appearance. She took me for a restorative coffee and pastry at a smart café round the corner. In return I regaled her with tales of my adventures and my enthusiasm for my gastronomic discoveries. Glowing with the pleasure of discovery, I told of the glorious figs that I had eaten in Adrano only that morning.

Ah yes, she said. Those figs were *passaluni*, very special. There were trees on Etna, and only on Etna, that have two fruiting seasons, one in the spring, now, and one in the autumn. The autumn ones are good, but the spring ones are better, the best in all Sicily. She said this in a matter-of-fact throwaway manner. It was common knowledge, common experience.

As I made my way to the airport, I wondered what would happen if I wandered into a motorbike shop in, say, Birmingham or Basingstoke, and asked the person at reception whether they thought Allison's Orange or Ashmead's Kernel was the better apple at a particular season.

∞ Crespelle ∞

Signor Reitano was quite offhand when giving details about his splendid street treat. A little research and consultation with my board of Sicily advisors has produced this recipe.

Makes about 60 *crespelle*
30g fresh yeast • 900g plain flour • Salt • 60 anchovy fillets/300g fresh ricotta • Fat for frying – ideally sugna *(pig fat), but lard or even vegetable oil will do*

Dissolve the yeast in 6 tbsp warm water. Then heat water in a saucepan. Just before it boils add all the flour at once and beat vigorously. Allow to cool. Add a pinch of salt and the yeast. Mix thoroughly. Turn out onto a dry surface and knead vigorously with oiled hands until smooth and silky. Put into a bowl, cover with a cloth and leave to rise until twice the size. To make each crespelle, heat the fat or oil, break off a walnut-sized piece of dough and form into a plump sausage. Press an anchovy fillet or a teaspoon of ricotta into the surface and fold the dough around it. Fry until golden brown and crunchy on this outside. Fish out and drain on kitchen towel.

∞ Melanzane ammuttunati ∞

This and the following three recipes actually come from the Antica Stazione di Ficuzza. There wasn't room at the end of Chapter 3 to fit them in, but I was loath to leave them out as they produce terrific dishes and closely resemble other dishes I ate along the way.

Serves 6
1 bunch mint • *3 garlic cloves* • *200g* caciocavallo *cheese* • *6 large or 12* melanzane *(aubergines)* • *400ml extra virgin olive oil* • *1l* sugo *(tomato sauce)* • *Salt and pepper* • *Basil*

Chop mint, garlic and *caciocavallo* finely. Wash the *melanzane* and take off the stalk. Make 2 small 1cm cuts into the *melanzane* and fill them with mint, *caciocavallo*, garlic and a little salt and pepper. Heat most of the olive oil in a sauté pan and fry the *melanzane* until brown all over. Add the *sugo*, season and simmer for 10 minutes.

You can serve this hot or cold, with the remaining olive oil and torn basil leaves.

∞ Carciofi alla viddanedda ∞

Serves 6

6 artichokes • Juice of 1 lemon • 1 bunch parsley • 200g caciocavallo cheese • 100g extra virgin olive oil • 3 garlic cloves • 50g salted anchovy fillets • 100g la mollica *(fresh white breadcrumbs)*

Wash artichokes and take out their chokes. Cut the artichokes into slices and put in water with the juice of one lemon to stop them from going brown. Finely chop the parsley and grate the *caciocavallo*. Heat the oil in a saucepan and fry the garlic and anchovies. Add the artichokes. When the artichokes begin to turn brown, add the breadcrumbs, parsley, *caciocavallo* and a glass of water. Cook for another 5 minutes. You can eat it hot or cold as you prefer.

∞ Canazzu ∞

Serves 6

2 aubergines • 2 peppers • 4 potatoes • 1 onion • 200 ml extra virgin olive oil • 1 fresh tomato • White wine • 500ml vegetable stock • Salt and pepper • 1 bunch basil

Wash aubergines, peppers and potatoes. Peel the potatoes and cut everything into big pieces. Peel onion and slice finely. Heat oil in a large saucepan and fry the onion until soft. Peel and deseed the tomato and add to the onion. Add all the other vegetables and cook for 10 minutes. Sprinkle with white wine, dry off the wine and add the vegetable stock.

Season with salt and pepper and cook for 20 minutes until all the vegetables are softish. Serve with olive oil and torn basil leaves.

La Pescheria, Catania

CHAPTER SIX

Draught of Fishes

๏๏

Catania

It was Sunday afternoon in late September. The air smelt of dust and spices, and had the soft balm of the end of a hot day. I was back in Catania for the second part of my Sicilian odyssey, which would take me all around the coastline of the island, and who knew elsewhere as well. Already England, and its bellowing confusions, manias and obsessions, was infinitely remote. Sicily seemed older, less ephemeral, more complex, and more interesting.

An old man and his wife were sitting beside a makeshift stall in a side street off the Via Etnea selling dried chestnuts, chickpeas, peanuts in their shells, roasted corn nuggets and pumpkin seeds. Filled with missionary zeal to explore the full range of Sicilian eating practices, I said:

'I'm an English journalist writing about Sicilian food, and I—'

He said something in incomprehensible dialect.

'... was wondering if these were typical ingredients for Sicilian cooking?'

He nodded.

'What sort of dishes do you use them for?'

He nodded less vigorously.

'And can you eat like this as well?'

He nodded imperceptibly and then turned his head.

'Who buys them?'

He didn't nod at all and kept his head turned. His wife looked up at me with an expression it was impossible to read. I abandoned my forensic cross-examination and, crestfallen, walked on. It didn't seem an auspicious beginning.

At the end of the first journey, in June, I had felt exhilarated and puzzled in about equal measure. I think it was Sean O'Casey, or someone equally unlikely, who once wrote of the *palio* in Siena that only a dead person could fail to be moved by the excitement and drama of that event. I felt the same about Sicily. The food, the warmth of the people, the hypnotic beauty of the landscape made up a piece of theatre as dramatic as any opera, although perhaps more in the verismo style of *Cavalliera Rusticana* than the high-flown romance of *Norma* by Vincenzo Bellini, the Catanesi prodigy. They had all taken their place in my interior geography. At the same time, the way these elements balanced, how they worked together, how Sicilian society organised itself, its tides and currents, the Pirandellian side of the island, still seemed as obscure as it had when I first set off.

Quite why I wanted to deconstruct Sicily in this way, I am none too sure. In part it was to try and make sense of the hold it had had over my imagination and memory since I first visited it, in 1973. The only trouble was that the island was proving pretty resistant to whatever intellectual firepower I had managed to focus thus far, which had more in common with a cap gun than the bazooka I obviously needed.

And so I wandered around the city, scratching my head and

pondering these matters and wondering where I might find an ice cream.

The streets were largely deserted. There were few cars and not that many people. Not having to grapple with the molten flow of traffic and the haphazard nature of the road signs, it was easier to appreciate the spacious quality of the city, its elegance, openness and lightness. In contrast to Marsala or Caltanissetta, say, Catania was a modern European city, laid out to an orderly grid, rather than an accretion of streets around a knotted heart of narrow, winding lanes, the legacy of Arab municipal development. The city had been completely rebuilt after its destruction by an eruption of Etna to the north in 1693. The main roads were long and wide, like boulevards, and paved with blocks of caviar-coloured basalt. There were open spaces, too, piazzas and two opulent gardens, the Orto Botanico and Giardino Bellini, in which trees and shrubs grew with extravagant luxury.

Catania was a city of nice proportions. Nothing was too large or too high or out of kilter. The buildings seemed to have been constructed to accord with the golden ratio, the measurement that dominated architecture and design until the Bauhaus theories that stimulated the architectural imagination in the twentieth century. Buildings, rooms, doorways and windows were all predicated on a 6-foot measure, the height of the idealised human (although most humans were, of course, well under 6 feet at the time). That is why the dimensions were so pleasing. They were human, related to our spatial senses and to our eyelines.

The buildings in the old part of the city struck a carefree balance between the formality of neoclassicism and the extravagance of baroque. Some had been pebble-dashed with silica, made from volcanic dust. The extensive use of Etna's outpourings might have given Catania a grim, foreboding aspect. On the contrary, however, the silica caused granite-grey surfaces to sparkle in the sunlight, like a sprightly widow who has turned the black weeds of mourning to fashionable advantage, and the cream or honey-coloured stones used to frame the window lintels, doors and decorative cornicing added to the city's elegance.

◎◎

It might have been Sunday, but that evening the Osteria Antica Marina in the old fish market was open for business. The tables were set up in a random fashion outside, under two soaring basalt arches. The ground beneath them was as irregular as a choppy sea, causing the tables to tilt this way and that. There was a distinct smell of fish over a faint whiff of drains and of brine from the invisible sea.

'*Antipasto*,' I said decisively. '*Fritto misto e dolce. Non voglio il primo piatto.*' Remembering my conspicuous consumption on the first leg of my odyssey, I was wary of the kind of challenges that lay ahead of me, and had resolved not to have a vast blow-out in the first couple of days. Moderation was to be my watchword. So no *primo piatta*, no pasta, not even pasta Norma named after the heroine of Vincenzo Bellini's opera. In fact, I was going to follow the line of one of Bellini's other operas, and count myself among *I Puritani*.

My puritan supper started with crunchy little fried *polpetti*; *sarde a beccafico* lifted by intense cooked tomato; cold, chewy, vinous octopus *affogato*, with onion and potato in a white wine reduction; marinated anchovy fillets, soft as cooked pasta, light and sharp; peeled, baby pink prawns, barely cooked at all,

130

sprauncy with a hint of chilli; more octopus in oil, parsley and a trace of garlic; *sarde in agrodolce*, sardines breadcrumbed, fried and then marinated in vinegar and sugar with onions and sultanas. It wasn't elaborate or fancy, but each mouthful had a matter-of-fact precision, each method of cooking designed to tease out or complement the flavours of whatever fish or shellfish was being served.

Then came a *fritto misto* of tiny red mullet about the length of a matchbox, anchovies not much larger, and squid rings so brightly flavoured they make me realise how insipid most of the squid I get in England is. It made for a sparkling start. So much for moderation.

Although you find *fritti misti* all the way round the Mediterranean Adriatic coastline, the passion for deep-frying is another culinary debt Sicilians owe the Arabs. It's a perfect cooking method for sealing in the natural sweetness and distinct flavours of fish that have been twinkling in the sea a few hours before. The size and type of fish, small and gamey, lend themselves to this treatment. In a few years it may not be possible to eat them – not because they are fished out, although this is always possible, but because they will have migrated elsewhere and their place will have been taken by other species. I had met a French ichthyologist some months earlier, who told me that the eastern Mediterranean was being invaded by species from the Red Sea that had migrated along the Suez Canal, one of the effects of global warming, nudging what had long been held to be native Mediterranean fish further north. So where might these small, intensely flavoured fish move on to? Out through the Straits of Gibraltar to the coast of Britain? It is a tasty prospect.

My ruminations were interrupted by a discourse going on at the next table between two American tourists, a husband and wife, and their waiter. The Americans were eating grilled sea bass.

'Could I have a lemon to squeeze over the fish, please?' the husband asked the waiter in English. The American was built on the scale of an expansive country club beside the dainty bungalow proportions of the waiter.

The waiter demurred in Italian. The American repeated his request in a louder voice in English. The waiter stood his ground.

A young woman at a nearby table leant over. 'He says that lemon will interfere with the flavour of the fish,' she explained.

'Oh,' said the American, clearly baffled by the explanation. Such subtleties were outside his gastronomic experiences. 'OK. Right. OK then.'

'I also suggest you have a lemon or mandarin sorbet to finish,' said the young woman. 'That should do away with all the after-flavours of fish.'

'Right. Right. Thank you. That's really kind. We'll do that,' said the American. He turned to his wife, 'Won't we, dear?'

I finished with two slices of 'cake', one stuffed with a kind of rough pistachio cream and the other with a smooth almond paste. It seemed to me that the sponge base was much more in keeping with a French sponge than with other cooking traditions. Was this an echo of the *'monsu'* strand in Sicilian cooking, when the big houses employed French chefs in the endless round of one-upmanship that people with lots of money habitually indulge in?

Before I left I noticed that the American couple had taken the young woman's advice to heart and built on it. They had the sorbet and then they had cake.

☙☙

What was it that Walter Pater said about 'the solitary chamber of the individual mind'? Clearly he was a retiring old buzzard. Had his mind set on higher things, I shouldn't wonder. I wasn't in the Pater class. Never have been. When I went to bed that night I was invaded by a sense of being alone, of isolation, familiar to me from my other journeys. It wasn't homesickness so much as a feeling of insignificance, of not really being up to the job. After the first trip I was becoming all too aware of the complexities of Sicily and of the inadequacies of my personal resources. Not only did I not speak Italian very well, or not nearly well enough, but also I found Sicilian well-nigh impenetrable. I had a fairly clear – note the fairly – plan of where I wanted to go, but no real idea of where I was going to stay or what I was going to find as I went along or who I was going to speak to or, well, a host of other presentiments.

One of my female ancestors had been the first white woman to cross the Isthmus of Panama, or so family legend has it. It was certainly true that my great-great-aunt Gzaza Thompson, aka the Chimp on account of her remarkable resemblance to the primate, had survived life on a mine during the Gold Rush as the great San Francisco earthquake of 1906. Not for the first time, I wondered at the fortitude and mental strength of my female forebears. Something had gone missing down the line. Didn't they ever feel that travel is best experienced from the comfort of their own armchairs?

೯ల

In the morning the old Mercato dei Pescatori, a tiny corner of which the Osteria Antica Marina occupied in the evening, was in full raucous swing. It began in the square below the town hall, and ran out into the warren of streets around. The core was the fish market itself, around which had gathered butchers' shops and stalls, greengrocers, *salumerie*, like the rings round Saturn.

The first ring, the butchers, were carefully trimming, paring, slicing, chopping, arranging. Most specialised in just one meat – veal, lamb, chicken, pork. Their method of butchery was quite different from that in Britain, where a carcase is cut into individual 'joints' defined by the bone structure. The European tradition involves seaming out a carcase into its component parts defined by its principle muscles, so neat, integral parcels of meat were laid out in all their pink-grey glory. On one slab a fine set of intestines was displayed with a keen sense of visual drama, alongside a heart cut in half, liver, tongue and testicles. Another had a cat's cradle of thin, mottled sausage links looped from hooks. Most displayed as many 'value-added' products as they did pure butchery. These were not the spare ribs in an all-purpose sweet 'n' sour gunk, or unidentifiable lumps of chicken glowing in some virulent, Day-Glo glop, that we see shouting vulgarly in plastic tubs in Britain, but more considered items, such as thin strips of belly pork wrapped around small onions, and *involtini* of veal and cheese. Breadcrumbs were an almost universal ingredient, which was not only a useful way to use up old bread, but also helped to bulk out the dishes – a reminder of a time when thrift had been the spur to gastronomic invention. This had become so ingrained in the psyche of cooks and eaters that it continued even when such care was no longer necessary.

But the heart of the market was the fish area, which was divided into three parts. The local fishermen sold their catches from impromptu stalls set up on the glistening, wet, black, basalt paving blocks in the square immediately below the town hall. There were frozen-fish stalls under an arch that led to the third more orderly, commercial and less romantic area beyond.

Capone – Ray's bream – a fish shaped like a hurling stick, seemed to be the catch of the moment in the local fishermen's market to judge by the numbers being vociferously advertised to passers-by.

'*Caponecaponecapone!*'

'*Dueeurodueeuro!*'

There were buckets of small mixed fish for soup, a random kaleidoscope of shapes and colours; the odd silver and gunmetal grey sea bass; a box of squid with their tentacles hanging in limp resignation over the edge, and another of sauries, which contrived to be aggressive and boring; a deal box overflowing with silvery anchovies.

'*Pesce spadaaaaaeeeeeeh.*'

'*Cinqueeurocinqueeurocinqueeuro.*'

'*Freschissimifreschissimi.*'

The competition was fierce and loud. One old man was bellowing for all he was worth at the top of his lungs, although for the life of me I couldn't make out individual sounds, let alone a word of what he was shouting, so thick was his dialect.

On the other side of the arch at the back of the square with its frozen items, the range of fish was wider and was arranged with an eye to contrast and colour, the produce of bigger, more professional outfits. There was a little display of monkfish, their livers laid out beside them as if in mid-autopsy. Further along was a John Dory with its mouth fully extended like a cartilaginous telescope. Over here was one variety of red mullet, glittering like coral, and here another, *triglia bianca*, large, pale and yellow; and here a third, tiny, about the size of a finger.

Blocks of shiny mackerel, their sides cirrus-barred, flowed into pennants of orange, ugly gurnard, small hake, zebra-striped *pesce ombra* – a bream of some kind. There was a hillock of pink prawns, ready peeled. A fishmonger took drags at a fag between hacks at a colossal *cernia* (grouper) with his *mannaia*, a cleaver the size of an executioner's axe. The eyes of swordfish peered soulfully along the length of their swords to the sky above. The purple burgundy of tuna carefully dissected into the appropriate cuts glowed on several displays (so much for Nanni Cucchiara's prediction there would be no tuna at this time). There were flaccid octopuses, droopy squid, sprawling cuttlefish, scabbard fish, sardines, anchovies, *orati*, *spottri*, *dentici*, one, two, three kinds of prawns, sets of large flat containers holding five, no, six different varieties of clams and mussels, in sea water, spouting.

The freshness and quality of the fish were unvarying. I didn't see gills that weren't red as carnations, and some of the fish were stiff as wood, a condition that only lasts for a few hours after they are caught. Curiously, there was none of the ferocious buzz and excitement or ruthless vocal competition of the other square, none of the high-pitched voices vying for attention. The fishmongers seemed quite at ease with the bevies of tourists moving among them and the flash of cameras. The tone was steady and purposeful, voices orderly. I was more aware of the snicker of sharpening knives and the thwack of *mannaie* smashing their way through the bones of the bigger fish.

◉◉

Giuseppe Privitera was a measured repository of Sicilian food culture, history and practical observation. He was the size of a small wardrobe, dressed in black from top to toe, except for the

Slow Food slogan in white across the not inconsiderable front of his T-shirt. His large, handsome head was topped by luxuriant greying curls. The expression in his eyes behind his gold-rimmed glasses changed in the same way as water changes from light to dark and back to light as wind shifts broken clouds across the face of the sun.

Over lunch at Metro, a *ristorante-enoteca*, in Catania, he discoursed on how frying showed the Arab traditions in the west of the island (*'occidente'* as he put it), while *alla griglia* or *al forno* techniques prevailed in the east (*'oriente'*), and reflecting the influence of Greece and Byzantium, on how recipes followed trade or barter routes, such as the sheep and cheese recipes along the old *transumanza*, the route in the west, along which sheep were driven from the high pastures to the market towns, or the baking recipes of the corn route in the south. He moved easily and seamlessly from subject to subject.

His mouth moved with that enviably intelligent eloquence that all Sicilians seemed to possess. His hands curved through the air, describing expressive arabesques, more restrained, more elegant than the operatic energy of southern Italy. In Sicily, gestures seemed to be employed to amplify a conversation rather than act it out.

'The reason that you find more recipes for *stoccafisso* than for *baccala* in Sicily,' said Giuseppe, 'is because the Normans who came here in the thirteenth century preferred wind-dried *stoccafisso* over salted *baccala*. They were knights, you see, and travelled everywhere on horseback. The high salt content of salt cod often produced *emorroidi*, which would not have been easy if you had to spend many days in the saddle of a horse.' I decided that I had better watch the salt in my diet, considering the many hours I was would be spending in the saddle on my scooter.

I asked him whether he knew that Napoleon had suffered from such a bad attack of *emorroidi* during the Battle of Waterloo that he was unable to sit on a horse, and conducted the whole battle from a pallet bed? Because he couldn't sit on a horse on top of a hill he couldn't get the elevation to survey the battlefield personally, and so lost the battle.

No, Giuseppe didn't know that. He looked at me owlishly for a moment.

Course succeeded course – *bruschetta* piled with a confection of intense tomato braised with onion; spaghetti sauced with chopped fresh tomato, slivers of raw garlic and basil and olive oil; grilled *ombra*; a plate of puddings, including two cakes, a pistachio mousse and a fine, glutinous jelly made of red wine – and the conversation – my questions, his discourses – flowed on. He seemed to have the answers to everything I asked him, or comments on my observations.

I remarked on the extraordinary quality of the bread I had eaten everywhere. Was it all baked with flour made from the seas of wheat through which I had passed?

'Oh no,' Giuseppe said. 'Most of the flour from Sicilian grain ends up in North Africa and most of the Sicilian bread is made from Canadian flour.'

I found this rather disappointing. It led to a discussion about baking traditions in this part of Sicily. I remarked that so much of what I had eaten seemed to refer back to the Arabs. Take the sesame seeds, for example, I said, which clung to the crust of almost every piece of bread I had eaten.

'It could be Arab,' said Giuseppe. 'On the other hand it could be Greek. The old Greeks were very fond of sesame seeds.

And we owe a lot to the French, too,' he went on. 'Look at our raised sweet doughs, sponges, tarts, even savoury pies. What are they? French patisserie.'

Sicily was a land of contradictions, he said, and the key to its contradictions was to be found in the island's history. We sat in silence for a moment.

'What do you think of my project?' I asked. He paused before answering.

'*E un po' ambizioso*,' he said. A bit ambitious. Hmm. I scraped up the remains of my pudding. I didn't say that I thought so, too.

◎◎

Catania had a more purposeful air than Marsala, Enna or Caltanissetta. It didn't exactly bustle, but neither did it have the time-rich, easy-going nature of those other Sicilian towns. It was '*pui commercante*' as Giuseppe Privitera put it. But I liked the way the city revealed itself bit by bit. I mooched through the well-heeled, tourist-scoured, neat and tidy part of the old city, with the cathedral and the Piazza dell'Universita, the Via Etnea and the baroque churches, and the Mercato Antica.

Then, as I ranged further afield, I found sets of streets apparently given over only to specific products. One section was devoted to bridalwear, another was filled with hardware shops, a third with electrical items. It was like a medieval city in this respect, with discrete areas colonised by one guild or another. I found a second market, more diverse and less self-consciously decorative than the old fish market. And all along the way I was struck by the prodigious range of eating oppor-tunities: *paninerie, salumerie, alimentari, crespellerie, rosticcerie, trattorie, osterie, ristorante, bars,* cafés, *tavole caldas, gelaterie, chioschi,* chestnut roasters, offal boilers, and places selling roasted vegetables. There was even a fishmonger called Pesce Siamo Noi – Fish Are Us. It was a wonder that anybody did anything other than eat.

That evening I stumbled across yet another aspect of Catania, on the Via del Plebiscito, which curved through the western side of the city. The top half of the street was lined with cheap furniture shops. These gave way to a line of horse-meat butchers, unpretentious trattorias, street traders and shops dealing in other businesses' cast-offs. It was a harder, bleaker world. The people had a feverish vitality, forged out of a grimmer, more marginal reality. The faces were more pinched, bodies thinner, eyes brighter.

I passed a small stall, lit by a string of naked bulbs on a flex, at which a man was selling salted anchovies, olives and vegetables *sott'aceto.* Across the road, a merry-eyed matron was frying rissoles on a charcoal brazier outside a greengrocer shop. She dipped her hand into a bowl of water, scooped up a portion of meat from a mound lying on a square of waxed paper behind her, patted it into shape and dropped it into the sizzling, blackened frying pan.

'It's horse meat,' she said, with just the hint of apology in her voice. 'That's traditional around here.'

I saw nothing wrong with eating horse meat I assured her. But was there anything else in it?

'Onion, garlic, parsley, cheese and breadcrumbs,' she said.

'And these?' I pointed to a metal tray in front of her, loaded with carbonised vegetable lumps.

'Grilled peppers and artichokes,' she said. 'You eat the *carciofi* with a little oil and lemon juice and garlic, but the peppers you just peel and eat as they are. Very sweet and good.'

She smiled and turned the rissoles over. The night was filled with the sizzle of the meat, the rush of cars and their horns, and the rich, heady smell of frying.

'Would you like one?' she asked; but I was still too stuffed from lunch to be able to contemplate supper.

⊚⊚

I went back to the Via del Plebiscito the next day for lunch at the Trattoria la Vecchia. It was a spacious, plain eatery with paper tablecloths, basic cutlery, a random mosaic of random photos on walls, and plenty of people in overalls. It was without airs or graces of any kind, just cheery, chatty and good-humoured. People treated it as a canteen. There was an admirable matter-of-factness about the way they came, ate and departed. This was their normal, regular practice. In fact, customers were still coming in at 2.20 p.m. It was easy to see why. The food was cheap, filling and robust.

From the antipasto buffet I helped myself to warm, braised baby octopus; green bean salad with hard-boiled egg; a mush of violet cauliflower cooked with wine and olives; mussels stuffed with tomato and breadcrumbs; *melanzane* carpeted with béchamel sauce; a formidable dish of just *melanzane* and peppers, rich and oily, lifted by a touch of vinegar.

Spiedini di cavallo and *scaloppine di cavallo*, variations on horse meat, followed. The *spiedini* leaves of meat as fine as a paperback book cover were wrapped around cheese and dusted with breadcrumbs. Each tasted full and rich, the outside satisfyingly crunchy, the cheesy inside melting and squidgy. The *scaloppine* were mild, slightly sweet, delicate and rather refined, and distinctly chewy as you would expect of a meat with so little fat; they went well with a very good crisp, aromatic, faintly bitter salad of escarole, radicchio and fennel.

Horses had once been a regular part of the rural diet in the valleys, where they pulled ploughs and carried loads, just as donkeys had done in the mountains. In those days no one would have thought of turning their noses up at a potential source of protein, so when a horse died from natural causes or had to be destroyed or was found to be superfluous, it was eaten as a matter of course. Of course, it wasn't that long ago that horses were the main form of transport in Catania, too. As often seems to be the case, the diet of poverty had unexpected benefits. Like pulses and vegetables, horse meat was highly nutritious, low in fat, untainted by growth promoters and easy to digest; the perfect modern food you might have thought. I hummed, 'A four-legged friend, a four-legged friend, he'll never let you down,' words that Roy Rogers, the singing cowboy hero of my youth, used to carol, and changed the completing couplet to 'Tender and tasty right up to the end, that wonderful one-, two-, three-, four-legged friend'. For pudding I had a single yellow cling peach, honeyed and perfect, perfumed with late summer.

On the way out I had a chat with *la vecchia*, the old lady, who was in charge of the food.

'What was that star dish of *melanzane* and peppers?' I asked.

'*Caponata*,' said *la vecchia*.

'But I thought that *caponata* had to have celery and tomato in it, and yours didn't,' I said.

'No,' she said. 'This is the way I do it. This is my *caponata*.'

It struck me that Sicilian cooks seemed to feel a greater degree of freedom to interpret dishes than cooks on mainland Italy. Their recipes are handed down from mother to daughter and the object is to change them as little as possible. Recipes are replicated season by season. Each cook may have their own interpretation, but they do not claim it as such. It may be '*da qui*', from here, or even '*nostro*', ours, that is, our family's, but never '*da mio*', mine. Sicilians seem to be happy to claim personal responsibility for dishes in a way that other Italians don't.

၆၈

Porticolo Ognoni was just up the coast from Catania and just down the coast from Aci Trezza, the village where Giovanni Verga set *Il Malavoglia*, his masterpiece about a fishing family. It was 2.10 a.m. The small harbour was utterly deserted. There was just me, a couple of cats, and three white ducks asleep among the rubbish on the narrow, shingle shoreline, their heads folded back over their bodies and tucked under their wings. The area inside the harbour wall was a jumble of boats of all kinds and sizes, from big seagoing trawlers and *spumante* palaces down to the small, oar-driven fishing boats used close in to the shore. Between them glittered black-mackintosh water. Street lights made maze-like ribbons across it. There was a burst of voices and laughter from a nearby house. Unseen dogs barked in response. The odd car rushed along the coast road. Cicadas churred insistently. The air was cool. There was a stiff wind. The moored boats stirred uneasily, causing the mooring chains to squeak.

A battered Fiat 850 drew up and a man got out. He nodded to me.

'*Signor Urzi?*'

'*No. Non sono Signor Urzi.*'

He lit a cigarette and we stood in silence, a short distance apart. Little by little one or sometimes two other men turned up. Their cars were also battered. The first man greeted them. There were those brief flurries of very early morning conversation and then silence, as if the brief spurts of energy had exhausted their store of words. Presently the other men went off, and we were left, just the two of us again.

Then Carmelo Urzi appeared. He was a small man like a gnome, with a sweater and a scarf, and a woolly hat with a stunted peak on his head. His face had the stern look of a bulldog, perhaps because it was broad across the forehead and the corners of his mouth turned down. He smiled with his eyes and his voice was gentle.

Yes, he said, we would go fishing, for anchovies. The weather wasn't good – too much wind. But we would go.

After a brief discussion, he introduced me to the other man, Angelo. They unloaded the anchovy nets from the Fiat and carried them down to the boat. It was about 5 or 6 metres long, curving upwards slightly at either end. The wheelhouse, an upright shack, sat right in the middle of the deck. It was difficult to tell its colours in the orange light of the harbour lamps. It wasn't a pretty boat or picturesque or photogenic. It was a working boat, sturdy, sensible, decent, battered. Its surfaces were sticky with salt.

The engine boffed-boffed-boffed into life. The warm reek of diesel filled the air. Angelo and Signor Urzi went about making everything ready: coiling ropes, tying knots that would hold the more finely meshed anchovy nets to the bigger-meshed fishing ones with rapid, subtle deft movements, tugging hard to make sure they would hold. The anchovy nets looked like nylon gossamer.

It hadn't been a good year for anchovies, said Signor Urzi. Last year had been good, but not this year. There had been very few anchovies, and they had been small. Now it was getting towards the end of the season. And the wind wasn't good, either. The weather had an effect on the way the fish swam, when they swam and at what depth. The depth was crucial, he said.

'There aren't many fishermen left who fish for the anchovies, only one in my family, my nephew.'

At 3.15 a.m. we backed carefully out into the main channel and headed into the dark. The shore lights dropped away. Overhead I could see stars dotted about between rags of clouds. The wind seemed to have dropped slightly. The fresh smell of the sea blended with the warm smell of diesel. The surface of the water had the crinkled, polished sheen of black, industrial plastic sheeting.

Signor Urzi guided the boat from the wheelhouse. Angelo pulled on a pair of orange waterproof dungarees and lit a fag, the flame from the lighter briefly illuminating his face in the dark, the chiaroscuro of a Caravaggio painting. Men had been leaving these shores to go fishing for thousands of years. The reek of diesel and the chug of the engine were all that had changed. And the cigarette.

About 3 kilometres out Signor Urzi slipped the engine into neutral. We pitched and yawed. The sea was corrugated into heavy black bars. I could still see the coastal lights, except where there was a long stretch of absolute darkness – the open sea – but I had no real idea where we were in relation to any of it. Signor Urzi said that the depth was about 60 metres here, and the net must sit just above the seabed to catch the anchovies.

He heaved a marker buoy with a pole sticking out of it, and a winking light attached to the pole, over the side. It waggled away into the darkness. Angelo paid out the nets, hand over hand. A light mounted behind the wheelhouse threw a phosphorous-yellow beam over the deck. Angelo worked with extraordinary rapidity, pausing occasionally to shake out a fold in the nets with the complex hand-jive of an on-course bookie. They looked like very old net curtains – 1.3 kilometres of them, Signor Urzi said. He squinted into the darkness and juggled with the controls to keep us heading up into the wind. Neither man said a word. We were still yawing quite markedly.

'We usually lay the nets at night,' Signor Urzi said presently. 'But there are times when you can set them during the day. It all depends on the weather. The weather says when the fish move and how.'

It was 4.15 a.m., and the last of the netting slid over the side. Angelo paid out the final length of rope, attached to another marker buoy with a flashing light, to the very end of the nets, and we headed back for the harbour, gulls following us just above the boat, rising and dipping, swooping away and then back, ghostly bits of white paper shadowing us in the darkness.

The traditional fisherman's breakfast turned out to be an espresso and a *cornetto con crema* at an all-night café also patronised by Alitalia air crews. During breakfast Signor Urzi insisted I call him by his Christian name, Carmelo. After that, we went back to the harbour at Ognoni, and I fell asleep on the harbour wall until Signor Urzi woke me gently at seven o'clock to say we were going back to pick up the catch.

The sun was well up. Grey, pink, primrose, apricot clouds were scattered untidily across the chalcedony sky like bits of discarded clothing. The wind had died down. The sea had only a faint ripple. It was a metallic grey-black, liquid granite. There were a few inshore boats already out; squid jiggers, said Carmelo.

He is 80, he told me. 'And a little more. I remember the war, the Second World War.'

'Why do you still do this?'

'Because I have to do something, I have to keep active. It's good work.'

'But you don't get rich.'

'No, you don't get rich. That's true.'

Angelo spotted the marker buoy and hauled it aboard, winding the lead rope around an arrangement of revolving drums that hauled in the nets. Carmelo stationed himself behind the drums, Angelo at the stern of the boat. As the drums revolved, Carmelo took the netting, hand over hand, pulling out some of the fish trapped in the mesh before feeding the nets on to the floor behind him. Angelo drew them to the stern, taking out the fish Carmelo hadn't managed to extricate, and piled the netting up neatly. It was a system they had worked at day after day after day.

A good-sized *nasello*, hake, appeared soon after the netting began to rise up out of the water. Using a small lever, Carmelo stopped the drums while he pulled it free and threw it, with little ceremony, into a large plastic container half full of sea water. The fish was dead, its swim bladder burst. It floated belly up in the water. A flick of the lever set the drums revolving again. It was some time before the next fish appeared.

The sun began to warm up the world. The light grew stronger. The drums continued to go round and round. There was something stoic and noble and timeless about Carmelo's features below his woollen hat, now pushed back up his forehead. The sun caught the lower half of his face, turning it orange-gold. He could have stepped from the pages of *Il Malavoglia*. There was something about this work that pared existence down to essentials. Its simplicity was monumental.

I looked over the side of the boat and saw the netting billowing below us in the opal green water. Deep down there was a flash of silvery-white, the belly of another fish. And so it continued, the putter of the engine and the easy rumble of the revolving drums, the drips from the wet nets running over them; there were pauses as a murky grey-green saury, coral-pink red mullet, a slate-grey pinhead hake, bream with single smudged black spots on their sides, and a fish varnished with silver-pink, silver-blue scales and pale gold fins, which I didn't recognise, came up, and were dragged over the drums, yanked out and tossed into the plastic container. The largest might have made a kilo. But none was too small to throw away. There was no sentiment about this work. This wasn't about conservation. It was about survival. Fishermen, Carmelo and others like him, would go on taking fish out of these waters until there are no fish left, and then there would be no fishermen left.

An hour went by, a second hour. No anchovies. A squid appeared, rose-brown, tentacles entwined with the mesh, eye with black centre and nacreous iris. Carmelo yanked it out and tossed it into the plastic container. A crab came up. He wrenched at it, its limbs and claws flying off. He bit it in half, straight through the shell, chewed it, eyes gleaming with pleasure, before spitting the crushed remains overboard.

The last stretch of netting came in at 9.40 or so. Its 1.3 kilometres formed two mounds on the deck, at the stern. The sun was hot. We turned and made our way back to Ognoni. We had about 4 kilos of fish today, Carmelo reckoned. That was better than most days; 3.5 kilos was the usual catch.

When we got in there was a small group of people waiting on the slipway in the shade, customers, controlled by a single shaven-headed fisherman. 'We sell direct to consumers,' said Carmelo with a smile. Other fishermen had been before us. There was a small plastic bowl of silvery anchovies. Carmelo looked at them.

'Not good,' he said. 'Few and small and not good quality.'

Our fish were decanted into deal boxes, which allowed the water to drain away. The catch filled three of them before it was sorted by size and kind, 4 kilograms on the nail.

'How much is that worth?' I asked.

Carmelo shrugged. 'We'll have to see,' he said. 'It depends.'

He and Angelo still had work to do. We shook hands and I left them to it. I felt sad. If I came back here in ten years time, I doubted whether I would find any fishermen. The world was passing them by.

∾ Octopus affogato ∾

Serves 4

1 octopus (1.5 kg) • 200g onions • 250ml dry white wine •
2/3 cup olive oil • Salt and pepper • 500g waxy potatoes

Clean the octopus if needs be, rinse it, and chop it into chunks. Chop the onions. Combine all the ingredients except for the potatoes in a pot and mix well. Cover the pot, putting a weight on the lid, and bring the contents to a brisk boil over high heat for 15 minutes. Reduce the heat to a simmer and cook for another 1¼ hours. Peel and cube the potatoes. Add them to the pan 20 minutes before the end. Cool and serve.

∾ Broccoli con olive ∾

Coming from a country where cauliflower in cheese sauce is seen as the acme of cauliflower cooking, the range of cauliflowers and the resulting dishes came as something of a revelation. And that's something of an understatement.

Serves 4

1 head of violet or green cauliflower • 1 onion • 2 garlic cloves • Extra virgin olive oil • 12 green olives • 125ml white wine • 70g grated pecorino

Break up the cauliflower into florets. Chop the onion and finely chop the garlic. Pour some oil into a saucepan and gently fry the onion and garlic until soft. Add the cauliflower florets, olives and the wine. Cover and simmer very gently until the cauliflower is soft. Cool, sprinkle with grated pecorino and serve.

∾ Polpetti di carne di cavallo ∾

I think this is a fair stab at the little tennis balls of horse meat that the lively lady was cooking beside the Via del Plebiscito that evening. The only problem will be getting hold of the horse meat.

Serves 4

1 onion • 1 bunch chopped parsley • 250g minced horsemeat • 75g minced pork • 50g pangrattato *(dried breadcrumbs) • 50g grated pecorino • salt and pepper • Groundnut oil*

Chop the onion and the parsley. Mix the meats, *pangrattato*, pecorino, onion and parsley together and season with salt and pepper. Form into small balls. Fry in the groundnut oil until cooked through and crunchy on the outside. Serve with grilled peppers or a salad.

∾ Polpetti di alici ∾

Had we caught a few anchovies, Carmelo Urzi would have eaten them boned, dipped in egg and breadcrumbs and fried in oil. And if he caught a lot he would have made these fishy equivalents of the horse meat balls above.

Serves 4
200g fresh anchovy fillets • 3 eggs • 20g flour • 1 dsp pangrattato (dried breadcrumbs) • 50g grated Parmesan • Salt and pepper • Olive oil

Chop up the anchovies very finely. Put into a bowl and mix with all the other ingredients except the oil. It should result in quite a stiff mixture with which you can make the anchovy balls. Fry the balls in hot oil, turning them over to make sure they are crunchy all over. Drain on kitchen towel and eat immediately.

La Finocchiara (The lady with the wild fennel)

CHAPTER SEVEN

Sweet Reason

֎֎

Catania – Siracusa – Noto – Vendicari

I collected Monica and it was up, up and away, the joys of the
open road again. Monica responded like the thoroughbred
she was, easing her way through the traffic. Occasionally she
shied like a skittish nag when I heard the hiss of the brakes of
an articulated lorry like some monstrous anaconda just by my
left ear, and felt the perceptible drag towards those 18 wheels
whirling level with my head just a few inches away. How
refreshing were the deep breaths of diesel and petrol fumes,
how merry it was to be reacquainted with the mystery of road
signs – where there were road signs – and bafflement where
there were not. And, ah, that uneasy sense that I had taken the
wrong turning or missed the right turning and hadn't any idea
where I was heading for; and the heavy flak of insect life flat-
tening itself on forehead, cheeks and – sod it, not again – eyes.
It all came flooding back.

And the map: how I struggled with the bloody thing. It
had an independent will, never opening conveniently, shut-
ting up tidily, returning to its original shape, content to be
folded so that the section I needed was readily viewable. Not

ever. Finally I discovered the secret of how to use a map on a Vespa. I simply tore it into smaller, neat, tidy, convenient, biddable bits.

But then, turning from the main roads to my preferred B and C roads, away from the endless groves of lemons and oranges, I found the sense of ease and freedom again, swooping into the curve and out, out of shadow into light and back into shadow again, the warmth of the sun, the cool ripple of wind up the arms; picking out the details of buildings and landscape, picking up the smells of wild fennel, sheep, manure, sweet chestnut. In places pink cyclamen ran in seams among the crannies in the stone banks at the side of the road. There were stands of valerian, bushes of oleander, cascades of vulgar cerise bougainvillea, white jasmine. The profusion of spring flowers was long gone, but those that remained were more noticeable now, more valued.

I had a sense of freedom, of independence. I was commander of my destiny. The day made me wish that Tom and I had had the wit and courage to have whizzed around on scooters. But then romance and daring of that sort had never been one of the family's marked characteristics. Indeed, it said much for the sense of romance and foolishness in middle age that I was doing this now.

I climbed towards Lentini, passed through it, took a smaller road to Buccheri, turned off that to a yet smaller road to Ferla on a high plateau. Much of the land was utterly barren, but where the earth was deep enough it was ploughed and cultivated, producing a fine crop of stones as far as I could tell. In some places the stones, gleaming white and irregularly shaped, had been heaped into great mounds. These were obviously used to build the drystone walls that divided up the land so precisely. Fitting these products of nature together must be a far cry from the drystone wall techniques of Gloucestershire, where I lived, and where the stone was quarried and cut for the purpose.

Dropping down into the Anapo valley below Palazzolo Acreide was like coming across a particularly beautiful and fertile oasis in the desert. It was steep-sided, enclosed and secret, and its base, around the river, was green with groves of walnut trees, stands of ilex, sessile oak, chestnut trees, olives, and peach, nectarine and apricot trees – as if they had just grown there, lush and fresh. Vegetation spread up the sides of the valley, thick and robust, and where nothing grew the brightness of the limestone made a welcome change from the lowering, masculine basalt around Catania.

So, little by little, I passed through Floridia before easing into Siracusa, city of Archimedes, Theocritus and Elio Vittorini, battering my way through the usual girdle of shoddy shops, factories and the scabby detritus of modern towns to the perfect historical centre.

@@

The pink of early morning washed over the golden buildings. Two men were dibbing a sardine swaddled in twine down the quay wall by the Porta Marina. Light from the sea rippled on the stones of the quay and on the faces of the men as they bent over the coping at the edge, watching intently whatever was happening in the water at their feet. One man had grey hair and dark glasses. The other had dark hair combed over the dome of his head. They were both smoking. Somewhere Ennio Morricone's theme from *The Good, the Bad and the Ugly* played on pan pipes chirruped. A large shoal of very small fish cruised restlessly backwards and forwards, a shadow just beneath the surface of the water. Suddenly they scattered, flashing silver-white bellies and sides.

Presently the man with the dark hair jerked the line and rapidly hauled it up. At the end, still clinging to the sardine swaddled in twine, was a large octopus. It waved some of its tentacles in a vague and ineffectual manner, like someone whose breakfast has been rudely interrupted by the arrival of the bailiffs. The man with the dark hair rapidly detached the octopus and shoved it into a plastic bag with little ceremony.

ᘓᘔ

Maria Paola Uccello was an agricultural adviser employed by the regional government. I had sat next to her at a dinner at Don Camillo, the smartest restaurant in Siracusa, the previous night, and, with the kindness and thoughtfulness that I was beginning to see as an integral part of Sicilian manners, she invited me to a honey tasting the next day at an *azienda agricola*, Pozzo di Mazza, not far from Siracusa. Unlike on the mainland, honey has an important part to play in Sicilian cooking. It's used to sweeten *cannoli*, nougat and various *biscotti*, as well as providing the *dolce* in several *agrodolce* recipes.

The tasting began in a leisurely fashion. Six judges and I limbered up with a light breakfast at the Pozzo di Mazza. I havered over orange, bitter orange, apricot, cherry, lime, and fig and almond jams, unable to decide which to have with the bread. In the end I gave up and tried the lot. They were made on the farm and were very good, with just the scintillating taste of the fruit and none of the cloying sweetness that mars most commercial products. I overheard some German tourists sitting at a nearby table begging not to be given so much to eat today. I had some sympathy with them.

I was handed a sheet divided into four sections devoted to Look, Smell, Taste and Texture. Each section was subdivided into further parts with further columns in which to register marks and defects in quality. Clearly it wasn't going to be a matter of 'Where the bee sucks, there suck I'. It all bore an uncomfortable resemblance to the exam papers of my youth – 'You must answer one question from Part A and two questions from Part B.' For a ghastly moment I thought I might have to fill in all parts of the form, in Italian, but, thank the Lord, I was spared this humiliation. As it was, I was completely out of my depth.

It turned out that Maria Paola and her colleagues from Siracusa, Catania, Palermo, Messina and the Nebrodi were in the process of deciding which honeys would represent Sicily at the honey olympiad in Bologna in December. The honeys in question, 11 in all, came from the Nebrodi, a mountainous area on the north of the island, east of Palermo.

Each judge had their own table in a large cool room upstairs in what must have once been a barn. Aside from the marking sheets, there was an apple, a bottle of water, a bowl piled with multicoloured plastic spoons of the kind used to eat ice cream, a glass, and a foil tray on which were small plastic pots, marked with letters and numbers, that held the honeys.

I don't want to get overtechnical about this, and anyone who isn't hugely interested in honey may wish to skip the next few paragraphs, but I'd better explain that there's a strict etiquette governing honey assessment in Sicily, and elsewhere for all I know. First of all, we used plastic spoons because metal ones interact with the honey and alter the flavour. Secondly, we didn't just dig the spoon in and whip it up to our mouths. As Maria Paola showed me, we had to smear the honey vigorously round the inside of the plastic pot, the better to release the perfumes and flavours. Then it was sniff and savour, and only after that were we allowed to taste. We refreshed our mouths between each honey: water if the honey was quite light and multifloral; water, a slice of apple and water again for the heavier, single varietal honeys. And to think I had assumed it would be just a matter of spooning the stuff into my mouth and going 'nyumnyumnyum'.

There were honeys said to be made from a single flower source, chestnut or cardoon, say, as well as general purpose, *millefiori* honeys, literally, honeys of a thousand flowers. And this was where the problems began. When one particular flower predominates in an area or a season it is reasonable to suppose that bees will go for that flower and take the nectar from it, so the honey will taste of that flower – chestnut or cardoon. But you can't train bees, and they obviously have a tendency to wander off piste occasionally and include other nectars in their scavenging – citrus for example, or eucalyptus. The bee-keeper puts 'chestnut' on the label of the pot in all good faith, and then experts get sniffing and sipping and saying 'Now hang on a minute. This seems a bit *millefiori* to me.'

In fact, there was a great deal of discussion about what was and what was not *millefiori*, some of it quite heated.

'*Questo e castagno*. This is chestnut,' asserted one lady.

'*Non. Questo e un millefiori buono*. This is a good wild-flower honey,' said Maria Paola.

'*Equilibrato.* Balanced,' said a man across the room.

'*Ma non e castagno.* But it isn't chestnut,' said Maria Paola.

'*E castagno, ma non e castagno.* It's chestnut, but it isn't really chestnut,' said another lady.

'*L'analisi organolettica dica.* The organoleptic analysis says—' said the first lady.

I am pleased to say that neither the *analisi organolettica* nor the DNA analysis counted as highly as human judgement.We moved on to another honey.

'*Castagno.* Chestnut,' declared Maria Paola. '*Per me non e fresco.* I don't think this is fresh.'

'*Scusa-mi, Maria Paola,*' said a very forceful lady with stiff hair, '*ma secondo a me, questo non e castagno, e millefiori.* Excuse me, Maria Paola, but as far as I am concerned, this isn't chestnut, it's wild flower.'

But Maria Paola was not so easily crushed. '*No,*' she said. '*E castagno, ma non e buono.* No. It is chestnut, but it isn't a good one.'

Honey has the effect of turning normal sane, balanced individuals into intense, fiery-eyed obsessives. One of the judges confessed to being so passionate about bees that he went out on his wedding day to rescue a swarm.

I thought G2 smelt of lime, and was rather chuffed to discover that it was, indeed, *agrumi* – citrus. I mean, these people were real experts. They could tell if there were trace elements of cardoon, eucalyptus or orange in there. So to be told I had got the citrus right gave me a bit of a boost. But we agreed that it wasn't very good citrus.

The next smelt of dandelions to me, and the one after that of dog shit. Well, that's what it seemed to me, but I didn't like to say so. It was chestnut, I gathered. Not very good, not fresh.

The maker claimed it was oregano, but it wasn't. That was all right then.

Now here was a really good chestnut: intense, slightly bitter, like burnt caramel. There was no dog shit about that one. We all liked it.

And here was one that really was *millefiori*. Oh yes, there was myrtle and chicory and cardoon and, yes, a hint of chestnut, too. Very nice. I was getting a bit of a sugar high. I wondered how the members of the panel managed. They had been at it all week, working their way through over a hundred honeys.

And so we came to an end. None of the honeys was spectacular, it was agreed, but some were good, sound. Maria Paola gave me a pot of thyme honey from Hyblea, and even I could tell this was in a different class. There was the perfume of thyme, and a delicate web of flavours fading into each other as the limpid liquid glided over my tongue. No wonder Virgil and Theocritus were partial to the stuff. 'Eat only honey and the best dried figs,' was Theocritus's view. Clearly he was something of a gourmet.

Now it was time for lunch. We'd earned it. So we sat down outside in the shade on the terrace. First up there was *sgombro*, grilled mackerel spruced up with raw tomatoes, capers and lots of juice. Then there were strips of *melanzane*, cooked in vinegar with slices of celery and crunchy carrot, and doused in olive oil; and salami with pistachios shining like emeralds in it. And squid stuffed with breadcrumbs, ham and pine nuts, with *bobbia* – potatoes braised with peppers on the side. There were sharp black grapes and sweet muscat grapes for pudding, and *biscotti* with a glass of malvasia just in case we hadn't had enough. I made that two glasses of malvasia. I hate to see waste.

One of my fellow judges, Illuminato Sanguedolce, came up

to me and said I should look him up if I was thinking of paying a visit to the Monti Nebrodi on the northern side of the island. I said I thought I might do that very thing.

☙

I didn't hang around in Siracusa. Oh yes, it been the greatest and richest Greek city when Magna Graecia was Magna Graecia. It had been the most important port on the Mediterranean for aeons, the playground of philosophers, princes and tyrants. I rather liked the sound of Dionysus II, son of the Dionysus, the first tyrant of Siracusa, who was given to 'loitering in the fish markets and squabbling in the streets with common women'. And the city was stuffed full of remains and remarkable buildings.

But Ortygia, the seductively beautiful old part of Siracusa, was choked with an astonishing number of buses, which disgorged shoals of tourists to trail around each other in an endless sequence of discrete groups, like shoals of coral fish moving from one spot to another to graze for a while before swirling on to the next cultural monument. As a tourist myself, I couldn't very well object to their presence. I just wasn't convinced that there was enough room for them and me. Besides, reams had been devoted to the glories of Siracusa, to its Greek theatre and Roman amphitheatre, Federick Hohenstauffens's Castello Maniace, the cathedral built over the Great Temple of Athene, the Palazzo Beneventano del Bosco, and so on – the usual bewildering array of historical glories. There were times when I felt a positive surfeit of antiquity. More to the point, I didn't feel I was going to make earth-shattering gastro-discoveries in Siracusa.

So I leapt aboard Monica and, directed by Maria Paola, headed south and slightly inland.

@@

I found the Az. Ag. Saccolino with some difficulty, at the end of a long track more suited to motorcross than a ladylike Vespa like Monica. Surrounded by olive, apricot, nectarine and almond trees, it sat on the side of a hill in the middle of nowhere in particular, south of Noto and just above the coastal plain that runs down to Pachino.

It was an odd place. Had there been guests, things might have been different, but I was the only person staying and the only person dining, except for the proprietor, his wife and children, and the man who I took to be the manager, who doubled as chef. Fulvio – I never discovered his surname – was large and shambling with long, thinning hair and a luxuriant moustache. There was something deeply melancholy about him. He came, he said, from Friuli on the mainland, and wrote for various newspapers. He spoke of Spain, Spanish food and the Spanish newspaper, *El Pais*, with a nostalgic longing. He was a mine of opinion and information on culinary matters. I say information, but sometimes what he said sounded more like stream of consciousness than considered communication and I found it extremely difficult to follow his train of thought.

As far as I could make out, he never left the place. Certainly, he never did in the two days I was there. He drifted about like an ungainly, melancholy ghost. When he cooked he donned full chef's gear – white jacket, spongebag trousers and a floppy toque that fell over his head like a large pancake. He was a creative cook, which is not the same as saying he was a good one. Some of his dishes were distinctly idiosyncratic.

Nevertheless, there was a certain magic about Saccolino, about its surreality, the oddity of its occupant, and the olive and almond groves and apricot and nectarine orchards around it, about the pale, creamy gold of the land, the craggy steepness of the surrounding hills, the way the evening light suffused everything, turning the world a dainty pink; and the peaceful quietness through which, on my first night, I could hear children singing far away, and a call and response conversation between unseen figures, and birdsong.

@@

There were times when Sicily appeared to be one gigantic kitchen garden in which everything grew in magnificent abundance. Around Saccolino it was almonds. The trees had blossomed in January, and the fat fruits with their velvety, jade green skins were now ready to be picked. The area was the centre of the island's production of almonds which, in various forms, play a central role in Sicilian cooking, as they had in Arab and even Greek cooking. The almonds of nearby Avola, *pizzuta d'Avola* (*pizzuta* means sharp-tongued in dialect and refers to the sharp point of the almond shell), are revered for their shape and for their eating qualities. They are quite different from the Spanish Marcona almonds, so fashionable among chefs and foodistas in Britain. The kernel inside (almonds are not nuts, but kernels, strictly speaking) is plumper than the Spanish equivalent, and, for my money, far richer in benzaldahyde, the mundane compound that gives almonds their haunting perfume and flavour. But if you're looking for an almond to grind and put into puddings and pastries, the Romana di Noto is your almond. And should you want a good all-rounder, go for Fascionello.

Wild almond trees have been in the Mediterranean since time immemorial, and there is evidence of domesticated versions as early as the Bronze Age. Certainly the Mesopotamians were busy cracking almonds open in 1000 BC. I think it is safe to assume that they arrived in Sicily quite early on. However, it was the Arabs who started exploiting their qualities ground up in pastries and puddings. Almonds became widely used by cooks to the great houses during the Renaissance, going into such dishes as *biancomangiare* – blancmange (not at all the same dish as the much loathed staple of school lunches in my youth) – mixed with mashed capon. There is a whole subculture of marzipan, into which I won't go, largely because I dislike marzipan almost as much as I once did blancmange.

I passed through almond groves on my way to Noto, World Heritage Site and perennial favourite among British lovers of high baroque architecture. It's true that there is something fantastical about the frothy mass of buildings in golden-red stone, but for me there was a touch too much of the theme park about the place. Noto was too perfect, too tidy, and seemed to know it. It could do with a bit of ruffling up, I thought.

My appreciation was further dimmed when I discovered that my real objective in going there in the first place, the Caffe Sicilia, as famous for its traditional pastries and ice creams as the rest of Noto is for its visual theatricality, was closed. Disconsolate, I wandered about aimlessly, and it was in this fashion at last I found what I had been searching Sicily for: an ice cream worthy of celebration.

If ever the world owed a debt to the Moorish maestros of the kitchen, it is for the ice cream and the sorbet. I am not talking about Häagen Dazs or Ben & Jerry's here – overrich, oversweet, oversized – still less about Magnums, Wall's and other lesser breeds of ice cream, formed from a marvellous compound of fat, sugar and air, that so beguiled me when I was young. I can still remember the shock of tasting my first Italian ice creams in Cervia on the Adriatic coast at the age of 11. Nothing in life had prepared me for their subtle softness or for the purity of their flavours, which were neither rich nor cloying: strawberry ice cream tasted as if all the strawberries in the world had been distilled into each slow, indulgent lick; *nocciuola* tasted more of hazelnuts than hazelnuts; and chocolate was more chocolatey than seemed possible or real.

And then, as experience broadened my horizons, came *granite* and *sorbetti*, or sorbets, the corruption of the Arabic sherbet, those icy, crystalline essences of orange or lemon or coffee that cleaned away the heat and dust of the day and made my teeth and temples ache.

Whatever its history, the true importance of ice cream lies in its ubiquity and its democracy. It is an utterly classless food, and in one sense at least represents the most enduring and far-reaching example of Arab culture. It's received wisdom that Sicily, as the former bridgehead for the Arabic ice cream invasion of the rest of the world, is the place to find the finest examples of the genre. That's what you're told. But selfless research suggested otherwise, and God knows, I'd eaten enough ice creams.

I had found a halfway decent one in Marsala, but when I made an appointment with the resident *gelataio* to get him to explain the arcane mysteries of his craft, he cried off at the last moment. Caltanissetta, Catania and Siracusa had all proved a disappointment. I licked my way through numerous examples of chocolate, coffee, strawberry and pistachio in an effort to rediscover the heady beauty and excitement of my boyhood, but to no avail. It wasn't that they were bad. It was just that they weren't good enough. None had been worth the challenge of finishing them before they melted in the hot sun and ran down all over my hand, making it irritatingly sticky for the rest of the day. None had touched my G (for *gelati*) spot. Perhaps it was true, as Maria Paola maintained, that all ice creams were made with an industrially produced base these days. That would have accounted for their similarity in texture. The standard was good, but boringly uniform. So what made a killer ice cream? Did such a wonder exist? It was a mystery to me.

That was until I came to the Caffe Mandalfiore, tucked away on one of Noto's side streets, unremarkable from the outside. But one cone of almond ice cream changed it all. It was filled with the airy perfume of the nut, the silky soft cream studded with crunchy toasted almond shards that exploded when I bit them. *Pizzuta d'Avola* assuredly. I had one of those moments of epiphany that light up even the darkest days.

@@

In the other direction from Noto, towards Pachino (famous for its tomatoes, which, it is said, owe their unique flavour to the salted earth on which they grow; it's difficult to find them locally because they're too expensive and tend to be shipped off to high-end greengrocers in Milan or Turin), was an even rarer and, for my money, more rewarding treasure than Noto: the nature reserve of Vendicari. This ran for several kilometres along the coast, with one or two shallow, rush-fringed lakes that attracted migrating birds in numbers. I was particularly taken by elegant pink flamingos, heads down, chomping away at whatever flamingos chomp at. There were ibises, too, and any number of small waders, energetic brown bits of fluff, pecking away at the mud like tiny, industrious cleaners.

Part of the reserve was bounded by a long, curving bay, on one side of which stood an abandoned *tonnara* – a tuna processing factory – that looked like a Greek temple from far off, with its long, raised floor and twin lines of tall, upright columns of creamy golden stone which had once supported the long-disappeared roof. Behind them a slender chimney stretched up into the sky, graceful and exquisite. Beside it was the lowering, stolid mass of a Swabian tower facing gloomily and purposefully out to sea.

The greater part of the Vendicari was made up of low scrub, thorny and aromatic, and myrtle, thyme, rosemary, acacia, through which a well-maintained path ran to a dream-like cove, a tongue of clear blue water slipping lightly on to a curve of beach the colour of lightly toasted breadcrumbs. There were a number of families and couples already in residence when I arrived, so the possibility of surrendering to my pagan self, and swimming naked as a sprite (all right, more like Old Silenus, a roly-poly, Bacchic figure) was set to one side. Perhaps it was just as well. The dimpled whiteness of my form marked me out from the lean, tanned figures around me.

Then it struck me that I had been here before. I took out the notebook in which I had a few notes of the trip I had made in 1973. I realised Tom and I had swum here then lunched on grilled fish and salad somewhere nearby – where was it? I couldn't remember. There were just a few tantalising hints: 'The wind sucks and blows. The sea licks the lip of the rock, the constant, repeated, slightly shifting pattern of sound; partially sunk bottle lifting lightly in the transparent, sun-mottled sea. Mellow with sensations growing with food and wine. Grilled octopus, grilled fish of some kind; warm, slow, moving freckles of light on water; painted boats, stubby raised bows, dropping away to low sterns; heat, breeze; mind increasingly undecided; widening sense of grace and humour that alcohol at its best brings; Saki at lunch after a morning of Hemingway.'

Oh my God. These were the words of a chap half-pissed over lunch, awash with fancy writing but rather short on essential detail, such as the name of the place where this splendid meal had been eaten. Not for the first time I cursed the inadequacies of my youthful self as a note-taker.

Thirty-three years before the beach had been a secret place. Tom and I had had it to ourselves. Now I watched the families as they alternated long periods of sun-soaked inertia with leisurely bursts of sun-cream anointment or sorting out something to eat. I felt a node of resentment at the occupation of my paradise. Then I felt ashamed. It was mean-spirited in comparison to the generosity with which I had been treated. A deeply bronzed bald man, his blue-grey triangular bathing trunks moulded around his genitals, detached himself from the group to which he belonged and made his way with studied nonchalance, carefully holding in his stomach, down to the water, waded in and began swimming with a flashy crawl. Presently a woman in a glittering, paradise blue costume followed him. She slipped easily across the little bay like a blue porpoise, passing the man without pause or effort.

I took out my battered paperback copy of the *Odyssey*. The beach seemed the right place to stagger through another chapter. Reading the book had been my intellectual undertaking for the journey. The trouble was that I had only to open it to fall asleep, which I promptly did.

When I woke up, the beach was deserted except for a couple of diehard families. I went for a last swim. A flock of flamingos sauntered by overhead, their wings flashing first pearly pink, then white edged with black, and then back to pink again as they wheeled above me in the pure azure sky. I could almost touch my past.

∽ Sgombro alla griglia con capperi ∽

The first of three dishes from Az. Ag. Pozzo di Mazza, after that memorable honey tasting. Each was notable for the clarity of their flavours, no mean feat when your taste buds have been drowned in the sweet stuff all morning.

Serves 4
2 large or 4 small mackerel • 4 very ripe tomatoes • 50g capers in salt • 1 lemon

Slash the sides of the mackerel and grill them, keeping all the juices that run out. Deseed the tomatoes, but do not peel them. Chop them roughly. Rinse the capers thoroughly then drain them. Put the mackerel into a deep serving dish and plaster them with the chopped tomatoes. Scatter with capers. Pour the mackerel juices over and squeeze the lemon over everything.

∽ Insalata di melanzane ∽

One of the many virtues of this dish is the contrast in textures.

Serves 4
500g melanzane *(aubergines)* • *Olive oil* • *White wine vinegar*
• *2 medium carrots* • *2 sticks celery* • *2 garlic cloves* • *Salt and*
pepper

Wash the *melanzane* and cut off their stems. Cut them into
slices and the slices into strips. Put the strips into a colander
and sprinkle with salt. Leave for 30–40 minutes, then wash
thoroughly. Drain and dry them carefully. Fry in olive oil until
soft. Drain and sprinkle with white vinegar. Slice the carrots,
celery and garlic, and blanch briefly in boiling salted water. Mix
with the strips of *melanzane*. Season with salt and pepper and
dowse in olive oil.

∽ Bobbia ∽

No one I have spoken has even heard of bobbia. However, that's
what it was called, and this is it.

Serves 4
500g waxy potatoes • *500g mixed peppers* • *2 garlic cloves* •
25ml white wine • *Olive oil* • *salt and pepper*

Peel and cut the potatoes into cubes. Deseed the peppers and cut
into strips. Peel and slice the garlic. Put everything into a frying
pan and mix around. Add the white wine and splash liberally
with olive oil. Cook gently, stirring from time to time to prevent

sticking, until the potatoes are cooked through and the peppers are soft. Season with salt and pepper. Eat while warm.

∾ Almond ice cream ∾

This is not the almond ice cream I slurped down in Noto, but it's one that gets pretty damn close.

Serves 4 people
200g whole peeled almonds • 350 ml double cream • 3 egg yolks • 100g caster sugar • A few drops of vanilla essence

Briefly soak the almonds in hot water. Dry them carefully. Lightly heat 150g of the almonds in a pan so they give off their oils, but be careful not to colour them. Grind them in a mortar. (Use a food processor if you must, but in short bursts. Take care you don't liquefy them). Mix a little of the cream into them to make a paste.

Beat the yolks with the sugar in a bowl until pale and frothy. Slowly stir in the remaining cream, and then add the almond mixture and the vanilla essence. Set the bowl in a saucepan over water and heat it over a low heat, stirring, until it begins to thicken (don't let it boil). Remove it from the heat and let it cool. Chop the remaining almonds into slivers and toast until brown and crunchy. Make the ice cream following the instructions given by the manufacturer of your ice cream machine. Scatter the shards of toasted almonds over the top when you serve it, or you can add them to the ice cream mixture when you churn it.

Lina, il laboratorio della Casa Don Puglisi,
Modica Bassa

CHAPTER EIGHT

There's Always Time to Pay and to Die

@/@

Noto (St Paolo) – Modica

It was easy riding from Saccolino, heading inland away from the coastal plains, climbing up on to a fertile plateau, the fields neatly marked out with white stone walls, the stands of frothy olive trees and single tousle-headed carob trees. It was an orderly landscape, apparently richer than further inland towards Caltanisetta and Villalba, but no more inhabited. Indeed, it seemed populated more by cows than humans. At least, they were the only animals or crop of any kind that I saw.

The sun was high in the heavens. I was in no rush. Every now and then a waft of warm, fetid cow, or wilful wild fennel or some other sweet, unidentified perfume washed over me. My shadow ran before me on the road. Really, there was nothing wrong with life.

Aside from the absence of lunch, that is.

It was another day when I didn't get my timing quite right. My passion for the winding byways didn't seem to cross-reference with Sicily's centres of gastronomic excellence. Or gastronomic anything, as it turned out. Of course, had I been the experienced, careful voyager I would have stocked up with tasty goodies before setting off – a little salami, bread, cheese, fruit – but somehow I couldn't be bothered. I made the assumption, rash as it turned out, that I would find something along the way.

First of all, there were precious few towns or even villages of any kind on the roads I had chosen to follow. There was the odd *masseria*, looking like a small, walled village, but on closer inspection most of them turned out to be deserted; and, with my usual lack of resolve, which I portrayed to myself as considerate good manners, I felt it would have been a bit rude just to drop into any of those that were occupied and demand to be fed.

I found one hotel with a restaurant into which I clumped, only to be turned away by the old biddy on the door with the asperity of a dowager duchess being asked for money by a tramp. So I had to make do with memories of the last meal I had eaten at Saccolino, one of my erudite friend Fulvio's more idiosyncratic offerings – a slice of spinach and tomato fritatta; penne with smoked *scamorza* cheese, raw tomato and chilli; veal escalope *al marsala* with copious and incongruous fennel seeds – and with anticipating the dinner that lay before me. To be honest, missing the odd meal was not going to do my figure any harm. It was more mental disappointment than physical deprivation. The last time I was truly hungry was probably in about 1980.

And then I dropped down into Modica.

It was rather a shock after days in the high, wide and handsome flat landscapes to find myself descending precipitously into what appeared to be the centre of the earth, following a road that wound down and down. I could glimpse bits of the town here and there, but nothing prepared me for the full picture. It was as if I had stumbled across a lost civilisation still in full swing.

There were two Modicas, in fact: Modica Alta at the top of the gorge, which I never explored properly, and Modica Bassa at the bottom, into which I headed, and by which I was instantly captivated. Like much of the area, this part of the town had been completely rebuilt after the immensely destructive earthquake of 1693. And it must have been built with extraordinary speed, resulting in a beguiling homogeneity. As you know, baroque is not my favourite style of architecture, but here it was elegant, confident and handsome. Beneath all its twiddles and scrolly bits and adornment, the underlying structures had strong classical proportions that gave it a sense of balance and purpose to offset the worldly frivolity.

But what this rather bald description cannot convey – I am not sure that any description could ever convey – is Modica's air of fantasy, the way the houses clambered up the sides of the tremendous gorge, almost as if they were stacked on top of one another like card houses: uneven tier upon uneven tier, slightly staggered, strung along a series of tiny winding streets and steep flights of steps. Wherever I was in Modica, I either looked up at the rusty cream façades of the houses above, with their pedimented windows and doors, and balconies resting on stone scrolls or animals, or down on roofs, the tiles of which were tightly curved and the colour of stone.

Modica had its individual splendours, too. The guide-books go on at some length about the Chiesa di San Giorgio, reached via a monumental flight of 250 steps and regarded by one and all as being among the most remarkable baroque churches in Italy. I found it a fine building, not as pleasing as the duomo in Caltasinetta; and, oddly, its pale blue and gold interior reminded me of the synagogue in Casale Monferrato in northern Italy. It was the smaller, less celebrated details elsewhere in Modica that caught my eye. There was a lovely Arab doorway in the Via de Leva; a handsome, unnamed building, the windows of which reflected the various past influences on Sicilian architecture – a kind of neo-everything hodgepodge with pointed Norman and scallop-edged Moorish arches, each on a different storey; and a huge art deco structure that looked like a monumental garage, its curving roof interrupted at various points by four vast, grimacing heads. It was all rather bizarre.

In mood, too, Modica proved a delicious contrast to the edginess of Catania, the tourist-infested beauty of Siracusa and the self-regard of Noto. To me, the baroque splendours of Modica were no less striking, or not much less striking, than those of Noto, but they were less grandiose, less imposing, moderated by everyday life. People lived in these buildings as well as keeping them in admirable condition. More, the town seemed very comfortable with itself. It was a decent place full of decent people who enjoyed living there, like the man who made things out of tin, the man weaving baskets and carving whistles, the woman running the bread shop. Passing by one rather fine open door, I heard music being played. I peered in on a group of children, between eight and 12 years old, puffing and sawing away at their instruments for all they were worth under the firm guidance of a large man listening keenly to the sounds they made.

'I went away when I was a teenager,' said the man who checked me into the hotel. 'I worked all over the world. I was very lucky. Then I got married and we decided it was time to come back here. And now I am lucky again.'

๏

Modica turned out to be as blessed with foods as it was with beauty. Among its finest gastronomic blessings I would count *il cioccolato modicano*. I couldn't miss it. Every bar and shop seemed to specialise in the stuff, always *vero, artigianale, originale* it seemed.

I had been tipped off that if I wanted to investigate the real, proper, authentic chocolate I should go to the Azienda Bonajuto, makers of *il cioccolato modicano*. There I found Paolo Ruta, son of the owner, in a bit of a tizz. His desk was buried beneath a mountain range of files, papers, magazines, computer disks and the other office scree. Clearly it conformed to some kind of internal order imperceptible to the untrained eye because, after some energetic burrowing, he was able to locate files, or in this case a letter, without any difficulty.

The reason why Paolo Ruta was in such a state of excitement was that a chocolate producer of Barcelona in Spain had written to him. From his letter, which Paolo Ruta thrust at me, it appeared that the Spanish chocolatier had concluded that he and the Azienda Bonajuto made their chocolate in exactly the same way, to the same effect – including rolling and crushing the raw cocoa in the way that the Aztecs prepared their chocolate when the Spaniards first reached Mexico in the sixteenth century.

Not surprisingly, Columbus and other brave Spanish explorers couldn't wait to share the products of their discoveries with the patrons back home, and chocolate soon spread throughout other corners of the Spanish empire, of which Sicily was one. Indeed, Modica had been part of the fiefdom of a Spanish family, the Cabreras, who had been responsible for rebuilding it after the 1693 earthquake. So perhaps it isn't surprising that this other chocolate producer in Spain was using the same techniques.

Paolo Ruta explained that the secret to *il cioccolato modicano* lay in the heat used to make it. The cocoa was melted at a very low temperature – 50°C – which meant that the sugar used to sweeten it never fully melted. This particular technique also meant that the spices used to flavour the chocolate – vanilla, cinnamon, chilli, carob were popular – could be added at the beginning of the process without being altered or destroyed by the heat. The qualities of the chocolate were very addictive. It had the crisp snap and faintly granular texture of what I consider to be properly cooked fudge.

Of course, the ultimate quality of the chocolate doesn't depend just on the way it is made. Although Paolo Ruta was too much of a gentleman to suggest it, I had heard from other sources that most of the places advertising traditional/artisanal *cioccolato modicano* used any kind of industrial cocoa – even, horror of horrors, stuff from Nestlé.

This would not do for the house of Bonajuto. It got its cocoa from Principe, a small island off the west coast of Africa, where an obsessive and saintly Tuscan, Claudio Corallo, had created an idealistic enterprise to encourage local farmers to grow cocoa. The end result was unquestionably artisanal and of the highest quality. The farmers produced cocoa which, if the Bonajuto chocolates were anything to go by, had limpid flavour, harmony and balance. I could taste it lingering around the crannies of my mouth a good half an hour after the last tablet had vanished.

☙☙

Sergio Savarino could have been a character in one of Italo Svevo's novels, a man of the world in a small town. Perpetually swathed in the fumes of a Toscano Antico cigar, he was well turned out, cultured, languid, given to good humour and sardonic observation. His conversation was spotted with references to writers such as Salvatore Quasimodo, who had been born in Modica, Elio Vittorini and Cesare Pavese. He ran a successful men's outfitters in Modica. And, it turned out, he had an encyclopaedic knowledge of local foods. Would I be interested, he asked, in going see how the great cheese of the area, *ragusano*, was made? I thought I would. Very well, he said, he would arrange for us to visit Rosario Floridia, champion cheese-maker and breeder of the very rare Razza Modicana cows. *Ragusano*, Sergio explained, could only be made with milk from Razza Modicana cows.

The next day we met at the Bar Italia on the high street and breakfasted on delicate, refreshing *granita di mandorla*, almond granita. The Bar Italia was a modest, unremarkable place, but if you were looking for a granita it was the place to go, said Sergio. In fact, the bar dealt in a sophisticated range of frozen fruit refreshers. Aside from granitas, there were various *sorbetti*, and *cremolate* which I had not come across before. In part, the difference between them was a matter of the size of the ice crystals, those in a *sorbetto* being smaller, and so smoother, than the ones in a granita. A *cremolata* differed from a *sorbetto*, it seemed, because it was made of just the fruit plus a little sugar, whizzed up in a food processor and then frozen to a semi-liquid state. (I was so taken with the delights of the Bar Italia that I went back there in the evening for *cremolata di gelsi* – a smooth, velvety slush of mulberries, perfumed as an orchid and tasting intensely and purely of the fruit.)

We climbed out of Modica in Sergio's rickety Fiat, and

scooted along the back roads. His elbow rested on the window frame. There was a Toscano wedged between his first two fingers. For once it was out.

I recognised some of the roads from the day before, but we soon turned off into a maze of lanes that twitched across the flat, fertile, stone-strewn plateau with its white, drystone walls, carob trees and olive trees. Suddenly we whisked into a farmyard that was immaculately clean and orderly in the brilliant morning sun.

And there they were, several Razza Modicana specimens, gathered in a pen at the end of the yard, waiting with bovine patience in the shadow of a large barn for their turn at the troughs full of shiny, cinnamon brown carob pods. They were handsome animals, a deep russet-chocolate brown, glossy, with huge, languorous dark eyes and curved, sharply pointed horns. They looked the way cows should look, like Guernseys and Jerseys, as if the milk from them will have a particular richness and creaminess.

'Are they good for milk or for eating?' I asked Sergio.

'Not really for either,' he replied, lighting up his Toscano. 'They only produce about 3000 litres of milk a season, as opposed to the 9000 litres a Friesian cow gives. And the meat tends to be quite tough because they don't carry a lot of fat.'

'Perhaps that's why they're so rare,' I said.

'Maybe,' he said, 'but the milk is of a very high quality, ideal for making cheese. The protein content is high, and the fat content gives the cheese its rich flavour.'

'How many cows has Signor Floridia got?'

Sergio puffed at his Toscano and cocked an eyebrow. He replied that Signor Floridia would never say how many cows he had. It was, he suggested, not so much a trade secret as one to be kept from the prying eyes of bureaucrats.

The dairy was large and airy, and full of stainless-steel machinery. It smelt soft and milky, with a lingering acid note. Signora Floridia was snipping up wild rocket to later stir it into one batch of cheese, along with *peperoncino*, chilli, one way of extending the product range. The Floridia daughter was stirring a batch of milk with an implement like a medieval, flanged mace. The milk had set to a junket-like consistency in a large stainless-steel tub. Rosario himself was working on a mass of what would become, at the end of a long process, a 14-kilogram block of *ragusano*.

And it was work. At this stage, the cheese looked like a shiny, white pouffe. Rosario turned it over and over, pressing its surface, squeezing it, pushing, turning it in on itself, patting it into a homogeneous mass again. He was a handsome man with white hair brushed stiffly back from his teak brown face. His eyes were strikingly bright. He was not tall, but he was strongly built, the muscles on his wiry arms sharply defined, his hands muscular and sensitive at the same time. At times it was almost as if he were fondling the cheese.

He kept up the massage for half an hour at least. Then he lifted the rounded mass out and dumped it into a *masciella*, a coffin-shaped wooden box, ramming a wooden block up against the side. He placed another block on top with the insignia of the maker, in raised letters on its surface, placed next to the surface of the cheese to brand it. The cheese would stay like this for 24 hours. At the end it would look like a large, old-fashioned block of soap.

From the *masciella*, the cheese would be taken to the maturing room beneath the dairy, to be strung up *a cavallo* – with a length of thick cord tied around its middle – and suspended from a beam. The blocks of cheese would stay suspended in mid-air, marvellously higgledy-piggledy mobiles, for up to two years, turning from white to creamy gold to pale amber, gradually drying out and intensifying their flavours.

Yes, Rosario said, they made cheese 365 days a year.

'What, on Christmas Day and Easter, too?'

'Yes, on Christmas Day and Easter too,' he said. 'The cows don't take holidays. They don't stop giving milk, do they?'

'I suppose not,' I said.

'Why do you do it?' I asked

He looked surprised that anyone should ask the question.

'Because I have to. I feel obliged to,' he said. That was all.

And besides the *ragusano*, he said, they also made *Tuma*, *provola* and ricotta. That was what his daughter had been making, from the whey left over after they had made all the other cheeses. Ricotta is produced by heating the whey to 100°C, which causes the final small clots of curd to rise to the surface where they can be scooped off and drained in plastic tubs with holes. Once the tubs would have been made of rush or withies. EU regulations had seen them off.

The best cheeses, Rosario said, were made from November to March, when the grass was at its greenest and richest. It was curious, I thought, how the seasons in Sicily seemed exactly the reverse of those in Britain. We think of winter as the deadest time of year, when animals have to come in and be fed on silage gathered during the summer. In Sicily June, July, August, and even September, are the lifeless months when the searing heat stops all growth.

Rosario invited us to sit down in a large room that did duty as the farm canteen and sale room. He was making a great attempt to speak Italian to me, but every so often he would slip into Sicilian and I would be lost. Sergio had told me that Italian was a second language for Sicilians. They spoke their own language as a matter of course.

First we had a bowl of ricotta, so fresh that it was still warm from the whey being heated. It was a delicious sloppy broth, comforting, digestible, delicate, almost neutral; not as eggy as sheep's milk ricotta. We were given bread baked on the premises, compact, almost dry, with a curious, smooth, brown crust, and wine also made on the *azienda*. The wine was cold, and tasted of damsons and cherries. Signor Floridia began by breaking up his bread and dropping the bits into his bowl of ricotta. I did the same with my bread. It immediately softened and became an unsweetened bread and butter pudding. This must have been the way shepherds would have eaten.

Then we tasted the *ragusano*. The first example was five months old. It had a spongy firm–soft texture, like Gruyère, and tasted slightly caramelised with a modulated tang of warm grass. There was a kind of civilised wildness to it, and layers of flavour, subtle and distinct. It was a cheese that hung around a long time in your mouth.

But not as long as the two-year-old *ragusano*. In this, the flavours had intensified, becoming powerful, penetrating, concentrated and focused. The texture had dried out, become closer to mature Cheddar, but it broke up into flakes or stratas, like shale. It was a cheese to produce a craving. By tasting back and forth I could trace the qualities of the first cheese in the second one, but they seemed to occupy different worlds.

While we tasted, Rosario subjected Sergio to a discourse on the inequalities of life. He waxed eloquent on the matters of bureaucracy, ridiculous legislation, price, the inequitable behaviour of middlemen, the unscrupulous way in which some of his fellow cheese-makers were trying to bend the DOP (Protected Designation of Origin) regulation. The problems of farmers seem to be the same the whole world over.

When his jeremiad had run out of steam, he took us to see the sultan of his herd of Razza Modicana cows, and the sire of their progeny, which was kept in a fifteenth-century byre a kilometre away with a small harem of broody cows. There was no soulless artificial insemination for la Razza Modicana. The bull was a majestic animal, massive not just in his proportions but in his manner. He moved with massive slowness, lifted his head with massive disinterest, followed a cow waiting to be served with a massive friskiness. They disappeared out of the yard where they had been standing and vanished round a corner. Shortly afterwards we could hear his massive bellows of passion; but, dear reader, I must leave the scene to your imagination because some rare sense of decency prevented us from watching this majestic love-making, and we returned to Modica.

☙☙

Sergio took me to La Rusticana for dinner, where we were joined by his wife. She was a lively, engaging woman who taught the piano. A beguiling sense of affection shone through a skein of lively banter.

La Rusticana was a very basic trattoria with very good food, the closest I had found so far to what I imagined to be true *cucina dei contadini*, even if the number of courses was rather greater than would have been seen on the table of the average Sicilian farmhouse.

They went like this:

Antipasti:

* Salad of dried broad beans with celery stalks and leaves, and vinegar. The beans had been cooked so that some of them had burst and thickened the texture of the salad, but most remained moist and whole. The vinegar and celery leaves helped lighten the mixture.
* A kind of *millefoglie* pie made of layers of pastry, one layer stuffed with tomato pulp and oregano, and another stuffed with ricotta and parsley.
* A plate of pecorino, *salsiccie*, dried tomatoes and olives.
* Bruschetta with partially dried tomatoes.

Primo piatto 1:

* *Maccu*, a thick soup of dried broad-bean purée with pasta the size, thickness and texture of a chipolata sausage.

Primo piatto 2:

* *Frittata di ricotta* (a fine fluffy omelette rolled around ricotta) like an eggy, cheesy Swiss roll.

Secondo piatto:

* Rough-hewn lumps of pork braised in tomato sauce loaded with tomato extract.

Fruit:

* *Ficchi d'India* (prickly pear)

Pudding:

* *Biancomangiare* (blancmange)

A woman from Chicago, Charlotte Gower Chapman, lived in a Sicilian village in the 1920s and 1930s and wrote a remarkable book, *Milocca: A Sicilian Village*, based on her experiences. In it she gives a picture of life in rural Sicily at the time, which gets its vividness from the patient accumulation of detail and accuracy. 'Pasta is usually served at only one meal a day,' she wrote, 'usually in the evening when the man of the house is back from the fields. During the day each member of the family satisfies his hunger when it makes itself felt, by taking a piece of bread and fruit, nuts, some cheese, salted sardines, or possibly an egg, with or without a swallow of wine. The untranslatable word *campanaggio* refers to any of these things which are eaten with bread. The man in the fields may cut himself a raw artichoke or a bunch of grapes, or his employer provide something in the way of cheese, onions or boiled greens.

'At present,' she goes on, 'most of the families of Milocca manage to afford spaghetti manufactured at the mill. In former days this was luxury.'

On this basis, the scale of the dinner at La Rusticana put it firmly in the luxury category, but there were plenty of people still alive who would remember the conditions Charlotte Gower Chapman described, not least because they persisted until relatively recently.

It wasn't lightweight fare. Filling was the word that sprang to mind, along with hefty, robust and stonking, particularly in the flavour department. This came as no surprise to me. If you had walked 7 or 8 kilometres to work and 7 or 8 kilometres back – not unknown for agricultural labourers up until the 1960s – and had spent ten or so hours under the broiling sun or in the chilling rain, the dinky British version of the

Mediterranean diet – a dainty cheese and tomato salad with a grilled fillet of sea bass served with a splash of extra virgin olive oil – wouldn't have cut much ice. Not that people would have been able to afford fresh fish, even if it had been available this far from the sea; meat, too, would have been a rarity. As the grannies of Villalba had said, many families would not have eaten meat more than a few times a year, so vegetables, pulses, bread and pasta were needed to provide bulk as well as nourishment – and even these were limited for many people. The dishes they cooked revealed an extraordinary versatility and ingenuity when it came to livening up dull ingredients.

With some difficulty, I heaved up yet another large chunk of succulent, chewy pork, rusty red with tomato sauce the same colour as the resplendent buildings outside. I remarked to Sergio that I had yet to see a pig in Sicily.

'That's because they're all inside in intensive units,' he said. 'Do you want to see one?' I thought probably not. The conversation turned to Sicily, its past and present ills.

As we walked down the street afterwards, Sergio offered the same view as Nanni Cucchiara: that Garibaldi had been little better than a bandit, and that things had been better before Sicily had become a satrapy of northern politicians and businessmen. I pointed out that things hadn't changed much in this sense since the days of the Roman Empire. Would they ever change? I asked. He thought not, he said, puffing at his Toscano.

⊛⊛

Not all Sicilians were fatalists. Lina wasn't. Lina was a pragmatist.

She was a woman of … well, I couldn't tell her age and I didn't have the courage to ask her, but in a way she was ageless.

I felt that she had always had this mild, kindly, sensible look beneath her white bonnet, and a stout, sensible body under her white coat and sensible feet in sensible shoes. At the same time there was something formidable about her, a sharpness about her eyes behind her spectacles, a sense of a powerful will, a feeling that Lina had only one gear and that was forward, at her own speed and in her own time.

'What's your surname, Lina?' I asked her when I first met her.

'Everyone just calls me Lina. No one uses my other name.'

'Right. I see. OK. Good.'

When I came into the *laboratorio*, the production centre of the Casa Don Puglisi in Modica, two large rooms off a steep backstreet just around the corner from the Casa Don Puglisi shop, it was filled with the comfort of warm sugar and chocolate. Lina was taking scoops of melted chocolate from a large tub of the stuff, and plopping a scoop at a time into rectangular moulds. These rested on scales so that she could check the exact weight going into each one. Never once did I see her take out any part of the chocolate she had put into a mould, or add to it. It was scoop, plop, scoop, plop, scoop, plop every few seconds, 100 grams on the nail every time, hundreds of times.

The Casa Don Puglisi was a *dolceria*, which is different from a *pasticceria*. A *pasticceria*, according to Lina, specialised in cakes and creamy confections, whereas a *dolceria* specialised in biscuits and dried baked goodies – *nucatoli*, *mustazzoli*, *taralucci savoiardi*, *anicini* and the curious, sweet pastry particular to Modica: *'mpanatigghie*. The Casa also produced *pasta di mandorla*, blocks of almond paste, and *latte di mandorla*, almond milk. And, inevitably, there were the blocks of *cioccolato modicano* which Lina was ladling out now with such precision, born of daily practice. There would be 2000 blocks by the time she had finished.

The Casa Don Puglisi functioned as a normal commercial business, but in many ways it wasn't. That is to say, it was commercial but it wasn't normal. It was part of a network of businesses set up to make use of products grown on lands confiscated from Mafia bosses – the best known is Libera Terra. The Casa was a co-operative that grew out of the work of a priest, Don Giuseppe Puglisi, who had ministered to the people of the Brancaccio, a slum quarter in Palermo, until he was murdered by the Cosa Nostra in 1993. An orphanage in Modica had grown up out of his work and the pastry business was set up to give women who had been cared for there skills and an occupation.

One of the characteristics of Italian and Sicilian artisan food production is that the people who actually make it don't turn their noses up at modern technology, as long as it doesn't interfere with the quality of the end product. So there was a battery of grinding machines, mixing machines and machines for melting chocolate, not to mention a computer-controlled oven for baking. The ingredients – *materie prime* – were sourced with care, the rough work was done by machine, and the critical processes and finishing work were done by hand.

While Lina was measuring out the chocolate, Gabriella was grinding the almonds that would be made into that day's batch of almond paste to go into the *'mpanatigghie*. The almonds still had their skins on because, Lina said, this was *'piu saporito'*, tastier, and the untidy brown flakes of skin don't show up in the *'mpanatigghie* mix. Later Gabriella ground skinned almonds for *biscotti di mandorla*, or to be formed into blocks of *pasta di mandorla*, wrapped and sold as such for home use. In the other room, with its high, vaulted ceiling and cream walls Giuseppina and Maria were tapping the ingots of solid *cioccolato modicano* out of their plastic moulds, and wrapping them first in grease-proof paper and then in display paper before tying them up with string.

After doling out the chocolate for the *cioccolato modicano*, Lina's next job was to make the *panetti di pasta di mandorla*, one of several different almond items that would be made during the day. She took the skinned ground almonds and mixed in the sugar. Slowly, she worked the egg yolks into the ground almonds – no egg whites at this stage – and then added water, working at it until it formed a stiff dough and was ready to go into a rolling machine. The dough was rolled over and over again, five, six, seven times, egg whites were added from time to time and it was rolled again until it had reached the right homogeneous state – a soft, tight, almost crumbly texture. The flavour was delicate, quite unlike the aggressive marzipan I was used to, but, whatever Lina said, it was sweet.

Over in the other room the wrapping of the *cioccolato modicano* went on rhythmically and the neat stack of ingots mounted higher.

'No you can't be precise about quantities', Lina said. 'The size of the egg yolks varies. The almonds vary. Experience, that's what tells you when it's right.'

She had been running the *laboratorio* of the Casa Don Puglisi for 13 years, she said, and had had a *dolceria* which she ran with her sister before that. Her arms were as muscular and wiry as those of Rosario Floridia, a testament to a lifetime of labour.

I asked her where the recipes came from.

'*In testa*,' she said, tapping her forehead.

Back in the first room, Gabriella had been joined by Giuseppina to make *biscottini*, little waved S-shapes of egg, flour and water baked to a sandy brown, to be dipped into coffee for elevenses or whenever. There seemed to be different pastries for each hour of the day. Giuseppina took the extruded dough from the machine in short lengths and handed them to Gabriella, who laid them out on the baking tray. When one tray was full, she started another. There were four, five trays, each with 30 or 40 little pastry Ss on them. All the while, Gabriella and Giuseppina carried on a lively discussion as they went on working with deft automatism.

Gabriella slid one of the trays into the oven and pressed the timing controls. Presently the smiling smells of molten chocolate and honey were joined by the vanilla and wheat of freshly baked biscuits, which crumbled to a slightly sweet, wheaty powder as I ate one, two, three.

Right. It was time to start making the filling for the *'mpanatigghie*. Oh, no it wasn't, because it was time for the doctor, who had turned up to check the blood pressure of one of the girls, so work stopped for that.

The *'mpanatigghie* is a curious pastry: a crisp case like a small pasty filled with a mixture of fried minced veal, chocolate, almond paste and cinnamon. The nearest equivalent I can think of is a mince pie, which, come to think of it, had originally been made with spiced mincemeat. Lina called it *un dolce da viaggio*, a sweet for a journey. It was Spanish originally, she said. The name itself is a Sicilian version of *empanada*.

To make the filling, Lina began by pushing fried mince through the rolling machine, which crushed it dry and turned it a kind of mushroom colour. She added several scoops of liquid chocolate to it, and then almond paste, mixing in each ingredient very thoroughly. She worked with complete assurance without measuring anything.

'And what are the qualities for being a *pasticciere*?' I asked.

'*La pazienza*,' she said. Patience. She made it sound as if it were a command.

'You can't hurry *dolce*,' she said.

She began working the dough for the casing on the stainless-steel surface. It had already been stirred by machine for about two hours and Lina began to add egg white to it, turning it over and over. Finally, she judged it to be ready for the rolling machine. When it had the right texture, she scooped the pastry into a ball and moved it back to the stainless-steel worktop, carefully dusting it with flour first. She broke off a lump the size of an apple, and began to roll it rapidly by hand with a wooden rolling pin about a metre long.

'*Questa pasta e delicata*,' she said, turning it 45 degrees, flipping it over, and rolling it again until the dough formed a circle about a metre across, and was so thin I could see the worktop through it.

She took a brass cutter the same shape as a hand bell, and cut circles out of the pastry with considerable force – bang, bang, bang. Gabriella stripped away what was left over and squeezed it together with the rest of the unused dough. Lina put a squirt of the filling on to the centre of each pastry round. Gabriella folded the rounds over and sealed them. Lina squeezed the seals still further, and then created a dog-tooth pattern along the sealed edges using her thumb. She did this with eye-baffling rapidity. It had the same fascination as watching a croupier shuffle cards. Gabriella put a twist of sugar on to each '*mpanatigghie* with her fingers before they went in the oven for 15 minutes.

And out they came golden-brown little puffs, too hot to eat for a minute or two – time to dust a little cinnamon over them as they cooled so that the heat didn't burn off the perfume of the spice. And now they really were ready and, crunch, a light bite broke the thin casing with a puff of almond in it. The filling was still molten, rich, layered – chocolate, cinnamon, sweetness, almonds and on and on, the perfect *dolce da viaggio*. I said my goodbyes. Lina and her young women put together a bag of other pastries for the road, and I steered out of Modica, and up on to the high plateau again.

∞ Insalata delle fave con sedano ∞

A fine, filling, healthy dish from the Trattoria La Rusticana in Modica. The celery gives lightness as well as crunch.

Serves 4
200g dried broad beans • Red wine vinegar • Salt and pepper • 2 celery hearts • Extra virgin olive oil

Soak the broad beans overnight. Then put into a pan and cover with water. Do *not* add salt. Bring to boil and cook until the beans are soft. Drain, keeping some of the cooking liquor. Puree about a quarter of the beans, lightening the purée with some of the cooking liquor and a tablespoon or so of vinegar (to your taste). Mix the bean cream and the whole beans. Season with salt and pepper and Add a little more vinegar if you like. Finely chop the celery heart, leaves included, and stir into the beans. Serve cold with some extra virgin olive oil dribbled over the surface.

∾ Frittata di ricotta ∾

All you need are good eggs, good sheep's ricotta and good-aged pecorino. Easier said than done, but worth it.

Serves 2

2 dsp aged pecorino • 4 eggs • Salt and pepper • 1 dsp butter • 200g sheep's ricotta

Grate the pecorino. Break the eggs into a bowl. Add the pecorino and season. Beat until light and fluffy. Melt the butter in a frying pan over a low heat. Add the beaten egg and cheese mixture. When it begins to firm up, spread the ricotta over the whole surface. Cook for another couple of minutes, then roll up like a Swiss roll. Turn out onto plate. Eat warm or cold.

∾ Biancomangiare ∾

This banished the hideous memories of my schooldays. It makes an easy and better alternative to the ubiquitous *pannacotta*.

Serves 4

150g peeled almonds • 50g caster sugar • 30–35g cornflour

Chop 125g of the almonds finely. Put into a saucepan with 300ml of water and leave to soak. After half an hour, pass through a muslin cloth, squeezing it thoroughly. Very gently heat up almond milk in a pan. Add the sugar and the cornflour. Blend to a paste and continue cooking gently until it is lump-free. Pour into four moulds. Cool and then pop into the fridge for at least an hour. You can decorate with the remaining chopped almonds or pistachios.

∽ 'Mpanatigghie ∽

I can't pretend that my 'mpanatigghie comes close to Lina's. I've only got about another 50 years of practice to go.

Makes about 12 'mpanatigghie
Pastry: *350g 00 flour* • *120g* sugna *(pig fat) or butter* • *5 egg yolks* • *A pinch of bicarbonate of soda*
Filling: *500g minced veal* • *100g* cioccolato modicano *(or high quality plain chocolate plus a little sugar to give the right sweetness)* • *100g cocoa powder* • *600g roasted, ground almonds* • *500g caster sugar* • *4 eggs* • *3 egg whites* • *A pinch of ground cloves* • *½ tsp ground cinnamon*

In a bowl mix all then ingredients for the pastry with enough water to form a firm dough. Leave to rest in a cool place for a couple of hours at least.

Fry the minced veal gently in a frying pan until grey. Melt the chocolate and mix into the veal carefully. Add the cocoa powder, ground almonds and the sugar. Add the eggs one by one, mixing in thoroughly. Add the egg whites, the ground cloves and some of the cinnamon. You should have quite a firm paste.

Preheat the oven to to 220ºC/425ºF/Gas 7. Roll out the dough until quite thin. Cut out circles about 12cm across. Plop a dessertspoonful of the filling in the middle of each. Fold over and seal the edges carefully with a little water, folding them over and pinching them to form little wave patterns along the join. Make a little cut in the top. Bake for 20 minutes or until the 'mpanatigghie are golden brown. Dust with a little more cinnamon as they cool down.

Cesarina Perrone, bread maker & teacher, Marsala

CHAPTER NINE

Big Eats

֎

Modica – Porto Palo – Marsala

As I sped Monica from Modica to Mandranova, just east of Agrigento, I found a few crumbs of *'mpanatigghie* lodged in the corner of my mouth. It was a happy reminder. Making biscuits and sweetmeats may seem antediluvian in the age of IT literacy and global finance, but it seemed to me that anyone can acquire those skills. It takes a rarer sense of application and craft to make these *biscotti*.

It was a long haul along tedious main roads. Not for me the Biblioteca Buffalino at Comiso or the excavations of the Greek fortifications at Capo Soprano. I was spared the hideousness of Gela, a vision of hell from the road, with its cracking towers, articulated piping, and all other expressions of oil-refining technology. I had to get on. Places to go. People to see. Food to eat.

A scooter is an exhilarating mode of transport just so long as a) the sun shines; b) it doesn't rain; c) a stiff wind doesn't blow in your face; d) you have remembered always to top up your tank at the last petrol station; and e) you don't have to spend more than six hours in the saddle on any given day.

Longer than that and I became prone to a) underpant rucking, which became progressively irritating, uncomfortable, distracting and finally unbearable, whereupon I would have to stop at some secluded spot to readjust my undercarriage; b) discomfort caused by said undercarriage becoming hot and sweaty; c) a depressing sense of just how limited my mental equipment was. Locked away inside a helmet, you can't listen to Radio 4 or 5 Live. I suppose, had I been a bit more technologically literate, I could have got iPodded up and bathed my brain in the classics, but I was stuck with my own store of thoughts which, after a few hours, seemed depressingly familiar.

When she was little my daughter, Lois, liked to watch a video called *Rosie the Hen Went for a Walk*, and so she did, over and over again, not two or three times, but ten or 15 times. I felt much the same about my thoughts. They seemed to be on a kind of rather short loop, repeating every hour or so. They covered what I had eaten the night before; where I was going to find lunch; increasing panic if it looked as if I might not find lunch; what I was going to do if I didn't find lunch (again); what I was going to eat for dinner; attempts to tease out some telling insight from what I had eaten; considering the state of my underpants; curiosity at some passing sight; general irritation at my inadequacies as an informed observer; wondering whether to stop to consult the map; wondering whether I was where I thought I was; wondering turning to doubting; doubt turning to anxiety; anxiety turning to panic; finally consulting the map again; so where had I gone wrong; and where was I going to find lunch ...

The mental loop had run so many times that I was drained by the time I came to Mandranova, hard by Palma di Montechiaro. It was a handsome estate in an unlikely spot, burnt hills and olive groves all around and a bloody great main road streaming practically past the front door. The olive harvest was in full swing, the state-of-the-art press in an outbuilding producing a steady stream of rich green-gold oil. The air was thick with that grassy smell of the stuff. It was the dream creation of Giuseppe di Vincenzo, a merchant banker in a former life, and his wife Silvia. Tiring of the demands of Mammon, as he told me over a glass of wine that evening, he had given up the life of first-class air travel and morning meetings in favour of planting 10,000 olive trees and making oil. He said he had had to go back to banking for a time, until his trees started producing. Now they were, and the oil from them was winning prizes and gurgling out of the pipe into the waiting bottles.

To begin with he was full of the technicalities about this variety of olive and that, *biancolilla, cerasuola, giarraffa* and *nocellara*, their organoleptic profiles and acid levels, but presently the conversation moved on to a more metaphysical level.

'I didn't start up this enterprise,' he said, 'to become rich. I could've made more money as a banker. But this land was owned by my father and he won prizes for his sheep. I want to make something of quality. I want to change an idea that the outside world has of Sicily.'

'So what does Sicily mean to you?' I asked him.

'There are many Sicilies,' he said. 'The Sicily of history, the Sicily of the *contadini*, the Sicily of the Mafia, the Sicily of politics.' He went on: 'I want to create an idea or image of Sicily that isn't corrupt or stained by the Mafia or marked by incompetence, a Sicily that stands for a certain idea of quality, in the same way that Dolce & Gabbana sell an idea of fashion.'

I mulled over the Dolce & Gabbana parallel as I rode to Licata, about 15 kilometres away, for dinner. It was true that Domenico Dolce had been born in Palermo, but I wasn't sure that Giuseppe's challenge wasn't of a rather higher order than establishing a high-end fashion house. Sicily was a great deal more complex and more fascinating at every level, even if I couldn't quite get the measure of its complexity and fascination. Perhaps dinner would help. It frequently did.

Licata is not a pretty town by night. Nor by day, I suspect. A bit like a Sicilian Margate was my impression. But in this unpromising spot, I had been told, was La Madia, and so to La Madia I went for dinner. It turned out to be rather more of a proper restaurant than I was used to, smart and orderly, with brilliant white napery, gleaming cutlery, high-pedigree glasses and attentive waiters. To be honest, it was quite refreshing, although, even in my smartest gear, I was a touch shabby compared to the other diners. Not that the attentive waiters batted an eyelid, or treated me as anything other than an eccentric millionaire.

I began with *puzze di insalata mediterranea, 'scatoletta di sgombro sott'olio con aqua di pomodoro verde*. Ultra-thin, dried slices of tomato and onion had been laid on the base of a soup plate. A small piece of dried bread rested on top of them. A chunk of cooked mackerel marinated in oil sat on top of that. A small dab of mayonnaise seasoned with *bottarga*, tuna roe dried in the sun, lay on top of the mackerel. The tail and bottom section of the fish rose up like a sail to one side. A waiter poured what appeared to be water into the plate. It turned out to be clear tomato juice of tingling intensity. The dish was utterly sublime, light, delicate, refreshing. I could taste each of the component elements individually, like chimes, but each balanced with each other and worked together in intricate counterpoint. It had come a long way from bread and tomato salad, that very basic Mediterranean staple from which it was obviously derived. Ay up, I thought, this is pretty damn fine stuff, and woke up to the fact that I was in the hands of an exceptional chef.

Next was *fiore di zucchini con ricotta con crostino di pomodoro*. A zucchini flower was stuffed with superfine ricotta. There was a little bunch of tiny, partially dried tomatoes still attached to a stem; and a very thin slice of crisp bread rolled around some tomato confit. The tomato acted as a foil to the light eggy creaminess of the sheep's milk ricotta, and there was a contrast between the butterfly-wing friability of the bread and the softness of the stuffed flower. It was a dish of exquisite judgement and balance.

The third course was *lo spiedino di polpo verace, passatina di ceci, salsa al rosmarino*. A single octopus tentacle was coiled on top of chickpea purée surrounded by a trail of golden olive oil. The octopus was tender to the point of softness, but it had been seared and caramelised on the outside to increase its natural sweetness. The chickpea purée was lustrous and silky, creamy and nutty to taste. The vividness of the *salsa al rosmarino*, olive oil infused with the herb, lifted and focused the other ingredients. The total effect was masterly.

By this time I was getting into the swing of things, and was ready for *la spatola a beccafico, caponata di verdure e cipolla rossa*. I wasn't sure what fish *spatola* was (on further research it turns out to be paddlefish), but whatever its identity, it was stuffed with breadcrumbs, herbs and pine nuts on a layer of *caponata*, and red onions. The fish was chunky. The breadcrumb stuffing had been lightened with a liberal dash of lemon juice The *caponata* was refined almost beyond recognition. The clarity of the flavours, the subtle distinctions in textures, and the way the whole dish hung together, was exhilarating.

The chef, Pino Caiutto, had the gift of being able to take

recognisable Sicilian dishes, and through a personal alchemy transform them into intricate, delicate compositions in which the elements of the original were held up to be admired individually. I might not have been getting on with sorting my way through the endless paradoxes that seemed to make up Sicily, but, stone me, I was having the finest dinner I had had in a very long time.

La melanzane perlina con ricotta e pomodoro was up there with the rest. A couple of very small, slender *melanzane* had been roasted, the flesh taken out and mixed with ricotta and then put back inside the skin. The *melanzane* had been wrapped in a cocoon of cooked tagliatelle as thin as threads, and roasted again so that the pasta had turned *croccante* – crunchy – around the soft, smoky filling. It was sauced with tomato passata sweetened with a tiny amount of honey. It is possible to get too carried away about these things, but there was the soft, smoky stuffing, the crunchy wheaty pasta, and the honeyed fruitiness of the sauce, and a whiff of herbs, and, well, loads of stuff going on.

The sixth course: *lo spaghetto fatto da noi con fegatini di sepia*. Who's ever heard of squid livers? Not me, for one. Not that I cared a jot. Here were perfect strands of spaghetti, silky and submissive, sauced with the quiddity of marine life, rich, subtle, deep, mineral and iodine. I floated on a sea of sensations.

Il filetto di manzo lisciato all'olio di cenere was almost the last hurrah, and Signor Caiutto's inspiration showed no sign of slackening. There were several slices of beef sirloin, generously cut, on a bed of crunchy lettuce and very small roast potatoes and glistening with an oil infused with charcoal – barbecued beef with roast potatoes and salad. Ah, but such beef, with the texture of velvet and the flavour of roses. A few leaves of iceberg lettuce slightly wilted. Crunchy roast potatoes. Lightly acrid burnt edge you get from a proper chargrill. Clever, funny and very, very good.

Dinner came to a theatrical finish with *le cornucopia, cialda di cannolo con crema di ricotta e marmellata d'arance*, as unreconstructedly, old-fashionedly Sicilian as the other dishes had been refined and elegant. Creamy, crunchy, soft, sweet, sharp, luxurious, over the top, ludicrously indulgent. Heavens, yes.

And that was it, one of the finest meals I had ever eaten in my life – delicious, clever, humorous on occasion, and true to its roots. There was nothing extraneous to any dish, no bit that had me asking why it was there. Each element functioned perfectly in its own right and in relation to all the other elements. Each dish was exquisitely balanced and carefully thought through. Nor did I get the impression of bravura cooking for its own sake. The presentation was very refined in many cases, but never at the expense of the flavour. And while all the dishes were the epitome of creative modern cookery of the highest order, nevertheless they had their roots in identifiable Sicilian originals, even the beef. It made most British cooking look posturing and prosaic.

Pino Caiutto turned out to be a serious young man. I told him what I thought of his food. He seemed pleased. He had trained, he said, in the north of Italy, in Piedmont. What brought him to Licata? I asked. He held out his right hand and pointed to his wedding ring. I wanted to say more, but I was too full. I went off into the night suffused with a ringing sense of well-being.

◉◉

I was tempted to go back to La Madia for lunch, the imperative of the road called me on. The threat of rain hung in the air. But on I had to go. There were times when I resented the tyranny of travel, the need to get to the next place. Wouldn't it be very nice just to loaf around for a few days, potter about, treat the whole thing as a romp? But no, the imperative of the odyssey commanded, and the truth was that I was always curious about the next place.

So after a decent breakfast I headed for Porto Palo, via Canicatti, Racalmuto where Leonardo Sciascia, the great chronicler of Sicily's interlocking moral mazes, had been born, Aragona, Raffadali, Siciliana. It was overcast and cool, but it was a joyful route all the same, climbing up from the coast through rolling hills that got steadily steeper and steeper. They were heavily cultivated, with fields of tomatoes left to dry on their vines, strips of artichokes among stands of vines grown on pergolas and neat plantations of olive trees. One line of hills was dominated by walnuts, another by lemons.

The land had some of the lilt and sway of further inland, but on a more intimate scale. The holdings were smaller and the land a quite different colour than in spring. The browns had turned to duns, the greens were tinged with yellow. In places the earth had been tilled, ready for the next crop. The towns were small and pretty, not in the picturesque style of places on the mainland, but curious and lively. They didn't have the same depressed, uncared-for air that I had felt going through the towns of the deep interior, such as Salemi, Corleone, Caltanissetta and Adrano.

The sky remained overcast, but the threatened rain didn't arrive. It was getting towards 2 p.m. I was going to find lunch at any cost. I was not going to be caught out again. Absolutely not. Happiness depends on sound sleep, orderly bowels and regular meals. In Siculiana I hit on *scacciata*, a kind of bun of springy dough coiled round bits of sausage meat and studded with black olives in a *salumeria/tavola calda*. It might just have been my hunger, but it was splendid convenience food, exactly the kind of food a chap in the saddle needs. Sadly, so urgent was my desire to eat it, I failed to make a note of its name.

No longer panic-stricken on the lunch front, I sailed blithely on. Not long afterwards I passed two cheery biddies picking something beside the road. I stopped.

'What are you picking?' I asked. They looked a bit askance.

'Fennel,' said one.

'Wild fennel,' said the other.

'*Molto buono*,' said one.

'*Molto saporito*, very healthy,' said the other, and held up a plastic bag bulging with green feathery fronds. There were snails clinging to some of them.

'With snails,' I said, remembering the *babbaluci* hunters of Godrano.

'With snails,' they said together, as if the snails came as an unexpected bonus.

'Very good,' said one.

'What do you do with the fennel?' I asked.

'Make it into broth. Very good,' said one.

'Very good with the snails,' said the other. 'With just a little onion and garlic. Not too much.' And she gave a quick demonstration of how to prepare the fennel fronds.

'Or to make a sauce for pasta,' said one.

'What kind of pasta?' I asked.

'Any kind, long or short,' said one.

'It doesn't matter. They are both good. With the fennel,' said the other.

And with that they got back into their car and drove on, and I made my way to Porto Palo.

☙❧

I sat on a terrace of Da Vittorio in Porto Palo. The sun was setting in a blaze of cerise to my right and the violet sea rolled into the beach in long, low parallel lines in front of me. I ate my antipasti: a plate of raw prawns, fat, floppy, pink commas in oil, lemon juice and chopped parsley; a bruschetta of crisp cooked prawns on polenta with raunchy tomato; a bowl of mussels in a resonant sauce of tomato and chilli; a plate of sharp, silvery, marinated anchovies.

Bloody marvellous, I thought. This was as remote a corner of the coast as it is possible to find, I thought. All to myself. Peace and quiet. Time to meditate on matters and take stock. Long walks on the beach. Play in the sea a bit. The world to myself.

A group of seven or eight settled down at a nearby table, chatting in that casually intense manner of executives on a brainstorming outing. It took me a little while to work out that they were Irish. And executives. On a brainstorming outing. So much for the lost corner of paradise, I thought, so much for the thrill of discovery. I felt like the bloke who had slogged through the jungle on the Thailand/Burmese border for days to make contact with a tribe untouched by the outside world, only to find that Michael Palin had dropped in by helicopter with a film crew the week before.

Thoughtfully I ate a plate of *spaghetti con ricci*, spaghetti with sea urchins – a massive plate of very al dente pasta (Sicilians seemed to prefer their pasta stiffer than they did on the mainland) with what appeared to be a whole seabed of sea urchin's roes.

It's a rum old life, I mused. Tom and I had had the island to ourselves in 1973. The cholera epidemic in Naples had scared off all but the most dedicated or ignorant of travellers. Now there was no cholera to keep the hordes at bay.

Presently, a busload of German tourists filled up another

long table, clearly ready to party. Four of them had substantial beards. I couldn't remember seeing so many beards en masse before. There seemed something oddly significant about them, but what, exactly, I couldn't imagine.

I ate my *secondo piatto*: a whole small sea bass; a large slice of swordfish; six large prawns; all bronzed under the grill.

Why do people travel in herds? I wondered. The more of them you are with, the greater the barrier between you and the people among whom you are travelling. Perhaps that's why. Tourists don't really want to have contact with the country immediately around them, only with its food and its monuments. Organised tourism is about travelling within your comfort zone, and being protected from engaging with the untidy realities outside it.

I ate my pudding, a little crisp warm pastry filled with ricotta sweetened with honey. It took me back to Marsala. *Cappidduzzu? Cassatedda? Raviola?*

I was tired of travel and thinking, so I went to bed.

☽

The alluvial plain between Menfi and Selinunte was fizzing with agricultural activity. This may be something of an exaggeration, but it fairly bustled compared with the desolate emptiness of inland Sicily earlier in the year. The fields were straight-sided, as if they were so many pieces of a jigsaw designed by a compulsively orderly mind. Small tractors pulling large trailers piled high with grapes puttered along the road. Groups of men and women gathered underneath the olive trees, peering upward, or bending down, in unison in some oddly choreographed dance. Single figures moved among rectangles of artichokes where serrated sword leaves sprouted out of the earth like lines of dusty grey fountains.

I stopped at Selinunte for a rare excursion into sightseeing. I first came here with Tom in 1973, and the great temple to Hera has remained my favourite Greek temple, almost my favourite monument of any kind, ever since, a place made perfect by memory.

෨෨

I have a picture of Tom standing between the pillars, a tall, gangling figure in T-shirt and jeans, his dark glasses pushed high up on to his abundant wavy hair, fat sideburns flowing down either side of his face. The sky above him is an ethereal, eternal cobalt. I could remember the sticky breeze off the sea. It didn't seem that long ago.

With the exception of an orderly car park, a smart modern building housing the ticket office and gift shop, and excavations further along the coast, nothing in essence seemed to have changed since I first came here. The sky was still the same, and the sticky breeze that blew in from the sea. And the temple was still perfect, high on a headland, sideways on to the sea, mono-lithic, solitary, sublime both as an artefact and as a ruin; horizontal order of steps leading up to expansive base, vertical mass of the great, honeyed cream pillars, grasses and creeping plants growing in the cracks between the massive blocks, black crows resting and nesting in the crevices at the tips of the pillars. And around it the tumbled remains of other temples, the low, flat land running down to the sea, tufted with scrub, bushes, pines and the wild celery, that gave the place its name – *selinon* means wild celery in ancient Greek.

It represented another Sicily, long gone, when the island was the centre of the civilised world. Then it was part of Magna Graecia – the richest part of it, too, hub of Mediterranean trade, prosperous if not independent. But then Sicily has never been independent in three thousand years, and while that might suit Sicilians in many ways it has meant it has never been possible for a civil society to evolve naturally as it has in other places. Perhaps that was why so much about contemporary Sicily appeared so contradictory and confusing; and why the monumental beauties of the past appeal so much. They represent a simpler, nobler aspect of the island, easier to assimilate, safer to respond to. I headed back on to the main coastal road to Marsala.

@@

It was John Dickie's fault. When you're next in Marsala, he had said, you must get in touch with Cesarina Perrone. She's a schoolteacher, he said. She knows everything there is to know about local food. And she'll show you how to bake country bread in a traditional wood-fired oven. So I called her up. Wonderful, Cesarina said, Lorenzo and I will meet you at the Porta Garibaldi. Fine, I said. Lorenzo? Obviously her husband.

It was a brilliant day as I tootled into Marsala, familiar to me from the first leg of my odyssey. The air was full of the familiar keen edge of iodine and salt from the sea. I parked by the great arch, and waited for some nice, mumsy, middle-aged matron with her hair in a bun and a pipe-smoking husband. So who was this slim, sexy woman dressed in jeans, a shirt with a Burberry band round the inside of the upturned collar, and seriously fancy shoes, walking towards me? And the pipe-smoking husband of my imagination turned into a smooth banker, suave and charming and with long wavy hair.

'Follow us,' said Cesarina. 'It's just going to be a simple Sunday lunch. At our country cottage just outside Marsala. I hope that's OK with you.'

Er, OK, yes, I said. That would be fine by me.

The country cottage was a very substantial four-storey building standing in a fine garden with olive, orange and lemon trees, a persimmon and a kitchen garden.

'Relax,' said Cesarina. 'Make yourself at home.'

'Righty ho,' I said. 'But what about the bread?' I wanted to get things on to an orderly track as soon as possible.

'Oh yes, the bread,' she said. 'We'll get to that in a moment. But before, there are just a few dishes we thought you might like to see being made. John said that you were really interested in real Sicilian food.'

'Oh, yes, I am, I am,' I said.

Things began quietly enough, with just her and Lorenzo, and Enzo, the guardian-cum-odd-job-man-cum-gardener-cum-baker-cum-teller-of-tales, and his wife Rosa, and sister-in-law Giuseppina, and Cesarina and Lorenzo's children. Presently, a couple of friends turned up. And then Lorenzo's mother and father. Each wave brought with them something to add to the feast. The friends brought quinces, to be peeled, cut up and stewed in syrup. The mother and father brought some *sarde al beccafico* and some roasted peppers. Everybody contributed, everybody lent a hand, and gradually, irresistibly, over the next three hours, the simple Sunday lunch achieved critical mass.

My lesson started with *ghiotta*, a fish stew. The base of this was *salsa di pomodoro*, tomato sauce. I'm not saying that all *ghiottas* are made this way, but Cesarina's was. Now here was the first point: *salsa*, that is straight tomato sauce, which looked uncannily like passata to me – '*e la bas di tutte le salse*', is the base of all other sauces, according to Cesarina, mentor, guide, tutor, coach and force of nature. And you make *salsa* with just tomatoes, onions and a little garlic. *Basta*. That's all.

Olio? Certo – of course. But you have to make sure that the tomatoes are the right ones, the little round ones.

Their name?

'*Pomodorini*.'

'*Pomodorini*? Is that a variety?'

'I'm not sure. They're just the little round ones. They come in July. They always come in July.'

I see.

But then, if you add meat to *salsa*, along with, naturally, more *soffrito* (onions and garlic), then the *salsa* is immediately transformed into *sugo di carne*, or *sugo di pesce* if you add fish, usually tuna, *sauro* or *sgrombo*.

'*Chiaro* – is that clear – *Matteo*?' I was completely undone by Cesarina's energy. She issued information bulletins in short, high-octane bursts.

Yes. Definitely. I think so.

The *salsa* had been made already. Small whole fish, gutted and their gills removed, were added to it and left to stew.

Meanwhile, there were more onions being fried, red ones, to make *cipolle in agrodolce* to go with little squares of fried tuna – *tonno con cipolle in agrodolce*. Taste this, taste that, cried Cesarina. 'But it's better later, warm or cold.'

And now it was time for the bread. Enzo took charge and led me outside to inspect the oven, a massive, proper brick kiln, just like a pizza oven. Wood was already crackling away inside. Enzo threw in a bundle of dry rushes to really get the heat going—

'Eh, Matt-hew? *Eh, Matte? Buon fuoco,*' he said, smiling broadly.

He lugged a large wooden bowl, in which the dough was to be mixed, into the house. It looked like one end of a barrel. It probably was one end of a barrel. He heaved it up on to two chairs placed at the end of the already crowded kitchen and Rosa got to work with a running commentary from Cesarina.

'*Prima, farina di grano duro.*' First durum wheat flour. In went four kilos. We were going to be making a lot of bread. It was pale yellow, the colour of primroses.

'What's the difference,' I asked, 'between *grano duro* and *semoula di grano duro*?' This was a mystery that had long puzzled me, the two being apparently interchangeable.

'They are the same, the same thing,' said Cesarina. That explained that. 'Now we make a well in the flour, and into that goes a little of the dough from the previous bread mixture, *lo spirito del pane*, the soul of the old bread. When you make bread every day or even every week, you can do this.' Into the flour went a large sponge of risen dough, followed by a small brick of *lievito*, natural yeast, mixed with warm water for good measure, and Rosa got to kneading with her fists.

And knead she did, for the next 40 minutes. Salt was added, measured by the tips of Enzo's fingers, and kneaded in, and then water. It was a right old squelchy business to start with, and hard work, very hard work, but Rosa was unrelenting. The dough took an awful pounding. Rosa shoved her fists into it as if it was an inert punchball, turning it over and doing it again and again, rhythmically and powerfully.

'Just flour, water and *lievito*,' said Cesarina. 'No, no oil. Oil's too expensive.'

Rosa just went on kneading and kneading.

'This is how the bread was always made,' said Cesarina. 'Once a week. Rosa still makes it once a week. The bread is good all week. In fact, it gets better after a day or two.'

Finally the dough was ready to be turned out on to a floured board and pushed flat by Rosa's fists, turned and fisted again until it is ready for the *bel letto all' pane*, 'the beautiful bed for the bread'.

A second table in the next room was covered first with a blanket and then with a sheet dusted with flour. Then the dough was broken up into pieces and shaped and rolled in *giugiulena*, sesame seeds. We all took a hand. My efforts were notably inexpert, producing a large, blobby mass. Everyone was very complimentary, but I noticed that Rosa, Giuseppina, Cesarina and Enzo turned out nice oval loaves with ease. These were carefully laid on the bread bed until half of it was covered by plump, pallid cushions of dough. The sheet was folded on top of them, followed by several more blankets and they were left to rise.

'How long for?'

'Until they are ready,' said Cesarina.

'Oh, I see.'

We went back to the kitchen. For a moment of repose? Oh, no. It was time for a lesson in pasta, and Giuseppina had taken over kneading duties and gone to work on a lump of pasta dough in the barrel bowl.

'Just flour and water this time,' said Cesarina. 'No *lievito* this time.'

'And a very little oil,' said Giuseppina. 'And an egg.'

'What pasta?' I asked.

'*Busiati*,' said Cesarina. 'And *gnoccoli* – gnocchi.'

I said something about how I made *gnocchi di patate*, gnocchi made with mashed potato and flour. Giuseppina stopped kneading for a moment and gave me an old-fashioned look, and then went back to kneading. She kneaded for another 20 minutes.

Many standard Sicilian dishes, Cesarina said, really started off as dishes for the rich and were adapted by the poor. Take *caponata*. That was originally served as a kind of vegetable accompaniment for fish. Fish was cooked *agrodolce*. But the poor dispensed with the fish or meat because they couldn't afford them and cooked the vegetables *agrodolce* without them.

'Or there's *pasta fuitta*,' Cesarina said, 'which is also known as *pasta con le sarde scappate*. You know about *spaghetti con le sarde*?'

I did. It's spaghetti with a weird wonderful sauce of bits of sardine, pine nuts, raisins, fennel, garlic and olive oil.

'*Spaghetti con le sarde scappate* just has spaghetti with raisins, pine nuts, garlic, parsley, breadcrumbs, and oil, but no fish. Because the sardines have *scappate*, escaped. The poor couldn't afford them.'

'Or the sardines scarpered,' I said.

'Scarpered?' she said. I began to explain but gave up. The complexities of a bilingual joke were a bit beyond my Italian, and, besides, there was too much going on. But I liked the way Sicilians managed to turn a dish of utter poverty into a joke, a clever, bitter joke.

And in the meantime there was a little something to keep us going: *cabbucce*. Rosa took some bread dough that hadn't made it to the *bel letto all' pane*, and cut it into small squares which she fried in olive oil until they puffed up and turned brown. She dusted them in sugar and cinnamon and we ate the *cabbuce* while they were still hot, crisp outside, and airy and springy inside.

The pasta was ready. It had that pleasing, smooth firmness, and dry, satin texture. Giuseppina broke off a bit and rolled it until it was as thin as a strand of wool. She broke this in half and rolled each half round a very thin piece of wood, the size of a thin knitting needle, with the casual legerdemain of a magician. Miraculously a coil of pasta appeared, like a pasta spring. This was *busiati*. She went on to make a pile of *busiati* before turning her attention to the *gnoccoli*.

'We are making *gnoccoli cavati*,' said Cesarina. 'You take a thin rolled-out piece of dough, the same size as for *busiati*,' and she did. 'And then you gently scratch your fingers over it, like a cat with its claws – *cavati*.'

A second pile of pasta shapes began to mount up.

'And if you make *gnoccoli con ragù di pesce*, you add *mollica* – breadcrumbs – to the *ragù*. You fry them in just a little oil and a little garlic. And salt and pepper, of course. And basil.' As she said '*e basilico*' her voice rose slightly, as if she was addressing a class. Yes, teacher, I thought.

Enzo came in to announce that the bread dough was ready for the oven. How did he tell when it's ready?

'You give each loaf a little tap and if it makes the right hollow noise, it's ready,' he said. He tapped a risen loaf. It gave off a faint echo.

We all followed Enzo and trooped out to the oven.

He had raked the ashes right to the front of it. With a good deal of ceremony he dipped the head of an old mop in a pail of water and wiped the floor of the oven. Then, with equal cere-mony, Rosa placed a plump, creamy loaf on a wooden paddle with a long handle, which Enzo held ready. He swivelled round and poked the loaf into the oven. A quick flick of the wrist, and it slid off the paddle on to the floor of the oven. It was followed in turn by all the loaves until the oven bottom was covered with them. Enzo propped a metal cover over the mouth of the oven and we all trooped backed inside.

'When will the bread be ready?' I said, ever the avid food researcher.

'When it's ready,' he said.

'Really, Enzo! An hour? Half an hour?'

'*Un' mezz'oretta*,' he said. A little half-hour, whatever that meant.

Five minutes later we trooped outside again to check on the progress of the loaves. It was clear that the oven was rather hotter that Enzo had gauged. Some of them were already looking a trifle burnt on top. Enzo frowned, and used the wetted mop to douse the glowing ashes a bit, while Cesarina gave the loaves a wipe with a damp cloth, as gently as a mother wiping a baby's brow, before they were popped back in the oven.

In the event, the *mezz'oretta* was more like 15 minutes, but the loaves looked as they should – brown toasty hummocks – and their yeasty, wheaty, caramelly smell filled the air.

And then it was time for *sarde al beccafico*, another bitter Sicilian linguistic joke. The dish translates literally as sardines like fig-eaters. This is a reference to small birds – thrushes, sparrows, tits and the like – that feast on figs. In revenge for this, they were themselves once eaten – but by the gentry, naturally. The coastal poor invented their own version, stuffing sardines with *la mollica bianca* – the crumbs of a fresh white loaf – olive oil, salt and pepper naturally, chopped parsley, hard-boiled egg, chopped onion and pine nuts, with a little lemon peel in the *mollica*. That's how Cesarina's mother-in-law stuffed them at any rate, before placing them in a dish, tails in the air like plumes, with a bay leaf between each, and baking them.

There is a tome to be written about *la mollica* itself, '*Il Parmigiano dei poveri*, the Parmesan of the poor,' Enzo called it. There was a heated debate about which part, soft interior crumb or crisper crust, of which loaf was good for which dish; and on the difference between *la mollica* and *pane grattugato*, dried breadcrumbs. There were strict rules for all these things, according to Cesarina. Whatever the crumbs were used for, it still came down to thrift. Nothing, no part of any food, was thrown away. Everything left over – crust, crumb, scrap of meat, bone of fish – could be turned into something else, a titbit, something delicious, something sustaining, if you went about it with enough imagination. In Sicily I was eating richly on the products of the imagination and experience of millennia.

And now, finally, it really was time to eat. We retired to the upper terrace, where tables had been set up and covered with the products of our morning's work. We started with the freshly baked loaves, sliced in half horizontally and stuffed with tomatoes (and they have to be the right tomatoes: sharp, pointed plum-shaped ones) and olives and chopped salted anchovies and small bits of *caciocavallo* and a dribble of olive oil – *pane cunzattu*. And I had two helpings because nothing tastes so good as the bread you have baked yourself. Well, half-baked it anyway.

'What is this wine, Enzo?' I asked, as he sloshed some more into my glass. It was easy drinking.

'*Sfuso*,' he said. '*Il vino dei contadini*.' *Sfuso*. Wine of the peasants.

'Oh, great.'

'*Fa quindici gradi.*'

'What!'

'*Quindici gradi.*'

Fifteen degrees alcohol. Bloody hell. I'd already downed a glass of the stuff and here he was filling up my glass again, to the very brim.

'*Molto buono per i contadini.*'

Very good for the peasants. Pretty good for me, too.

I don't think it was just the *sfuso* that infused me with that unmistakable sense of warmth and content. This was the kind of day I had dreamed of when I set off. How could I not love such a family? They reminded me of my own, with an even greater emphasis, if possible, on food and its attendant rituals.

We settled down to *pipareddri'chini* – stuffed peppers; and *viole fritte* – tiny electric-blue fish with a violet line running the length of their sides, fried; *caponata*; and *sarde al beccafico*; and *tonno in agrodolce*; and cheeses, at least five of them; and *mele cotogne* – quinces – sliced and cooked in syrup to a beautiful glossy, glowing amber; and *fichi d'India*, prickly pears. And just when I thought I had finished, a ricotta and chocolate tart appeared, *crostarta di ricotta con ciocollato*. And just when I thought I had finished that, there were *tagliancozzi*, which were uncannily like *cantucini*, those dentally wheat and almond biscuits of Tuscany, made to go with a glass of marsala, and there were three glasses to try. So we did, and we all agreed that the *dolce* was the best with the *tagliancozzi*. And so the afternoon trickled away in conversation and eating until there was no energy left for either. And after that I was finished, for ever. I thought that I would never be able to eat again.

∾ Scacciata ∾

John Irving cannily identified this for me. It's a kind of coil of bread studded with whatever savory goodies you fancy. Sausage and olives seem to go very well. There are a good many variations on the basic idea. It's a fine snack for the road. Or for anywhere.

Makes about 8 scacciata
600g 00 plain flour • 20g brewer's yeast • 50ml extra virgin olive oil • Salt • 300g sausage meat • 20 stoned black olives

Preheat the oven to 190°C/375°F/Gas 5. Mix the flour, yeast, olive oil, salt and enough warm water to make a stiff bread dough. Leave to rise for 2–3 hours. Using your hands, roll it out into a long snake about 3cm thick. Coil into a round shape. Stud with bits of sausage meat and olives, tucking some down into the cracks. Place on an oiled baking tray. Bake for 30 minutes. Eat hot, warm or cold.

∾ 'Pipareddri'chini ∾

This recipe, and the two following come from Cesarina Perrone's kitchen. They are as delightful and vivid as the woman herself.

Serves 2
2 small peppers • 10 green olives • 2 hard-boiled eggs • 1 onion • Fresh basil leaves • 8 tbsp la mollica *(fresh white bread-crumbs) • 2 tbsp of grated parmesan • 2 tbsp of grated pecorino or of seasoned* caciocavallo *cheese • Cubes of cheese (provola, fresh* caciocavallo *or* primosale*) • Pinch of oregano • A pinch each of salt and pepper • Extra virgin olive oil*

Preheat the oven to 190°C/375°F/Gas 5. Cut a slice from the top of each pepper. This will form a 'hat' to keep the filling in during cooking. Remove the seeds and inside filaments, and wash and dry the peppers. Chop the olives and hard-boiled eggs, and finely chop the onion and basil leaves. Mix with the breadcrumbs along with the cheeses, oregano and salt and pepper.

Stuff each pepper with the mixture and reassemble it by sealing it with the 'hat'. Place them in a baking tin with a splash of extra virgin olive-oil (so that it's light and delicate) and bake until they have softened. Alternatively, for a more robust and full flavour, or fry the peppers in hot oil, turning them over carefully. Serve cold.

∾ Sarde a beccafico ∾

To be factually accurate this recipe comes from Cesarina's mother-in-law. You'll find *sarde a beccafico* all over Sicily, but each cook has their own version.

Serves 4
1kg of fresh sardines • 250g la mollica *(fresh white breadcrumbs) • 100g pine kernels • 200g* passulina *(or raisins softened in lukewarm water) •* Juice of 1 lemon • Oregano • Extra virgin olive oil • Bay leaves • Slices of oranges*

Preheat the oven to 180°C/360°F/Gas 4. Remove the sardines' backbones and heads and open them like a book. Wash the sardines in running water and dry them carefully. Mix the breadcrumbs, pine kernels, *passulina* or raisins, lemon juice and oregano. If the mixture is too thick, add a drop of olive oil. Place a teaspoon of the mixture on each sardine and roll each fish lengthwise. Dust a baking tin with breadcrumbs. Place the sardines very close to each other in the tin with their tails upwards to prevent them from opening. Alternate each sardine with a bay leaf and an orange slice, in order to obtain a more delicate and aromatic flavour. Bake for 15 minutes. Once the sardines are cooked, cover the tin with foil for half and hour (as Cesarina says this makes them taste even better) before serving.

∽ Tagli'gnozo ∽

Makes about 60 biscuits
500g of white flour • 250g sugar • 3 eggs • 1 egg yolk • 100g softened butter • A pinch of cinnamon • 400g toasted almonds

Preheat the oven to 200°C/400°F/Gas 6. Put the flour, sugar, eggs, egg yolk, butter and the cinnamon in a large bowl and mix it to make a soft and dense mixture. Cut the almonds into rather large pieces and add to the mixture. Make little ingots of dough like *panetti* (the Italian name for blocks of butter) about 5–6cm long and lay them in a line in a baking tin. Bake for about 20 minutes until they turn the right golden colour. Take them out of the oven, cut them into biscuits about 2cm thick, then cook them for another 15–20 minutes. Eat them cold: they keep a long time in aluminium containers. Wash down with marsala.

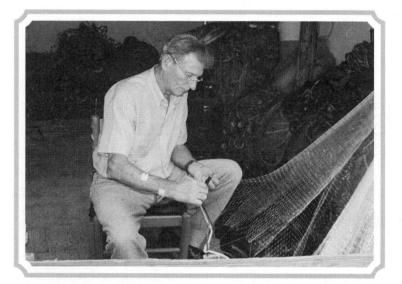

Fisherman mending net, Trapani

CHAPTER TEN

Bandit Country

❧❧

Marsala – Trapani – San Guiseppe Jato – Montelepre – Palermo

Feeling like a shriven saint, the next morning I visited Cesarina's school in Marsala. In the course of the previous day's Lucullan feast, I had asked whether it would be possible to see how it dealt with the turkey twizzler issue, and with characteristic energy she had promised to take up the challenge.

The school had once been a convent. It now housed several hundred three- to ten-year-olds, who dashed around, made as much noise and exuded as much cheerful energy as three- to ten-year-olds do everywhere. The building was ranged around a central yard in which grew a grove of lemon and orange trees, and the schoolrooms were bright and airy with high ceilings and big windows.

The headmistress was a square, cheery woman. When she heard of my interest in food, she immediately said how much she enjoyed the smells of cooking coming from the kitchens directly below her office.

'Of course you must visit them,' she said, 'and see what we

all eat.' I couldn't remember any of the head teachers at my daughter's various schools extending a similar invitation.

The kitchens weren't large, but they were well, and recently, equipped. The dinner ladies were a bright, energetic bunch, pleased, it seemed to me, to be doing what they were doing: preparing lunch. Today they were making a spinach frittata as the first course, they explained, with pasta with a cream and bacon sauce as a second course, and yoghurt or a banana to finish. There was no choice. Everybody got the same, including the teachers on dinner duty. If a kid couldn't eat the lunch, they could have a *panino* or organic bread stuffed with *panelle*, the ubiquitous chickpea fritter.

The ladies explained that they worked to menus and recipes that had been drawn up by the Trapani Educational Service. These covered the whole school year and had been designed by a nutritionist in consultation with cooks to be balanced and nutritionally valuable, and good to eat. On the first Wednesday of the spring/summer menu lunch had been gnocchi with tomato sauce, grilled veal, mixed salad and kiwi fruit. On the third Monday of the autumn/winter menu, the lunch had been pasta with lentil sauce; grilled swordfish; fennel; bread and a banana. Pasta featured heavily but not invariably. There was always a vegetable, and plenty of potatoes but no chips. Fish cropped up quite frequently. I began to feel hungry again, notionally anyway. I found it exhilarating to have contact with a society that valued good food, proper food as a matter of course. No wonder Sicilians grew up confident and knowledgeable about what they ate and expecting a high standard of cooking.

I thought of the controversy caused by the TV series *Jamie's School Dinners* in Britain, the land of burgers and chips with everything. In British schools choice was king, and choice, it seemed to me, was a large part of the problem (along with badly paid and undermotivated staff, inadequate investment and the general low esteem in which food and eating is held by all institutions in the UK). Give a child, or most adults come to that, a choice in what they eat, and they will choose what they had yesterday and the day before. They keep to their gastronomic comfort zones. This is bad in practice, and bad for the future. By the time they make their own food choices, people have had a very narrow band of taste experience, and will, in all probability, go on eating rubbish until they die – which will happen pretty quickly. It may seem paradoxical, but in this instance choice is the enemy of experience.

The obvious answer, as Cesarina's school bore out, is not to give kids any choice in what they eat, and to make sure what they are given is fine, tasty, decent grub. If they don't like it, too bad. They may go hungry for a day or two, but none are likely to die of starvation. The way things are at present, many will die of obesity. Of course, there are plenty of people who find this heretical, and will bang on with the old libertarian argument: 'You can't do that. You have to give children a choice over school dinners.' And waffle on about the nanny state. But why? Schools don't give children a choice over their history curriculum or what books to read in English literature. So why should they be given one with food, where the long-term consequences of a bad diet are so well documented? What on earth are three A-grade A levels and a starred first going to do for you if you have popped your clogs by 35 because you've eaten crap all your life? The bright and lively kids in this school in Marsala didn't seem to suffer from dictatorship in their diet.

I chewed on the *panino* with chickpea fritter that I had been given to keep me going on my journey. It was excellent bread and the *panelle* was hot. They came from a different world.

◎◎

The shore road out of Marsala heading north for Trapani was hideous, with an uncertain surface and lined with petrol stations, car agencies, builders' yards and other industrial detritus. Then I turned off this highway purgatory on to a minor road, which wound through a stretch of landscape not much more attractive than the main one, but of an utterly different nature. It was scruffy, semi-rural and semi-agricultural, fields and blocks of houses jumbled together at random. This was the *frazione* of Nubia, celebrated for its red garlic, *l'aglio rosso di Nubia*. The earth was a pale, milky-brown tilth in which not much seemed to be growing aside from a fine crop of weeds. But it was the wrong time of year to be looking for the celebrated garlic, which had been harvested in June and July.

I passed a large flock of sheep the grubby colour of a child's well-loved cuddly toy. They were grazing on a patch of ground between two blocks of buildings, heads down, ears flopped over their eyes, moving en masse like a living mower. A shepherd was watching them, leaning on a stick. He lifted his hand in gracious acknowledgement. It was a scene that could be taken from any one of the last five thousand years. Suddenly I came across a number of pens with ostriches wandering about in them. They looked as puzzled as I did.

Anyone who keeps only to the main roads in Sicily, dashing from celebrated monument to celebrated monument, and who doesn't absorb some of the Sicilian way with time and take an hour or so to potter off along the byroads, turns their back on many delights of this island of parallel universes. I must have been about 20 minutes from Cesarina's school in Marsala, but I had passed through several time and cultural zones. In Sicily, the remote past, the near past and the absolute present are jammed together or piled on top of one another.

A dirt track led from the winding road to the Museo delle Saline, a fine rectangular stone building with a windmill perched on top and surrounded by *basine*, salt pans, flat, geometric, watery, oddly pure; a queer area, right at the edge of the sea. An electric blue kingfisher hovered over one of the channels around the *basine*. All I could hear was the rustle of water and the flutter of wind. It seemed remote from Trapani, which was strung out along the horizon, an architect's model against the blue sky. Beyond Trapani, Erice crouched along the crest of its abrupt hill. The Egadi islands, Favignana, Levanzo and Marretimo, sat in the sea, mysterious, milky silhouettes. Beyond them sky and sea merged into one.

Salt is one of the key products in the history of commerce and gastronomy. Fortunes were made from it, wars fought over it. The Romans named roads after it – there are several Via Salarias in Italy, marking the ways along which the precious substance was brought from the coast to cities. It found its way into our vocabulary as salary, because wages were once paid in salt. And, of course, it has served to season, cure and preserve food.

The pans between Marsala and Trapani still produce mountains of fine marine salt through a process of evaporation that hasn't changed since the Phoenicians ran the coastline three thousand years ago. Channels let sea water into the *basine*, rectangular shallow ponds bounded by walls of golden, stone blocks, and sat there while wind and sun worked their magic, drawing off the water through evaporation. The increasingly saline and dense liquid was flowed from pan to pan until all that was left was the grey-white crystals that were excavated and piled in murky white tumuli covered with terracotta tiles. The didactic side of the museum was pretty perfunctory. Most of the building was given over to a basic but handsome trattoria. The room was long, with high beams, Arab-Norman pointed stone arches, white walls and terracotta floor. From the cool shade of the interior I looked out through a door on to a courtyard that was dazzling in the blinding sunlight. Blue water winked and flickered in the *basine* beyond.

I did not plunder the menu extensively, as I was still feeling pretty stuffed by lunch the previous day, not to mention the *panelle* bap from Cesarina's school. I managed a plate of antipasti, through which salt ran like a theme and variations: a chunk of salt-cured tuna, dense and fibrous as the bark of a wellingtonia; a salt-cured anchovy with a wild whiff of seaweed and ozone; sharp, pungent green olives cured in brine; bruschetta of tomato *salsa* mixed with ricotta *salata* and sprinkled with oregano. The oregano brightened the taste of the tomato and the salted ricotta seasoned each mouthful. It was of the place, and very satisfying.

After this I just managed a plate of *spaghetti con acciughe e mollica*. Well, the menu had said it was *acciughe e mollica*, spaghetti with fresh anchovies and breadcrumbs, but I couldn't detect the *acciughe* at all. I suspected that they had *scappate*. The chap looking after me assured me that they were all broken up and dissolved around the pasta, but he looked rather shifty when he said this. Still, it was a perfectly decent dish. I wouldn't complain too much as it cost all of 5 euros.

As I ate, a group of five or six smartly dressed men – dark trousers, dark jackets, blue shirts, no ties – and three very attractive women – dark suits, big shades – walked in at 2.10 to begin a business lunch. They were probably the city fathers and mothers of Trapani, but, immediately, I assumed they were Mafia. That's the way the diverse aspects of Sicily play uneasily on the imagination. Of course, they could have been both city fathers and mothers and Mafia.

It reminded me of an incident during my first visit to Sicily with Tom. On some coast road or other we passed a magnificent nineteenth-century house right on the edge of some cliffs. It had a shaded terrace over the sea. Pity we can't stay there, we thought. A little further on we saw a sign for the Hotel Concordia, and a track that obviously led back to the house we had just seen. The only problem was that there was a high mesh fence with a mesh gate between us and it. Then a big black Mercedes-Benz turned down the track and the gate swung open. Oh goody, we thought, and followed it through the gate and down to the hotel car park. It looked like an upmarket car lot, with more Mercedes, Rolls-Royces, Ferraris, Maseratis and the like cheek by jowl. Rather shamefaced, we parked our travel-scuffed rented Ford Escort, a dusty sparrow among birds of paradise, and went up to the hotel.

There was a door to the entrance. It was massive and wooden and it was shut. We knocked. It was opened by a man almost as massive as the door. Beyond him we could see the dazzling interior of the hotel filled with a mass of exquisitely dressed men and women in hats. It looked like Ascot on Royal Day, only a good deal smarter. Can we have a room for the night? we asked. The man looked startled, and then said the hotel wasn't open. But – we said. The door was shut decisively. There was a moment when we thought of banging some more. On reflection we decided that discretion was the better part of valour and went back the way we had come. When I got back to England I searched exhaustively for a reference to the Hotel Concordia in that part of Sicily, but I never found one.

@

'What is that?' I asked, pointing at soft, yellowish wrinkled slabs. The hideous by-product of some vile chemical process possibly?

'*Polmone. Polmone di tonno*. Dried in the sun,' said the man with a blue chin behind the counter of a stall beside the road that ran round the harbour in Trapani. Pretty, blue-painted fishing boats rocked against the harbour wall. The blue-chinned man specialised in tuna products. He had salt-dried tuna *sott'olio*, cooked tuna in oil, smoked tuna, tinned tuna, vacuum-packed tuna, tuna *bottarga*. No part of the tuna was wasted.

Tuna lungs? What? Really? I thought they had gills.

'What do you do with it?'

'You soak it and then cut it up and cook it in tomato *salsa* for a *secondo piatto*,' said the blue-chinned man.

'And this?'

'This' looked like a bundle of heavy-duty, black insulating tape.

'*Budino di tonno*.' He gestured vaguely at his stomach. Ah, yes, tuna intestine. 'You grill it or cook it in *padella* as an antipasto. Soak it first, mind.'

I asked him about the state of fishing in the area, as there was a sizeable fishing fleet in the harbour. Yes, he said. There were still plenty of fish in the sea. Not tuna, though. The *mattanza* wasn't like it used to be. It was the Japanese trawlers. They came when the tuna were migrating and tracked them with radar and caught them in nets and took all the best fish.

Still, I said, there are enough for you to sell here.

There were, he said, for the time being.

◎◎

Trapani was the town of a thousand balconies. There wasn't a house, it seemed, that didn't have a box of wrought-ironwork festooning its façade; some of the boxes were straight-sided and straight-laced, some bulging and blousy, some had geometric diamond shapes, some had filigree as delicate as lace. Much of the town had been reconstructed after being badly bombed in 1940, and again in 1943, but it didn't feel like that. Nevertheless, there was an odd disjunction about the place, as if two Trapanis were joined uneasily together.

There was the Trapani of cultured Europe, with handsome, wide boulevards – the Via Garibaldi, Corso Italia and the Corso Vittorio Emmanuele – lined with palaces that dated from anywhere between the sixteenth century and the eighteenth: Palazzo Milo del Barone della Salina; Palazzo della Duco Saura; Palazzo Burgo del Barone di Scurinda; Palazzo della Giudecca of the Cimbra family, that testified to an earlier, more tolerant Sicily; palazzo after palazzo. Really, they were more like town houses dressed up.

This Trapani was wrapped around a coil of narrow streets, much older, Arab, as tangled as the mesh of the fishing net I saw a man unpicking as I wandered through it. This part had the unmistakable feel of a suburb of Marrakesh or Tangier. The houses were low and brightly coloured, and had flat roofs, and the people had a Moorish darkness. This was the Trapani of *cuscusu*, a sloppy couscous served with fish, the local variant on the Moroccan original.

I wanted to find a shop I had heard about that dealt only in boiled sweets, an old Trapanese tradition. It wasn't so much of a shop, I had been told, just a table inside a space at the end of a building, manned by an old chap who cut up sticks of sugar syrup with garden secateurs. I found it eventually, but there was no old man at a table in the space. It had become a proper shop, glittering with different-coloured sweets with all the quiet good taste of stage jewellery. But the detail about the secateurs had been real enough. A young man was using them to cut up lengths of coloured sugar-syrup sticks.

'The old man retired,' said the young man. 'But I make the sweets in the same way. Just water and sugar and whatever flavouring, orange, lemon, mint, carob.'

He handed me an offcut from the orange-coloured stick he had been pruning. I could taste the sugar but not the orange. Well, maybe, just. Perhaps not all traditions were what they were cracked up to be.

Round the corner, 30 or so kids were lining the pavement listening to a singer who had just set up his keyboard, amplifier and speakers on the side of the road. He was a short, young man with glasses and gelled curly hair that twinkled in the sun. He sang the usual repertoire of syrupy ballads, overlaid with a heavy contemporary bouff-bouff beat, with heart-rending sincerity. A line of eight girls who were watching swayed and clapped in absolute unison, like a well-trained backing group. What a curious place, Trapani was, one foot in Africa, one foot in – well, where?

I bought an ice cream and sat in the shaded Piazza Lucatelli trying to eat it before it melted all over my hand. A bent old man pulling a handcart loaded with vegetables stopped on the far side of the square. He pulled out a *broccolo verde* from a box on the cart, unscrewed the cap on a mineral water bottle, and carefully poured water over the head of the *broccolo* before thrusting it into a plastic bag and carrying it off to a customer round the corner. He returned presently, hefted up the end of the cart and pulled it down the street, calling out as he went. He should have been in sepia.

☺☺

I left Trapani, heading north-east, away from the sea, towards Calatafimi-Segesta, pausing to visit the hill-top memorial to Sicilians who fell at the crucial Battle of Calatafimi in 1860. Here Garibaldi had his first serious encounter with the Bourbon army. It was nip and tuck for a while, but the great man's indomitable spirit, energy and military nous carried the day. It was hailed at the time as a spectacular victory, which indeed it was. It was curious how Sicilians now viewed him, as someone who had betrayed them.

The road suited my leisurely pace. I had to keep a careful eye open for the usual range of obstacles, but it was delectable riding. The country around changed from the long, rolling swells of further inland. It was steeper, the views sharper, lit by a rich, soft light that infused the earth with golden warmth. The fields were small and the duo-culture of vines and olives less marked, with the occasional outcropping of melons. Some had already been tilled, leaving the earth as if it had been combed. The landscape was dotted with white-painted, single-storey cottages, the same shape as Monopoly houses. It looked as if people lived off this land rather than made money from it. Perhaps this was a sentimental view of farming based on aesthetic criteria rather than the hard facts of economic survival.

Surrounded by such visual beauty, it was easy to forget the grim realities about which Giovanni Verga and Carlo Levi wrote with such dispassionate humanity. Whatever the inequalities and injustices of contemporary Sicilian life, and whatever the consequences of unemployment, which ran currently at about 19 per cent, the fact was that things were easier and better than they had been within living memory. It seemed almost impossible to believe that until 50 years ago ferocious poverty combined with complete social disenfranchisement. During the years when I was footloose and carefree in England just over a thousand miles away, when workers there were striking over pay and conditions, and successive governments poured money into the National Health Service and social services, all the work on this land would have been done by hand, back-breaking, will-sapping labour under a roasting sun for marginal returns.

Most fields were a long way from the nearest villages, or even *masserie*. It was not uncommon for the men who laboured on them to have to walk several kilometres to and from work. People lived with social isolation and ceaseless exploitation. Above them were ranged layers of authority: brutal, backward estate managers; absentee landlords; the Mafia; the Church; the government. They couldn't own land by law. They had large families to support. And then mechanisation arrived, and their labour was no longer needed. There was little industry in the towns to employ them and so they left in their millions.

I passed between Alcamo and Camporeale, following the curves of the road up the massively rounded hills, climbing to San Giuseppe Jato. I came round the edge of the town, and there was the valley of the Jato, verdant and immaculate; a colossal, billowing tablecloth covered with olive groves and vineyards, small forests of walnuts and persimmons and almond trees, and fields of tomatoes and *melanzane* and peppers. There were brown squares of tilled land and green squares of grass, the tinkle from herds of sheep and goats. It was scene straight from the world of Theocritus:

> *Sunburnt cicadas, perched in shadowy thickets,*
> *Kept up their rasping chatter*
> *A distant tree frog*
> *Muttered harshly as it picked its way among thorns*
> *Larks and linnets were singing, a dove made moan,*
> *And brown bees loitered, flitting among the springs.*
> *The tall air smelt of summer, it smelt of ripeness.*

All this stretched between stupendous escarpments rising sharply on three sides, and running away into the distance and mist on the fourth, rich and gilded in the afternoon sun.

☯

San Giuseppe Jato had the reputation of being another Mafia stronghold. Not that I was able to tell, or, indeed, was particularly interested. More to my liking was a man selling *cavolotti selvatici* in bags from the back of his van. The vegetable looked like a cross between radish leaves and rocket. The man was cheerily forthcoming.

'Where do you pick this?'
'In the hills.'
'And how do you cook it?'

'First you boil it and then you drain it and squeeze out all the water. And then you fry it with garlic and oil.'

'And how do you eat it? With pasta?'

'Oh, no. With sausages. It's very good with sausages.'

'Why sausages?'

'Because it's slightly bitter and that's good with sausages which are quite rich.'

Everyone seemed to have a precise knowledge of why this should be served with that, but not with that. Chewing this over, Monica and I hit the winding hill roads again, heading for Palermo by a somewhat circuitous route, via Montelepre.

@@

I had always wanted to visit Montelepre ever since I read *God Protect Me from My Friends* by Gavin Maxwell, as a boy. It was the story of Salvatore Giuliano, 'The King of Montelepre', a bandit and killer of considerable charisma and with a gift for publicity. The nadir of his reign came in 1947 when he and his band massacred 11 villagers who had gathered at nearby La Portella della Ginestra to celebrate May Day.

The reasons behind this piece of vicious violence – unusually brutal even in a land of unusual brutality – are labyrinthine and murky. There are plenty of clues and supposition, but no one has satisfactorily explained who ordered the massacre, or why. It is very probable that Giuliano was duped into carrying it out by a curious alliance of the Mafia and ultra-conservative Sicilian separatists (it would not have been the first or the last time in Italian history that the Mafia and right-wing extremists found common cause). The act provoked such an uproar that Giuliano himself became expendable. In those days, when Don

Calogero Vizzini's writ ruled the island's Mafia, direct confrontation with the state was not company policy, as it became under Toto Riina. Giuliano was betrayed and probably killed by his cousin when his public activities outweighed his usefulness. His cousin was poisoned in gaol shortly afterwards. It was dingy and nasty tale, as typical of one side of Sicily as Theocritus is of another.

The road between San Giuseppe Jato and Montelepre ran through a craggy, stony and remote land. Even in the airy sunlight, it was harsh, unyielding territory. The only sounds were those of the wind and the distant clonking of bells on the necks of sheep or goats, and the only evidence of human occupation were a few small, thin, glossy black cows. It was easy to see how Giuliano might have moved over this ground where he had grown up, avoiding capture.

However, it was curious how close this seemingly inaccessible fastness was to the commercial pastures that ringed the coast. Montelepre itself looked down on Mondello, the lush seaside suburb of choice for Palermitani, just 15 or so kilometres away, and yet these places occupied different worlds: Mondello, choked with hotels, restaurants, bars, shops selling beach gear and frightful knick-knacks, and busy with people glistening in sun cream and smart clothing, the image of contemporary commercialism; Montelepre, steep, narrow and winding, encrusted with balconies, draped with washing, with few people and fewer shops. It might have changed considerably since Giuliano's death in 1950, and there were a number of healthy-sized villas on the slopes around the town to suggest that it might not be quite as poor as it once was, but it still had the sense of inwardness, apartness and exclusion it must have had then. It did not encourage me to linger.

@@

On the way from Montelepre to Palermo, across the mountains, I saw a man standing on top of an outcrop of rock above the road. Just beyond him was a pen full of dusty, hairy, slate grey pigs. I turned up the path that led to the man, and stopped in a farmyard that would have made Cold Comfort Farm look like a model agricultural establishment.

'The pigs? They're wild boar,' the man said. 'They're not mine. I just look after them for someone else. Very good to eat. And for sausages.'

'And what about salami?'

'*Salamini*? Yes, certainly. Did you want any?'

'Yes. Why not?'

'Giacomo!' he bellowed. 'GIACOMO!' Presently a large man with a shaven head appeared. He looked like a mass murderer.

'This man wants to buy some *salamini*.'

'I've got some over there,' said the man with the shaven head, and he gestured to a building on the other side of the road, marked by a green sign that read Suino Genovese. It was just as ramshackle as the yard in which we were standing. We crossed the road and he unlocked a heavy door that opened into a very basic butchery with a very, very basic chiller cabinet piled with *salamini* of all sizes.

'What's in them?'

'Just meat. Salt. Pepper. And a little red spice.'

'*Peperoncino*?'

'No. Just red spice.'

'And how long are they aged?'

'Just a few days.'

He was not an expansive conversationalist.

I bought three small *salamini* for 5 euros, which was probably opportunistic on his part but seemed a small enough price to pay for the oddity of the episode. I ate one of the sausages later, sitting in the sunshine on a bridge over a trickle of water. It was finely meaty, soft, quite fresh, with a nice balance between meat and fat, studded with black peppercorns and with a snort of heat from the red spice. Cayenne, possibly, I thought, or more likely ground chilli.

As I sat there, a dark man clutching a mobile phone came up to me and asked if he could look at my map. Of course, I said. He studied it carefully and then handed it back.

'Where are you from?' he asked in Italian.

'England,' I said. 'And you?'

'India,' he said in English. 'Thanks for the map. Have a good day.' And he went back to chattering on his phone. I wondered what had brought him from India to this curious lost corner of Sicily. Somehow it didn't seem out of place. 'To an old Sicilian hand, as I believe myself to be,' wrote Norman Lewis in *In Sicily*, 'this is a Mediterranean island where the majority of public happenings are seen in one way or another to be bizarre.' I clambered aboard Monica and set off for Palermo.

☺☺

Palermo proved more elusive than I had anticipated, thanks to a slight map-reading error, the consequence of which was that, quite by accident, I found La Portella della Ginestra, the scene of the massacre carried out by Giuliano and his band. The road had climbed up and then turned over the lip of a valley into a natural bowl in the hills, resting between two steep, craggy peaks. The exact site was ringed by a horseshoe-shaped stone wall, divided by another low wall. On either side stood upright rocks, 11 of them, rugged and elemental, the body of each villager who had fallen. On the irregular surface of one of the rocks was carved:

1 MAGGIO 1947

QUI CELEBRANDO

LA FESTA DEL LAVORO

E LA VITTORIA

DEL 20 APRILE

SU UOMINI DONNE BAMBINI

DI PIANA S.CIPIRELLO

S.GIUSEPPE

SI ABBATTE IL PLOMBO

DELLA MAFFIA E

DEGLI AGRARI

PER STRONCARE

LA LOTTA DEI CONTADINI

CONTRO IL FEUDO

(1 May 1947. Here, while celebrating Labour Day and the victory of 20 April, the men, women and children of Piana S. Cipriello were struck with the lead of the Mafia and of the big landowners who wanted to put an end to the farmer's fight against the feudal landownership.)

On another was the names of all of those who were killed.

It was a reserved, windswept place, silent except for bird-song, the croak of a raven, and the swish of the odd passing car. It would have been desolate but for the sun, and the plum orchards all around. I found it deeply moving.

From here I had an easy run through Piana degli Albanesi before dropping down to Palermo.

∾ Spaghetti con acciughe e mollica ∾

Simple and delicious, like so many Sicilian dishes. The anchovies should cook down (but not disappear). The breadcrumbs give extra texture and body.

Serves 4

150g fresh anchovies • *Olive oil* • *1 garlic clove* • *Salt and pepper* • *100g* la mollica *(fresh white breadcrumbs)* • *350g dried spaghetti* • *Handful of parsley*

Remove the heads and backbones of the anchovies and cut up roughly. Heat the oil with the garlic in a frying pan. Fry the anchovy bits until just cooked through – a matter of a couple of minutes, if that. Season with salt and pepper. Take the anchovies out of the pan and fry the breadcrumbs until golden-brown. Cook the spaghetti in boiling salted water. Drain thoroughly and transfer to a bowl. Add the anchovy bits and the fried breadcrumbs. Chop the parsley and scatter all over. Serve immediately.

∾ Zucca gialla in agro-dolce ∾

This popped up at dinner one evening at the very smooth Casale del Principe, where I stayed while exploring around San Giuseppe Jato. I thought how very nice it was. It's those mint leaves. Very Arab.

Serves 4

750g yellow pumpkin • *Extra virgin olive oil* • *Salt and pepper* • *2 tbsp white wine vinegar* • *1 dsp sugar* • *2 garlic cloves* • *A handful mint leaves*

Peel the pumpkin and cut up in to similar-sized chunks. Heat the olive oil in a frying pan and fry the pumpkin until golden. Season with salt and pepper. Drain the pumpkin on kitchen towel, then put in a bowl and put to one side. Pour the oil out of the frying pan and replace it with the vinegar and sugar. Put it back over the heat and stir with a wooden spoon until the sugar has melted. Pour over the pumpkin. Crush the garlic and add to the bowl. Chop up the mint and mix in. Chill until needed.

∾ Zuppa di ceci e ditallini con cavolotto selvatici ∾

In the unlikely event of you not being able to pick your own *cavalotto selvatici* (a wild spinach), try that old English vegetable, orach. And, failing that, Swiss chard (the green bits only).

Serves 4
200g chickpeas • *Handful of* ditallini *pasta* • *2 small onions* • *Extra virgin olive oil* • *Handful of* cavalotti selvatici *or spinach)* • *Salt and pepper*

Soak the chickpeas overnight, then drain and place in a saucepan. Cover with water. Do *not* salt it. Bring to boil and cook until soft. Cook the *ditallini* separately in salted water. Finely chop the onions and fry gently in olive oil in a saucepan until soft. Add the chickpeas along with enough of their cooking water to make a thick soup. Add the *ditallini* and the *cavalotti selvatici*. Season with salt and pepper and heat gently. Serve with a splash of olive oil.

∾ Cassateddi di ricotta ∾

Ok, so it's not a million miles from *cappidduzzu* (or *cassatedda* or *raviola*), but it's a bit more sophisticated and the filling is very different. And you can't have too much of a good thing. Or I can't.

Makes 12–15 *cassateddi*
Peanut oil • Icing sugar • Ground cinnamon
Pastry: *300g plain flour • 100g sugar • 70g* sugna *(pig fat) or lard • 250ml white wine • vanilla essence • The grated zest of a half a lemon or a quarter of an orange*
Filling: *350g ricotta • 160g sugar • 120g cooking chocolate*

Make the pastry a day ahead. Mix the flour and sugar together and add the fat. Combine the ingredients, handling them as little as possible to form a dough. Wrap in cling film and pop into the fridge to rest for 24 hours.

Push the ricotta through a sieve and mix it with the sugar. Grate in the chocolate and mix thoroughly.

When you come to make the *cassateddi*, roll out the pastry very thinly. Cut out circles about 10cm across. Pop 1 tbsp of the filling in the middle of each. Fold over into half moons, taking care to press the edges firmly together. Fry in peanut oil until golden-brown. Dust with icing sugar and ground cinnamon.

Butcher, Mercato Porto Carini, Palermo

CHAPTER ELEVEN

Living with the Past

@@

Palermo

I sat at a table outside the Antico Caffe Spinato just off the Via
Roma in Palermo, sipping a Campari soda, nibbling on
pistachios, almonds and crisps, watching the world go by and
generally thinking that life was pretty ripper. I knew that the
pistachios came from Bronte and the almonds came from
Avola, because the bowls in which they were served said so.
Only the crisps lacked provenance. Suddenly a pigeon dropped
through a small gap between the umbrellas that sheltered me
and other devotees of the cocktail hour from the sun, settled on
the edge of my table and started helping itself to my crisps.
Startled, I flapped at it with my hand. The pigeon beat its wings
furiously. Between us we managed to overturn the bowl with
the crisps, and most of the contents fell on the ground. Four
more sinister, mottled, feral birds dropped through the same
hole, and started helping themselves to my crisps. I had just
been comprehensively mugged by a gang of pigeons. It was, I
reflected, the only time on the entire trip that I had felt any kind
of threat.

☯☯

Coming down into Palermo had been the usual nerve-shredding ordeal. Palermo may have lacked the sheer bewildering, multidimensional lunacy of Naples. Nor did it have the cobbles to provide a searching examination of scooter technique, balance and nerve, but it still made its own, very special demands on a Vespista.

On the whole, Sicilians had seemed to me to be relatively law-abiding drivers. It was true that they drove in a highly competitive manner – someone had told me that if you let someone get in front of you, it's taken as a sign that your mother was a prostitute; if true, it was clear that the virtue of Sicilian women was beyond reproach – but they did so with a very careful eye on other drivers. And they stopped at traffic lights – most of the time. And they tended to give me a wide berth. Having said that, they sometimes pulled over without warning, frequently pulled out without warning, thought nothing of reversing out into the flow of traffic, and had a tendency to park at 45 degrees to the pavement, so presenting an obstacle like that of a rock projecting into a stream, or, in the case of the traffic in Palermo, a raging torrent.

The most unaccountable part of this raging torrent was my fellow scooter *scuderia*, who manoeuvred their machines without any regard for a) anyone else; b) the rules of the road; c) self-preservation; d) the laws of physics. They – and there seemed to be an unaccountable number of them – buzzed in and out of the lines of traffic, wove between bumpers, squeezed between lorry and bus, on the outside, on the inside, over there, over here, regarding my attempts at orderly progress in a single direction with bemusement and/or contempt.

Then there was the problem of one-way systems, which appeared to have been carefully designed to guide me away from the place I was trying to reach, the absence of meaningful road signs and the speed with which I had to make decisions on which my sanity and my life might depend. The only response when faced with this bedlam was to enter the zone where my conscious mind had no part in the proceedings, took no account of the past or the future. I simply was – and trusted to England, Harry and St George.

◎◎

In spite of spending the next few days walking around Palermo, I found it hard to really come to terms with it. I wasn't the first person to feel this. When Goethe visited the city in 1787 he observed in his travel diary, with his customary open-minded acuity, that it was 'easy enough to survey, but difficult to know'. For him the problem was physical: 'easy because a street a mile long, from the upper to the lower gate, from sea to mountain, intersects it. And is itself crossed, nearly in its middle, by another. Whatever lies on these two lines is easily found; but in the inner streets a stranger soon loses himself, and without a guide will never extricate himself.' This remains largely true about Palermo, but my problem was different. It was the city's essential identity, its intrinsic, elemental character, that eluded me. Palermo seemed to be without a centre, either physical or metaphysical.

It has, in a sense, always been a place apart from the rest of Sicily, self-contained and resplendent within its mountain ring; rich, cosmopolitan, self-sufficient. I had the feeling that while the rest of Sicily looked to Palermo, its capital, Palermo only really looked to itself. At one time the area around the city, the Conca d'Oro, the Golden Shell, was the most valuable agricultural land in Europe, due to the lemons that grew there in abundance, and which were exported all over the world. During the lawless days that followed Garibaldi's eviction of the Bourbons and their agents, the landlords recruited security guards to watch over and protect their precious lemon groves. So effective were these upholders of law and order that they were in danger of doing themselves out of a job, until they hit on the ingenious idea of creating their own marauding bands against which to guard – a typically convoluted Sicilian variation on gamekeepers turning poachers. The gamekeepers/ poachers created a protection racket which gradually formalised into a culture that eventually became the Mafia, and Sicily has been reaping the bitter harvest of those lemons ever since.

Self-contained and self-sufficient it might be, but Palermo was about as unhomogeneous as it is possible for a city to be: light, shady, renovated, crumbling, ersatz, genuine, antique, contemporary, Arab, Norman, baroque, low rent, high rent, noisy, hushed, orderly, disorderly, rising up, falling down; long, wide, straight modern boulevards linked by knots of winding streets, each bent in on the next, trimmed with tiny workshops – tailors, barbers, metalworkers, *paninari*, cabinetmakers, workshops making plaster mouldings

It was lush, too. The air was lush: warm and balmy with a light dressing of humidity. The ground was lush: semitropical trees and shrubs grew with astonishing luxuriance, bursting over walls and through railings, fat, fleshy, dark leaves, vaulting palms bearing cascades of golden-brown dates, capes of brilliant, vivid, vulgar bougainvillea. Palermo seemed like one of those once-mighty cities of Central America or Cambodia, that had been rescued from rampant jungle and which the jungle threatened to reclaim.

Then there were the holes in the metropolitan fabric, caused by war and still clearly visible, in the Kalsa district in particular, after 60 years. And there were other rents in the metropolitan fabric, too, of a different kind: casual architectural brutality; blocks of flats and offices of eye-watering, brain-storming ghastliness. It is possible that the city's visual monstrosities could be interpreted as a reaction against the overpowering taste of those who had built the churches and palaces, a visual sod-you to the standards of the past, and as a three-dimensional statement that power now lay elsewhere. On the other hand, they could also have been simply the legacy of corrupt politicians, corrupting criminality and an utter disregard for taste or decency.

It's easy to wring one's hands at the despoliation of what had once generally been considered the most seductive of European cities: 'It is an ancient and elegant city, magnificent and gracious, and seductive to look upon,' wrote the Arab scholar and traveller Ibn Jubayr in the twelfth century, a view that persisted pretty much up until 60 years ago. Even now there are just enough Gothic-Norman-Arab-baroque-art nouveau remains among the sea of architectural detritus to evoke a glimmer of the charm, wealth and culture of the past. But charm, wealth and culture have not been enough to resist the barbarism of the post-war years, to deflect the philistinism of a corrupt political process and the crass venality of the Mafia.

In a sense, the Mafia represents the most refined form of free enterprise. Whatever its historical roots, today it has no moral basis, no philosophical foundation, no religious raison d'être. It simply is. Its existence is its justification. It is there only to exercise power in order to make money, and, as Anthony Sampson once wrote of the City of London's morality, good means profitable and bad means unprofitable. The Mafia has taken that basic premise to its logical conclusion, eliminating anyone who looks as if they might interfere with that process. Palermo was living witness to the effectiveness of its approach.

Still, I was in search of such taste and decency as was left, and there was more than enough for me. I saw La Martorana and San Cataldo and the duomo in the Catalan Gothic style. I admired the Palazzo dei Normanni and the Palazzo Valguarnera-Ganci where Visconti staged the great ball in the film of *Il Gattopardo*. I fell in love with the elegant roofless remains of the church of Santa Maria dello Spasimo and the enchanting Norman apse of the church of Magione. I found repose in the lush splendours of the gardens of the Villa Giulia until driven out by a blast of music for a children's fair. Palaces and churches, churches and palaces, religion and money, money and religion, both influences had plonked their marks all over the city.

In truth, I wasn't as interested as I might be in palaces and churches, or theatres and temples come to that. There were so many of them. I was feeling a bit saturated by history and visual culture, particularly of a religious kind. Philistine of me, no doubt, but I kept barking my shins on it, and sorting out its layers and the significance of those layers; trying to relate them to Sicily's food culture was making my head spin.

I tried the markets, starting with the Vucciria, once the most famous in Palermo, but clearly it had had its day. There was a skeleton crew of stalls, a kind of tattered remnant, enough for tourists to photograph who couldn't make the journey to the market at the Porto Carini – or face its naked celebration of food in its unsanitised, unadorned, unpackaged forms: bloody, mournful-eyed lambs, rams with their testicles still attached, chickens complete with heads and feet, coils of glossy, purple entrails, thunk of knife, bloody barreltrunks of tuna, curious snake-like zucchini; and smells – fruity, spicy, rank, dank, fishy, slimy, sharp, fetid, nutty, candied, aromatic; and the ripe, mulchy cough of the man running the tripe stall. This was closer to the 'wild seething place ... that gleams with theatrical vitality' that Carlo Levi had once found in the Vucciria. By contrast to the vivid vitality of the Porto Carini market, the stallholders in the Vucciria were going through the motions, subdued and mournful.

☙☙

The next day dawned bright and clear, and with it fresh purpose and fresh traffic gushing along the city's thoroughfares, and fresh inspiration at the Antica Focacceria San Francesco (1834) in the shadow of the Chiesa di San Francesco d'Assisi (not to be mistaken for San Francesco di Pola). It was obvious that the Antica Focacceria came high on the guidebooks' list of recommended eateries, but it was no less popular with Palermitani than it was with tourists, and for good reason. The food was high quality and high volume, and the service rolled it out with the same kind of no-nonsense, serious professionalism you find in the best Paris brasseries, the waiters and waitresses moving purposefully and at speed between the tables, sustaining smooth mastery irrespective of who they were serving.

I started with three very good *crocchetti* fine, thin *panelle*, chickpea fritters; a light and delicate *caponata*; *sfincione*, Palermo's pizza over which Palermitani will argue with the ferocity of fundamentalists of different persuasions; and that gastronomic depth charge, *arancini*.

At a table just across from mine was a couple. She had a youthful face, sharp, pointed, a trim figure and a pageboy haircut. He was a youthful-looking 50-plus. I would say, pouchy-faced and puritanically sensual. They were both wearing sensible shirts, sensible trousers and sensible sandals. They spoke to each other in short, sharp bursts with long periods of silence between each exchange, scarcely engaging the other's eyes as they talked. British.

Next to the Brits were a family of six, covering three generations. They hardly stopped talking at all, not for a single second. They didn't have the vivid, soaring, tumbling discourse of Neapolitans, but there was an irresistible flow about their conversation. It coursed, glided, eddied, burbled, ran onwards, not dramatic or demonstrative, but supple, constant, sociable. Palermitani.

Hardly had the empty antipasto plates been cleared away than Silvia, my charming, gum-chewing, knowledgeable waitress, smacked the *primo piatto* on to the table, *pappardelle con pomodoro e triglie*, as richly textured as an archbishop's cope, the pasta light, delicate and slithery; the little tomatoes from Pachino, whole and just softened in the heat of the pasta; the fillets of small, inshore red mullet firm, flaky and gamey. There was just enough acidity in the tomatoes to hold the opulence of the dish as a whole. The soft, indulgent sensuality of the pasta wrapped itself around the firmness of the fish.

On the far side of the little square, nearest the wall of the Chiesa di San Francesco that formed one end of the piazza and its fine Norman doorway with slender pillars on either side and dog-tooth decoration in four immaculate ascending arches above it – and a transept above them and a rose window above that – were two couples, jolly but eating carefully. Each of them seemed on be on a special diet: no meat for this, no fish for that, another not really approving of tomatoes, and none of them drinking wine, just Coke. Americans.

My waitress brought a plate of *tonno al ragù*. Now here was something: great meaty chunks of tuna, dense and compact, dotted with peas and mint. The sauce made it easy to swallow. The peas were probably frozen. And the mint … was that another echo of the Moors or from further back? Further back, I thought, because the herb was named after the Greek nymph, Minthe, who was caught in the arms of Pluto by his wife, Persephone. Persephone threw her, Minthe, to the ground and trampled on her. These days, of course, Persephone would have called a lawyer. The Romans were fond of the herb and liked to pickle it, and I seemed to remember reading somewhere that Archestratus of Gela had something to say on the subject of mint. That was the way with Sicilian food. There always seemed to be some antique voice chatting away in whatever dish I happened to be eating.

By now the British and Americans had departed, along with most of the other tourists, leaving the Palermitani to get on with conversation and pudding, and me with just pudding: sweetened ricotta, which tasted like condensed milk, with bits of dark, bitter chocolate and biscuit, hallucinagenically sweet, but edible down to the last smear on the plate.

I rose from my table and wandered off into the golden, slumberous afternoon.

☯

It was 5.30, give or take a minute or so, late afternoon, a nameless square where the Via Ettore Ximenes crosses the Via Archimede, in an area known locally as the Porto Vecchio. It was not a salubrious or scenic neighbourhood. Slapdash blocks of flats, and smaller buildings in need of serious attention, marked the boundaries. The traffic was incessant, the grating mosquito buzz of scooters against the base rumble of cars, horns of all registers tooting, people standing around chatting, shopping, eating.

Spread around the square and along various surrounding streets were four large fishmongers and a couple of local fishermen with impromptu stalls; five fruit and veg sellers; a man selling octopus boiled to order in a large pan; a man selling chestnuts coated in salt, which had been roasted in a cooker like a tall stovepipe hat; a taverna, a *panineria*, an *alimentaria*; two *salumerie*; two *panifici*; two *rosticcerie*; an *entoteca*; a man selling pizzas from the back of a van; another selling boiled calf's feet and tongues from a table; and more food shops along this street and that street. It was not so much a market as a simmering stew of eating opportunities.

I started the evening with a plate of boiled octopus. The thickset young man with dyed blond hair in the booth fished an octopus out of the pan of boiling sea water, dipped a long, thin-bladed knife into a bowl of unhealthy-looking water at his elbow, wiped it on a dubious-looking cloth, and carefully sliced a set of pinky-purple tentacles into bite-sized chunks. He placed them on a very large, incongruously elegant plate decorated with pictures of octopuses, and handed them to me, along with a chunk of lemon. No, he said, he didn't just do octopus. Sometimes he did mussels. Mussels and octopus, that was it. The octopus was chewy, slightly sweet rubber, with a wash of saltiness from the water in which it had been cooked.

The air began to thicken. The light bulbs strung up on flex above the stalls were glowing. The flow of people was constant. Booff-booff-booff-booff. The air shuddered from the bass of a stereo system in a car stuck in the middle of a melee. The scooters wove their way through the people and around the cars. Scooters and cars exchanged short poops on their respective horns as if they were talking to one another. They were, in a sense. Sicilians use their horns to let other drivers know they are about, and occasionally to express exasperation but never anger. I had yet to see an angry driver.

I spotted a man in a side alley selling something from a basket with a cloth on top. From time to time he lifted the top and fished out a mysterious morsel. He was surrounded by a group to which he was handing out whatever it was, sometimes in a bun and sometimes just on a square of greaseproof paper. There was something vaguely furtive about both the man and his customers, but they were all friendly enough when I went over to investigate.

'What's that?' I asked.

'*Frattaglie*,' said the man, lifting the corner of the cloth, and fishing out some of the contents with his fingers.

'*Frattaglie?*'

He gestured in the direction of his stomach. '*Di vitello.*
Want to try some?'

He handed me a scoop of frilly, mottled organs on a
square of greaseproof paper. The men gathered round looked
at me expectantly. It was delicious: greasy, slightly chewy,
delicate, a hint of caramel and meat, souped up with a dash
of pepper.

'*Buono,*' I said. '*Molto buono.*'

They all grinned. They shared my pleasure in their dainty
victual of choice.

'How's it cooked?'

'*Molto lavoro. Molto tempo,*' was all the *frattaglie* seller
would say.

A man arrived and bought all his friends a helping, as you
might buy a round in a pub.

Every stall was selling food people could take home.
Alongside the late peaches and early oranges, still green in
parts, and persimmons, the *broccoli verdi,* and *melanzane,* the
fruit and veg stalls had big containers of roasted peppers,
roasted onions, boiled potatoes, boiled beans and, at one, artichokes. The fish sellers had trays of *sarde beccafico, sgombri
marinati, polpette di pesce in sugo.*

At the hub of all this food retailing was Da Michele, a stall
with a vast barbecue. Earlier I'd watched Michele stoking up
the charcoal. Now he was laying out meat on wooden skewers:
spiedini – kebabs by any other name – and lamb cutlets and
polpette and veal escalopes for display in front. He was a
barrel-chested man. He moved with muscular certainty,
Toscano stogie clamped in his teeth. If I wanted fish, he told
me, I'd have to buy it from the stall next door and he would
grill it for me. A man came over and handed him a gigantic

cernia, a fine, muscular fish with a pouting mouth and sorrowful eyes. Michele slashed it diagonally on each side several times, sprinkled it with oregano and oil and plonked it on the grill.

'What time do you close?' I asked.

He'd carry on cooking fish until 8.30, he said, and close an hour later.

The smoke from a chestnut-roaster's stove rose up blue-white into the evening air. The sky was a dark blue, now, the colour of gentian. A young man in a blue overall put a bunch of small-headed yellow chrysanthemums into a sawn-off plastic mineral water bottle, and stuck it into a head-high bracket beside a small memorial plaque on a wall in a side street.

A couple of mothers pushed their baby buggies side by side, chatting away. Shoppers moved steadily from one stall to the next, disappeared clutching bags bulging with a couple of sea bass, a kilo of mussels, a head of broccoli, persimmons, whatever. Clusters of scooters criss-crossed the square. It seemed miraculous no one was hit. There was a sense of the vitality of everyday life, that this meant something in the lives of these people.

I found more food shops in another cross street. In it were two competing *rosticcerie* within a few yards of one another, bars, *paninerie* and a butcher's that dealt only in chicken. Another advertised itself as selling *carni specialita spiedini e salsiccie*, with neat clutches of plain pork sausages, pork sausages with cheese, onion and parsley, and pork with aniseed, thin ones for frying and fat ones for grilling.

It was seven o'clock now, almost dark, and each stall created its own zone of light into which people drifted, becoming suddenly visible, vanishing when they drifted out again. Smoke billowed from Da Michele's monster grill. I reckoned it was time for my main course, so I bought a single mackerel from the stall next door.

'For grilling?' said the fishmonger. He gutted and boned the fish, and flattened out the fillets still joined by the skin. It took him a minute. Then he wrapped the mackerel in a piece of paper, carefully folding in the ends so that I had a parcel to carry ten paces to Michele. He unwrapped it, dipped the fish in breadcrumbs and plonked it on the grill. I noticed a man asking permission to grill long, purple-and-white striped *cicoria di Castelfranco* from the veg stall. Certainly, said Michele, with the Toscano still clamped in his teeth. I decided I wanted the same. Michele organised that for me, splitting the chicory down the middle, placing the two halves near the mackerel.

'Do want to eat in or take away?' He gestured towards a dining area at the back, behind the monster grill. It had plastic walls, four plastic tables and plastic chairs and real windows.

'In, please.'

'Wine?' Michele was not a man to waste words.

'Yes, please.' Michele shouted at someone gossiping on the other side of the stall who dashed off to get the wine from the *enoteca* down the road.

I sat down in the dining area. A radio was turned up to mind-pulping volume. I watched Michele's customers through a veil of smoke that carried the smell of charring fish and herbs and oil. The man was a blur of movement, turning fish, dousing them with oil, sprinkling them with herbs and salt, talking, ordering, never taking the cigar out of his mouth.

The wine arrived along with a plate of grilled bread sprinkled with olive oil and oregano, and then the grilled mackerel with half a lemon on one plastic plate, with the chicory doused in oil and sprinkled with salt. The fish was perfect, absolutely perfect. The breadcrumbs gave it a crunchy coating, and the flesh was soft and oily and seaweedy as mackerel should be, the lemon juice flashing over it. Part of the chicory was soft and part was still crisp, its bitterness a foil to the richness of the fish. I finished both, and the wine.

It was time to go. As I left a couple of large black bream flopped on to the grill. Their expectant consumer peered at them. The stalls were still doing a steady business. The lights from the bulbs strung above them lit up the faces of the customers while their bodies were lost in darkness. The smoke from the grill drifted up, rolling across the façades of the surrounding blocks of flats, across the balconies draped with striped awnings, up into the velvety dark of the night sky.

∞ Sfincione ∞

Palermo's pizza. It's a brave cook who publishes a recipe as every version is debated with the intense passion of scholars of the Talmud, the Koran and the Bible combined.

Makes 2 *sfincione*, approximately 20–25cm across
Dough: *600g 00 flour* • *400g* semola di grano duro *flour* • *20g baker's yeast* • *50ml extra virgin olive oil* • *50g* sugna *(pig fat)* *or lard*
Filling: *1 red onion* • *200g* caciocavallo *cheese* • *200g* strattu *(very concentrated tomato purée)* • *30g anchovies in salt* • *1 tbsp* pangrattato (dried breadcrumbs) • *Pepper* • *Extra virgin olive oil*

Mix the flours together along with the yeast, oil, fat and some warm water (you shouldn't need more than a litre). Kneed until you have a fine, elastic dough. Cover with a cloth and leave in a warm place to rise for about 2 hours.

Preheat the oven to 220°C/425°F/Gas 7. Finely chop the onion and cut the *caciocavallo* into little strips. Stretch out the dough in an oiled baking tray. Spread the *strattu* all over it. Arrange the anchovy fillets over it and scatter the onion around and about, followed by the *pangrattato, caciocavallo* and pepper.

Bake for 20 minutes. Splash on some extra virgin olive oil when you come to serve it.

∾ Pappardelle con pomodoro e triglie ∾

Serves 4

16 small rock red mullet • 1 onion • Extra virgin olive oil • 1 garlic clove • 400g very ripe small tomatoes • 250g pappardelle pasta • Salt and pepper

Fillet the red mullet and finely chop the onion. Heat the oil with the garlic. Discard the garlic as it turns brown. Add the chopped onion and fry until golden. Add the red mullet fillets. Cook for a couple of minutes. Add the tomatoes, washed but whole. Cook until the skins begin to soften slightly and the tomatoes begin to give off their juices. Meanwhile, boil the pappardelle in plenty of salted water until al dente, drain thoroughly and place in a bowl. Season the sauce and pour over the pappardelle.

❦ Frattaglie ❦

Frattaglie is a generic term for most offal, although the offal referred to by the charming fellow in the market clearly had a very specific location. It might have been a variation of *pane cu la meuza*, beef spleen and lungs served in a bun, although the offal side didn't seem exactly spleen-like to me. It was too frilly for that. However, in the interests of offal lovers, here is a recipe for a kind of *panu cu la meuza*. Spleen has a delicate flavour and a refined texture, believe it or not. Use a nice soft bun. This is pretty unreconstructed.

Serves 8–10
500g calves' lungs • 1 beef spleen • 2 garlic cloves • 100g sugna *(pig fat) • Salt and pepper*

Blanche the lungs and spleen in salted water. Drain well and chop up. Peel the garlic. Heat the pig fat in a frying pan and fry the spleen and lung bits with the garlic gently for 30 minutes. Your *frattaglie* are now ready. Season them with plenty of salt and pepper. Especially the pepper.

❦ Insalata Pantesca ❦

Serves 4
4 good-sized waxy potatoes, unpeeled • 4 very ripe tomatoes • 1 red onion • 2 sticks celery • 100g green olives • 40g capers in salt • 1 tsp dried oregano • 1 tin of mackerel in oil • Extra virgin olive oil • Salt and pepper

Cook the potatoes whole in boiling water. Peel when cool enough and cut into squares. Peel, deseed and roughly chop the tomatoes. Thinly slice the onion and celery. Mix the potatoes, tomatoes, onion and celery with the olive and capers. Sprinkle with oregano. Drain the mackerel, break up and scatter over the top of the vegetables. Dress with as much oil as you think right and season with salt and pepper.

Illuminato ('Nato) Sanguedolce, assessore
all'agricoltura, Pettineo

CHAPTER TWELVE

A Joyous Start Is the Best of Guides

Palermo – Reitano – Gioiosa Marea

It was a long day in the saddle, or so it seemed, heading east-wards along the coast. It may have had something to do with minor irritations that dogged me weary hour after weary hour. My bag, so strategically placed between my knees, developed an inexplicable and infuriating knack of pitching sideways off the scooter at critical moments.

Then there was the indescribable inadequacy and general confusion of the signposting. It reminded me of the legend that the inhabitants of the Romney Marshes in Kent removed all the signposts during the Second World War so that in the event of an invasion the Germans wouldn't know in which direction they were headed. The authorities of Villabate, one of Palermo's satellite towns, through which I had to go to get to the sea road, had raised this practice to extraordinary levels of sophistica-tion. At one point, when I followed signs that clearly indicated the road to Bagheria, I found myself whizzing into a building

265

site, much to the mystification of myself and to the vast amuse-
ment of the builders who, clearly, didn't often get to see a portly,
sweating Englishman on a grossly overloaded Vespa, with
bloodcurdling oaths echoing from inside his helmet. They were
even more amused when, as I tried to turn round, my bag
lurched from its perch between my knees and landed on the
ground with a kind of theatrical dying fall for the umpteenth
time that day.

And when finally, at very long last, I found the right road
just as utter despair was engulfing me, there was the general
teeming, dusty, depressing dreariness of Villabate itself, and
the other villages along the road, to contend with. Above all,
there was the ruthless, relentless, competitive tidal race of
traffic, the most menacing components of which were, as
usual, other scooters appearing silently at my shoulder just as
I was about to negotiate a particularly vicious pothole, or a
double-parked car or, worst of all, one of those cars carefully
parked at 45 degrees to the pavement, causing me to come to a
sudden, juddering halt.

But eventually I escaped from this urban purgatory. The
road curved easily this way and that, elegantly following the
line of the coast. The sun shone. The sea winked and sparkled
to my left. Stands of cacti with buboes of *ficchi d'India* erupting
from the outer curve of their fleshy lobes rose up behind walls.
There were sudden cataracts of cool blue plumbago and boas of
spectacularly, appropriately flamboyant bougainvillea.

> *Give me the life I love,*
> *Let the lave go by me,*
> *Give the jolly heaven above*
> *And the byway nigh me,*

carolled Robert Louis Stevenson in *Songs of Travel*. Oh, yes, indeed, although I rather departed from him when he went on:

> *Bed in the bush with stars to see,*
> *Bread I dip in the river –*

I've never been able to see much wrong with a decent hotel and fine dining, myself.

I trundled along easily enough through Ficarazzi, Porticello, Santa Flavia, San Nicola l'Arena and Trabia. I passed by Bagheria, and the Villa Palagonia which Goethe hated so much; and La Certosa and the Galleria Communale d'Arte Moderna with its collection of paintings by Renato Guttuso, who is best known in Britain as the artist who illustrated Elizabeth David's book on Italian food. I waved at the excavations at Solunto and failed to bathe in the mineral springs at Termini Immerese.

And then the weather turned – cool and grey to start with, the odd spot of rain pecking at my face. It wasn't long before the odd spot had become a fine drizzle. Presently the fine drizzle turned into a heavy drizzle. The heavy drizzle became steady rain, the first I had hit in six weeks. It was a pity, because, according to the guidebook, this should have been an idyllic road, with majestic mountains rising up on one side and the azure Tyrrhenian Sea twinkling on the other. As it was, I was having difficulty staying on the road at all. The rain became more insistent and was joined by a fierce wind that seemed specifically bent on plucking me from Monica's seat and dashing me on to the road. It's odd how these things become personalised.

I remembered how my brother Tom emailed me on a previous trip marked by a similar hideous experience: 'Cheer up, Matty. Misery makes better copy.' Well, bollocks to that, I thought. I have never been much of a subscriber to the 'No pain, no gain' thesis. I'm never at my best in adversity. There comes a point when I am quite happy to trade even a small dash of misery for an ocean of dull prose.

We battled on, Monica and I, and I mean battled: pummelled and buffeted, soaked and sodden, frozen and miserable. The wind and rain didn't let up when we turned off the coast road, and headed for the next range of wood-clad, majestic Nebrodi, up and up. And so at last I came into Reitano, stopped and parked Monica beside the road. I was very cold, very wet and very, very fed up. There was a lorry parked on the other side of the road. The man sitting in its cab wound down his window and called out something to me.

'What?' I said.

'Your back tyre,' he said. 'You've got a puncture.'

So I had. I very nearly wept.

☙

Round about 4.30 in the afternoon the next day I lay down on the clover at the bottom of an ancient olive tree, rested my head on a conveniently shaped root and fell asleep as the voices around the table rose and fell and laughter came and went.

I had met Nato Sanguedolce at the honey tasting outside Siracusa. Nato had a bear-like physique and a warm, serious face. When you get to the Nebrodi, he had said, give me a call and I'll show you around. I took him at his word, and his word had led indirectly to my comatose state beneath the olive tree. 'Come and join us for lunch on Sunday,' he had said.

I am very fond of Sunday lunch, of long, cheery afternoons spent around the family table, full of food and chat and laughter. In my early days, it was preceded by a concoction called dragon's blood – many years later my mother confessed that it had been made of orange juice and green vegetable dye – while the grown-ups refreshed themselves with martinis, made in a jug with a glass core so the ice didn't contaminate the alcohol. We were allowed Coca-Cola with lunch, one small, glass bottle each, as a special treat. Lunch itself was classically British: roast meat, roast potatoes, at least two other vegetables, gravy, pudding. We listened to the conversations of the grown-ups around us, speaking politely when we were spoken to. As we grew, we moved on to beer and then wine and took over the conversation, and suddenly we became those animated, booming figures we had once been so in awe of. But the spirit of the meal remained the same. So Sunday lunch became one of the lodestones of life, essential, leisurely, laughter-strewn.

I did not know what to expect of a Sicilian Sunday lunch when Nato and his eldest son picked me up. It was 11.30 by the time we arrived at the building where we were to eat. It was more than a shack and less than a house, made mostly of unplastered breeze blocks lost beneath Virginia creeper and jasmine. It stood in the middle of an olive grove of incalculable antiquity, just below the town of Pettineo. Many of the trees were massive and seemed to be made up of different strands of trunk twisted together in dramatic stasis. 'Operatic,' Nato called them. Among them, and clustered thickly around the building, were other trees, lemons, medlars, a vast mulberry, providing shade and cover, and the earth between them was bright green with clover.

Preparations were well under way by the time we clambered out of the car. A log fire crackled in the clearing, with a very large pan of water in which to cook pasta standing in the middle of the flames. Slices of aubergine were grilling over a small metal barbecue. There were the introductions – Franco, Enzo, Melina, Gabriella, Rosalia and bands of children – both parties, as it were, rather uncertain about what to expect of the other. But there was the food to bridge the gap.

The principal room in the building was a large kitchen-dining room; a long table with benches and chairs down either side was already set for lunch. It was covered in cloths and set with bowls, each covered with foil. The foil caps were lifted. This is the *zucca a coniglio*, explained Melina. This is *cicoria*, said Gabriella and this is the *salsiccia di San Giuseppe*. All made at home, said Rosalia. Well, not the sausage, no, but everything else, said Gabriella. The dishes are from around here. The black olives, they're ours, said Franco, and the green ones, too, from these trees, around us. The black ones are very ripe and the green ones not so ripe, just cured in *salamoia* – salt and water with a little garlic and herbs.

'O my! O my! O my!' says Mole in *The Wind in the Willows*, when faced with the prospect of a picnic lunch with Ratty. I felt the same.

Each dish was accompanied by a blizzard of information and advice concerning provenance, ingredients, cooking methods. Roast green peppers. We only use green peppers for roasting, not the red or yellow ones. They use red and yellow peppers in Catania, but not around here. Green ones, long green, pointy peppers. They're called *cornetto di toro*, bull's horns. Melina, have you got a green pepper to show Matteo? You see, it looks like a horn.

And *zucchine a coniglio*, courgette like rabbit, there was another fine dish. It hadn't got any rabbit in it. It was like spaghetti *con le sarde scappate*; the rabbit had escaped. Instead of rabbit there was *zucchine*, courgette. Not any old courgette, of course; it was a special, long courgette, which was cut into strips and salted and dried in the sun so that it became very dense, leathery. And when you wanted to use it, you soaked it in lots of water and cooked it with dried grapes. No, not raisins, grapes that you have dried yourself in the sun. And green olives chopped up, and a little onion and *salsa* and oil, and you called it *zucchine a coniglio* because it felt just like rabbit. Tasted like it, too.

After the guided tour of the lunch, Nato, Franco and Enzo led me away through the olive grove with a show of mystery. I wondered what obscure, ancient ritual I was about to be subjected to. Presently we came to a vast old tree, still vigorous in spite of the fact that its trunk was completely hollow so that it formed a curved wall inside which I could comfortably stand. I was handed a piece of grilled bread sprinkled with salt and oregano. Olive oil – 'from this tree' – was poured over the bread and I ate it standing inside the tree, a kind of arboreal benediction. We all smiled and laughed and trooped back to the party.

The water for the pasta was ready, and in went the *maccheroni*, home-made of course, looking like wet washing, pasty and flaccid. The water seethed up. It was now about 12.45. A little later we sat down and the pasta was served on plastic plates with *ragù* –'con carne di vitello*, Matteo' – and sprinkled with *ricotta di bovina salati*. None of your grated Parmesan here. You see, Matteo, there are plenty of cows in the

Nebrodi. There are sheep as well, and goats, but most ricotta around here is made with cow's milk. It's got more flavour. It also has a creamier feel to it than Parmesan, I thought, and, yes, perhaps I would have had a second helping, although by now I was wary of second helpings, not knowing how many other helpings there would be. But it was so delicate and slipped down so easily.

Having disposed of the *maccheroni*, we started on the dishes that had been on the table when I arrived, the post-pasta I suppose you might call them. No one took very much, I noticed, just a spoonful of *pepperoni e patate* and a few slices of *salsiccia di San Giuseppe* and a forkful of slices of *melanzane alla griglia*. And no one took very much wine either, just a quick slosh into the plastic cup. But everyone had a top up from time to time, just as they refilled their plates. There was no rush, no bother. Take your time, Matteo. Take it easy. So I took it easy.

The children came and ate and went to play outside, and came back from time to time to refuel, while their parents talked and talked. If they ate a lot and steadily, they talked twice, ten times as much, with gestures as fluid and expressive as their voices. There was hardly a single moment in the whole after-noon and evening when there weren't one, two, three voices intertwined in conversation quite as operatic (although far less anguished) as the trunks of the olive trees outside. It was easy to see how Italian became the first language of opera. Duets, trios, quartets are the natural medium of communication.

Only Nato, Melina, Enzo, Gabriella, Franco and Rosalia didn't speak Italian, of course. They spoke Sicilian, full of sibi-lance and swallowed vowels and dialect words, so that I was frequently lost along the way. Every now and then they would pause and explain what they had been talking about in a kindly and patient fashion, before launching again on some discussion or reminiscence in which they all joined, roaring with laughter, while I surfed along on their conviviality.

There were no divisions, no hierarchies, when it came to conversation. All speakers held the floor, were shouted down, questioned, listened to with equal weight. When it came to the food, however, there was a distinct, traditional division of labour. Men minded the fire. Women minded the cooking and the washing-up. I was cheerily dismissed when I tried to help clear the plates away after one course. The men looked at me much as you might look at someone who had cracked a dubious joke at a Rotary club dinner party.

Later I asked what work the women did. This produced howls of laughter. 'We work at home,' said Rosalia. 'Much harder than the men work "at work".'

Melina explained that unemployment was high in Sicily. This was a poor area, and a great many men didn't have jobs, so what work was there for women?

'Anyway,' she concluded, 'we are happy to be at home. Someone has to care for the children. Someone has to make the meals.'

I wondered how these recidivist views would go down in England.

It was time for a second pasta dish, *tagliatelle con maccu*, tagliatelle with puréed dried broad beans as a sauce, copious, slathery, mild and nutty. And filling. Even so, Franco never stopped eating. He wasn't a large man. In fact, he looked wiry and fit, yet he hadn't stopped eating since we started – another little forkful of *cicoria*, and another spoonful of *zucchine a coniglio*, another slice of sausage, a second helping of tagliatelle.

I was awestruck. Here was a proper eater. He made me look like a dilettante. He kept on eating the other dishes even when we moved on to roasted chestnuts and walnuts and heaps of shells were piling up on his plate.

I've always thought there is something very companionable about eating chestnuts. It's a rite, breaking the shell, peeling, nibbling the part-charred, part-yellow, crumbly flesh. Chestnuts, it turned out, were also quite controversial in the Nebrodi.

'But chestnuts are just chestnuts,' I said.

No, no. There are different varieties of chestnut, and the chestnuts from around Pettineo are better than the chestnuts around Tusa.

'I saw a lot of chestnuts around San Giuseppe Jato,' I said.

Even the chestnuts around Tusa are better than the chestnuts around San Giuseppe Jato, they cried.

There were apples to go with the walnuts. They called them *puma* in dialect, like *pomme* in French. I spoke up in favour of the culture of English apples. We have 90 apples particular to Gloucestershire, where I live, I said. They looked dubious and impressed at the same time, and I felt a fool because it sounded as if I were proclaiming the superiority of English apples over theirs, which was an ungracious thing to do.

That's the end, I thought with some relief, as the apple chestnuts and apple cores were cleared away, but I was wrong. The *pasta reale* appeared, pale almond pastries baked at a very low temperature. A speciality of Mistretta, said Nato. And a set of other almond pastries just in case. And *la crema*, a cold milk pudding – 'with full-cream milk,' said Rosalia, who had made it. 'Skimmed is too watery' – set solid with cornflour, I think, or possibly arrowroot, and flavoured with lemon peel and dusted with cinnamon. That was the point when I decided that I needed a break even if they did not, and I headed for the olive grove leaving the discourse in full flow.

When I woke up some 20 minutes later, sunlight trickling through the tracery of lancet leaves above me, the voices were still rising and falling and the laughter was still coming and going. I went back to join the party. More friends had turned up, Nicola and Maria Olivia, with their daughter, and they were vigorously tucking into the remains.

At 5.40 exactly I was startled to see Franco raking glowing embers of charcoal out on the ground, Nato rubbing a grill clean with half a lemon he had picked from one of the many trees around, and two large bags of lamb chops – 'Castrato, Matt-hew' – being laid out on it, followed by a kilometre of sausage being coiled into a great Catherine wheel of meat on another grill.

I paled. Did they eat like this all the time? No, not all the time, said Nato, but when we have a chance, when we get together like this, three or four families, then we do.

While we waited for the chops and sausage to bronze up, I talked to Nato about his work as an agricultural adviser. Olives were his particular speciality. Although he didn't strike me as a particularly demonstrative man, his voice took on a particular tenderness when he spoke about the centuries-old trees, Sant'Agatese olives. But he loved all the things that grew in the Nebrodi, and there didn't seem to be a month when something wasn't coming into season.

'This month we have apples, pears, persimmons and pomegranates. Soon there will be oranges and mandarins. Then cherries and *nespole*, medlars. Melons after that, and peaches and nectarines. And the grapes.'

And this was just the fruit. He was, he said, in the process of putting together a complete record of all the different varieties of all the different fruits that grew in the area, because some were already disappearing, or only existed in small patches here and there.

'We have several different microclimates and microterrains,' he said. 'Some are good for one thing, some for another. And if we lose these fruits and vegetables they'll never come back, because the knowledge of how they grew and why they grew will disappear, too.'

He saw the whole pattern of life in the Nebrodi as interconnected and interdependent: the landscape, the things that grew in it, the people who grew them, their customs and rituals. 'It's important we don't lose these things. The Nebrodi isn't a rich area, like other parts of Sicily. People here are poor. Farming is mostly subsistence. Someone needs to care for it.'

It was difficult to reconcile his altruistic concern with the selfish exploitation of landscape and people so evident elsewhere, but I didn't say so. How could Sicilians treat strangers with such generosity, show such passion for their food and such care for each other, and still tolerate visual barbarism, political venality and criminal brutality? It wasn't that Sicilians were inert. To me they seemed heroically involved in life, in chiselling out happiness and pleasure with extraordinary energy and ingenuity. I tried to find English equivalents and couldn't.

As Nato spoke he tended the grilling meat, getting plenty of advice from all the other men present. Franco, in particular, was very precise in his judgement about when a piece of meat was actually ready to be eaten, putting some chops back over the fire for a minute at the most before judging them to be right.

So the late afternoon air was filled with the luxuriant, nutty, brown butter smell of meat over flame, and I was wondering where I was going to put one more mouthful, and at six o'clock we started eating again. Or perhaps we had never really stopped. The sausage was good, salty and sweet, and there was more bitter *cicoria* balancing its richness. The *castrato* – both male and female sheep were castrated, explained Franco – was tender and had a marked musky, feral flavour. I had a couple of persimmons to help it down. And what about another almond pastry? They'll all be gone soon. Why not? You can only die once of overeating. And let's have a final helping of *la crema* while we're about it. Hate to see waste.

Not surprisingly, there weren't many leftovers and they were shared out among all the families, along with a massive trove of *funghi porcini* that Franco had found in the woods on the other side of the valley in the morning.

And then it was goodbye. It was about 8 p.m. We all gathered outside, kissing cheeks and shaking hands.

'You've had a good time?'

'I've had a marvellous time, a bloody, bloody marvellous time. It's been like a miracle for me. Thank you. Thank you, thank you.'

'Just so long as you enjoyed yourself. That's what matters.'

☺☺

The next day Monica was restored to full fighting trim at no cost, thanks to Nato who lived up to the promise of his surname, Sanguedolce – Sweetblood. It seemed that the back tyre had picked up a splinter or thorn.

Mobile again, I set off early from Reitano to explore the Nebrodi further, hoping to see porcupines, wildcats and pine martens, said to thrive in the region, even possibly a griffon vulture – or at the very least the legendary *suini neri dei Nebrodi*, the black pigs of the Nebrodi, that ran wild, so I was told, in the abundant forests of oak, ash, beech, holm oak, cork, maple and yew. I headed towards Mistretta in bright sunshine, blithe with anticipation and the pleasure of being warmed by sun again. There were quails sitting on the telephone wires, like beads on a necklace.

I was slightly less blithe by the time I got to Mistretta, the source of the previous day's almond dainties. It was lost in cloud, and consequently rather chillier than sun-drenched Reitano further down the hill. I regretted not having more layers of clothing, but what the hell, I can take it, I thought, and went for a wander round the town, which was small but hand-some, with some fine baroque twiddly bits here and there. There were quite a lot of men with hooked noses, tanned complexions and cloth caps standing around, and a remarkable number of butchers. I counted six on the main street alone, and I never made it round the backstreets. One reason for cutting short my exploration of Mistretta was the attitude of the inhab-itants, which was not as cheery as I would have liked. Indeed, it was pretty offhand when I asked for directions and help. Enough of that, I thought; on, on, towards Nicosia.

And on, on I pressed, up and up. The cloud cover thick-ened. The landscape was bare and windswept, with outcrops of rocks, cropped grass, thickets of gorse, broom and brambles. Not unlike Exmoor, I thought. I passed flocks of grubby sheep and a herd of cows the colour of chammy leather or creamier, with large, lustrous eyes. And there were horses with odd-looking rounded noses grazing in a field. These I took to be the special breed of wild horses they have in the Nebrodi.

As I came round one corner, I was confronted by a line of donkeys stretched across the road. They stopped, surprised. They were joined by a small herd of cows with bells around their necks, a few inquisitive goats and four horses being driven along by a ruddy-faced old man in a cloth cap. He stopped, smiled beatifically and wished me good day.

'Where are you from?' he asked.

'England,' I said.

'England?' he said, and wrinkled his brow. I wasn't sure if England meant much to him. 'And where have you come from today?'

'Reitano,' I said. He smiled again and nodded.

'And where you going to?'

'Capizzi,' I said.

'Capizzi? Ah.' He smiled and nodded again. 'God give you a good day and a good journey,' he said, and continued on his way. He washed away the impression made by the people in Mistretta.

I kept dipping in and out of cloud, chilled and getting chillier. I turned off the road before reaching Nicosia and followed a smaller twistier one to Capizzi. The land was very bare, and khaki-coloured in the light. Quite a lot of it had been ploughed up, the earth a dun brown. There were majestic views, but unlit by the sun they were robbed of some of their magic. By now I was very cold indeed, and it was threatening to rain. How I regretted my hasty decision not to stock up with proper clothing. And I was hungry. I sang very loudly to keep my spirits up: 'John Brown's body lies a-mouldering in the grave.'

I abandoned John Brown as too lugubrious in present conditions, and tried 'My Darling Clementine'. Then I remembered that she fell into the foaming brine. I had to make do with

'There's a Hole in My Bucket'. That seemed to capture my mood, even though I was heading downhill at last.

Below Capizzi was a wide band of forest. The leaves were turning, the pale, washed-out yellows and golds of poplar and ash mixed with the more brilliant reds and purples of maples, a scintillating, shimmering kaleidoscope of foliage, although my ability to respond was being increasingly hampered by my sense that I was freezing to death. Even the sight of the verge studded with autumn crocuses did little to lighten my mood. I had never been so cold. I began to hallucinate about warm baths and crackling fires. I stopped and tucked the map under my biker's jacket as a means of deflecting the direct chill on to my breastbone. After a while I was aware that it had vanished, fallen out presumably, so now I had no map as well as no will to live. I stopped singing.

Below the mixed woodland came a wide belt of oak, small, mountain oak, carpeted with *funghi porcini*, I fantasised, with black pigs frolicking in the glades. And quite suddenly there they were, foraging cheerfully beside the road, a family of *suini neri dei Nebrodi*, the black pigs of the Nebrodi, quite small, svelte and charming. And no, I didn't have a film in my camera because I had used it up taking useless pictures of the bloody landscape. I could only watch and wonder as the pigs scampered off into the undergrowth. But I felt very pleased. It was like seeing otters or pine martens in Britain.

As I descended the oaks gave way to cork trees, marked where their bark had been cut away in sections. And were my senses deceiving me, but was that a flash of sunlight I saw, or thought I saw? It was, it was. And there was more of it. And I was heading into it and the world was getting sunnier and warmer by the second, and life was worth living after all, and

I had seen the black pigs and many other marvels; and the sunless uplands perhaps weren't so sunless after all but were really rather beautiful, very beautiful in fact, and yes, I could say as one with the poet Hopkins, look, we have come through.

◎◎

It was autumnal but sunny and clear by the time I hit the coastal road again, and headed in the direction of Capo d'Orlando and Brolo. It was a grand road for driving along on a Vespa, now that I was warmed through in the sun. Sometimes it clipped the seashore, but for most of the way it ran along the edge of the mountains, with a sharp wall of rock on one side, and on the other the almost inevitable river of dark, glossy, green citrus trees broken by blocks of blue-grey cabbages or droopy, shrivelled tomato plants, the tomatoes still clinging to them; odd blobs of brilliant red against the blotchy brown, reaching to the sea's edge. Seaside towns came and went, pleasant, nondescript, busy, with small signs pointing out bed and breakfasts, pizzerias, cafés, bars, the way to the seafront, tyre-repair shops.

I came to a large sign that pointed the way to Sinagra and I took it. The road was a rare thing in the Nebrodi: flat and leading inland. It ran parallel to a stream that flowed clear over a series of concrete weirs. There were pools in which ducks and moorhens splashed. It might have been a very English scene, but for the very un-English abruptness and height of the hills on either side and the very un-English goats, the white and butterscotch colours of caramel rolls, grazing on them.

But my objective wasn't Sinagra. I was heading beyond it, up in the hills, to the Trattoria Fratelli Borello, which Nato

Sanguedolce had told me was a repository of local foods. Soon the road began to climb into a layer of walnut and Spanish chestnut trees, their leaves tinged with tobacco yellow, and small vineyards and plots growing cabbages, fennel, peppers and *melanzane*. The steep, wood-clad hills were muffled in their thick, dense coat of greeny-gold. And then I was there, the Trattoria Fratelli Borello, proper and prosperous-looking, with a motley collection of local ancients hanging round the entrance. In fact, it was more than just a trattoria. There was a *salumeria* attached, selling local cheeses and various products of the *suin nero dei Nebirodi*, those perky black pigs whose rumps I had last seen bouncing skittishly into the oak forest.

Several groups of lunchers were already hard at it in the bright, sensible dining room, including a party of four smartly dressed young women, each with a mountain of gnawed bones in front of her. The whole scene gave me the feeling that this was a place where people came to eat. And eat I did.

The waitress's comment that the antipasti were '*abon-dante*' was an understatement verging on an outright lie. They would have been quite enough for lunch on their own. There were four plates: one of salami, prosciutto, *lardo* – cured back fat – and four cheeses; a second of strips of *melanzane* and green peppers *sott'aceto* and some green olives; the third of *ricotta fritta*, two large fritters of I couldn't decide what – dough I thought, perhaps local variants on *crespelle* – some rounds of smaller salami cooked with egg, and some very fine slices of raw, fresh mushrooms with a little vinegar poured over them and sprinkled with strips of cheese; and the fourth was a hot bowl containing bubbling *provola* cheese sprinkled with seeds of chilli.

The single slice of prosciutto was quite possibly the finest slice of ham I had ever eaten in my life, sweet, subtle, delicate, complex, penetrating with an exquisitely refined silky texture the quiddity of pig. The cheeses were all distinctive and distinguished. The pickled *melanzane* and peppers, which had considerable heat, acting as sharp foils to their lusciousness. And finally I fell before the simplicity of the melted cheese and chilli dish, gooey, fiery and indulgent. It was my kind of cooking.

I had not come across a lot of chilli in Sicily, which was odd considering how ubiquitous it was in Calabria just across the Tyrrhenian Sea. Like tomatoes, potatoes, chocolate, corn, tobacco and much else besides, chillies had arrived from the Central Americas when that part of the world, like Sicily and southern Italy, was part of the Spanish Empire. But while the Italians had taken to them with immense gusto and ingenuity, Sicilians used them sparingly. It may have been that the diet of rural Sicily was just slightly more varied than that of Calabria and Campania, where the vegetable/spice was used to liven up a whole raft of dishes that would otherwise be terribly boring; other spices were far beyond the means of poor labourers. Peppers grew easily wherever there was enough sunshine and water, and so universal did their use become that they were known as *la droga dei poveri*, the drug of the poor. Those innocent days seem rather far away.

A plate of *tagliatelle con funghi* was, mercifully, a small portion, of slightly slippery elegance, but the meat afterwards – sausage, several thin *castrato* lamb chops and *spiedini*, thin leaves of pork wrapped around cheese and crusted with breadcrumbs, with a salad and a plate of chips – was the usual hammer blow. The cook hadn't gussied up the ingredients but let their beauties shine out uninhibited.

In place of pudding I was brought a plate of chestnuts, two little chestnut *dolce* and a bottle of chilled *liquore*, a mix of puréed chestnut, cream and alcohol; a kind of Bailey's of the mountains, thick and creamy and tasting of chestnuts, and not at all sweet.

Like Nangalarunni, the Borelli brothers' food was rooted in the locality. It owed practically nothing to the outside world, not even the manner of its cooking. Everything I ate came from within a radius of 15 kilometres, probably less. They were the vegetables, nuts, fruits, mushrooms and animals that thrived in this terrain. This was the food people ate at home. It was the practical expression of Nato Sanguedolce's views on how the inhabitants, products, society and culture of the Nebrodi were intimately bound to one another.

I just managed to swing a leg over Monica, balance myself and head off down the hill again. I didn't get far. With rare good fortune, I found a dell beside a stream I had passed on my way to lunch, and lay down under a bush and went to sleep. When I woke up there was a long-tailed tit sitting on a branch above my head. I lay looking at it for a while, warm and dozy. The chilly rigours of the morning seemed a long way away, and I marvelled at my good fortune. Presently the bird flitted away and so did I.

◎◎

The next morning I had left the deserted anonymity of the Capo Skino Hotel at Gioiosa Marea on the coast, where I had spent the night, and worked my way further along the ss113. The world was delicious. The sea danced in the sunlight, and Monica and I danced along the band of tarmac as it unravelled hypnotically beneath us. A cooling wind ruffled my arms and over my back. We slid into shadow and out, swerved round the inevitable irregularities on the road with an easy sway. I was master of the road, the hour, the journey. For a moment or two, at least.

I stopped at Tindari or Tyndarus, depending on your classical allegiances, to look at the Greek-Roman temple and theatre, a rare excursion into remote antiquity for me. I preferred to do my excavating into Sicily's past on the plate. The remains lay just beyond a vast modern church – built to a much-venerated icon, La Madonna Nera, the Black Madonna – which appeared to have been sculpted out of ice cream with an ungodly lack of taste; a vulgar display of wealth and power compared to the fastidious beauty of the site. Tindari was set on a headland high above the shore, with umbrella pines, olive trees and sorbus, quite small and personal compared to the Olympian splendours of Selinunte. It was easy to understand why someone would want to build here, and the fine theatre must have the most beautiful view of any in the world, out over the true-blue sea (not ever wine-dark as Homer would have us believe; or perhaps he drank some very dodgy stuff) towards the island of Salina.

Rather uplifted, it was back to the road and on to Milazzo, where I had planned to have lunch in a restaurant praised in interesting terms in various guides. After a great deal of charging to and fro, stopping and asking, discovering that I was in the wrong part of town completely, chancing upon the right part of town, I finally found the place where I fondly imagined I was going to have a cheery guzzle. It was tucked away on some insignificant backstreet between Milazzo and Barcellona del Golfo. And it was shut, *per ferie*, for holidays. I was cross.

Disconsolate, I trailed back into Milazzo and went into the first place I came to, Il Porto del Marinai. Perhaps I should have been warned by the absence of other lunchers. I should certainly have taken heed of the appearance of crab sticks in the *antipasto di mare.* It was too late by the time the *spaghetti con granchio* – pasta with crab – arrived, pink, creamy, sweet, utterly revolting in every possible way. The dish left a profoundly unpleasant aftertaste that fouled my mouth for the rest of the afternoon and repeated with depressingly regularity. Of course there was a TV blasting away, too, just to leaven my mood. Sicilians and Italians have a morbid fear of death, and see solitude and silence as being synonymous with it. Perhaps the constant roar of television reminds them that they are still alive, although in the case of Il Porto del Marinai it might be a foretaste of hell. I suppose I was due something of the kind. The number of bad, or even indifferent, dishes I had eaten in the course of seven weeks in all could be counted on the fingers of one hand.

The beauty of the road that led away from the coast, up over a spur of the Peloritani mountains, was balm to the troubled stomach and mind. It wound like a double helix, with open views to start with and was then shaded by a forest of umbrella pines. Only a herd of flossy goats grazing peaceably on the verge, and a couple out mushrooming in the woods, broke my seclusion. Suddenly there was a break in the trees just before the road began to wind down to Messina, a window opening out on to a sweeping view from the city almost directly below my feet, across the Straits of Messina to Reggio di Calabria spreading like urban magma along the shore of the Italian mainland on the far side.

❧ Maccheroni con ragù di vitello e suino ❧

Nato Sanguedolce and his family have given me these recipes. He points out that all the recipes work better using the local ingredients. Well, yes. I couldn't agree more, but they're still worth trying if you don't happen to have a supplier heading for the Monti Nebrodi on a regular basis.

This is a main dish made with a fresh pasta made with Sicilian durum wheat that is flavoured with a *ragù* of veal with the addition of a bit of pork that brings out more flavour. The tomato sauce is made on the spot by simply cooking it without preservatives.

Serves 4 people
¼ onion • *4 tbsp of olive oil* • *200g minced veal* • *100g minced pork* • *White wine* • *300g* salsa di pomodoro *(tomato sauce)* • *Salt* • *2 bay leaves* • *400g* maccheroni,

Chop and fry the onion in some olive oil for a brief period, then add the minced veal and pork. After it has cooked for a bit add a splash of white wine. Allow it to evaporate before adding the tomato sauce, a pinch of salt and the bay leaves. Leave it cook for about an hour.

Once the *ragù* is ready, cook the *maccheroni* in boiling salted water for 15 minutes. Drain the water and add the sauce. Leave it to stand for a couple of minutes to allow the flavours to blend.

∞ Costata di maiale alla brace ∞

Pigs from different areas taste different and Sicilian chops tend to be thinner than ours. Still, that aside, the secret to this disarmingly simple recipe is anointing the chops with *salmoriglio* once they are cooked. According to Nato, *salmoriglio* should consist of olive oil made from Sant'Agatese olives, juice from Pettineo lemons and wild Nebrodi oregano.

Serves 4 people
4 tbsp of olive oil • 4 tbsp of lemon juice • oregano • 4 pork chops costate • Salt

Make the *salmoriglio* by mixing the olive oil, lemon juice and oregano together. Grill the pork over wood charcoal. Sprinkle a pinch of salt over the meat while it's cooking. Once the meat is cooked add the *salmoriglio*.

∾ Zucchine a coniglio ∾

This is a typical dish that is mainly served around the feast of San Giuseppe (March 19). It was one of the dishes that made up the *Virgineddi* meal (a meal prepared for the devotees of San Giuseppe). It's far too good to be eaten only once a year. You may have to use any old courgettes you can get your hands and dry the 'fillets' of courgettes (i.e. halved or quartered) in the oven.

Serves 4 people
400g fillets of courgette that have been salted and dried in the sun • Extra virgin olive oil • 30g dried grapes • 150g olives in salamoia (brine) • 1–2 tbsp wine vinegar • 1 spoonful of sugar • 20g pine kernels • 6 tbsp tomato passata • Salt and pepper

Rinse the courgettes in tepid water to get rid of excess salt and chop into bite-sized pieces. Leave the pieces of courgette to drip dry for around 20 minutes, then heat them in a pan on the hob and get rid of any remaining water. Heat some olive oil in the pan and fry the courgettes until golden. Soak the dried grapes in tepid water. Remove the stones from the olives, cut them into small pieces and fry gently in a little olive oil. In another pan warm the vinegar and add the sugar. Keep warm until the sugar has melted. Add all the various ingredients to the courgette chunks and simmer them gently for 10 minutes to acquire the sweet and sour flavour. The *zucchine a coniglio* can be served hot or cold.

∞ Crema di Latte ∞

Serves 4 people
1l full-fat milk • 200g sugar • 100g corn or potato starch • Ground cinnamon

Put almost all the milk and all of the sugar in a pan and heat gently. In a glass bowl stir the corn or potato starch together with the a few tablespoons of cold milk. Mix until completely smooth. Dilute the corn or potato starch mixture in the bowl by slowly pouring in and mixing the heated milk. Continue mixing the milk until it turns into a rich and velvety cream.

Pour the mixture immediately into a glass dish. Allow to cool. Sprinkle the top with a good amount of cinnamon.

Pino, il laboratorio d'Irrera, Messina

CHAPTER THIRTEEN

Supple Minds

@/@

Messina

'Messina leans against the mountains,' that energetic traveller, Ibn Jubayr, had written in the twelfth century, and
so it did. The Monti Peloritani rose like a wall behind it. The sea
lapped to the front. The town sprawled between the two, as if
lounging along the shore. But Messina had no old Arab quarter
with a knot of narrow streets at its heart that Ibn Jubayr might
have recognised, no rickety medieval quarter, no baroque
grandiosity even. The entire old city was destroyed in a few
seconds in 1908, when a hundred thousand people died in an
earthquake and the tsunami that followed it. Only one building
survived: the church of Santissima Annunziata dei Catalani,
which had been built on the ruins of a Greek temple to
Poseidon, god of earthquakes and the oceans. It still survives,
complete with a Byzantine dome – a marvellous mixture of
Norman solidity, Romanesque blind arches and slender
columns, and Moorish geometric motifs; it is as if most of the
history of the island has been concentrated into this delightful,
compact structure.

After the catastrophe, Messina was rebuilt with low houses and wide streets to minimise the possibility of another disaster on such a scale. It was unmistakably a modern city, laid out on a grid system, with boulevards and straight streets. This made it remarkably bright and open, and gave it a provincial, bourgeoise feel, placid and virtuous. These days we associate modern civic dynamism, progress and success with tall buildings.

Sadly for Messina, the careful city planning of a century ago was severely compromised by the effect of bombing raids during the Second World War, and by the rash of dully designed, badly built, utilitarian blocks of apartments, car parks, and office buildings that were put up to fill the gaps left by the bombs. But hidden away all over the city, like genuine gems among the disintegrating paste of cheap theatrical jewellery, are buildings of great distinction and beauty, like the church of Santissima Annunziata dei Catalani and the fine art deco house on the corner of Via Giordano Bruno, just off the Pizza Cairoli. It is a smart clothes store now, Muschio e Miele. I wondered what the ferociously pious Brother Bruno would have made of such a sensuous building dedicated to a wholly decadent commercial enterprise.

☙

Among the genuine architectural beauties of Messina is the house of the Rodriguez family.

In a sense, this journey began when I first met Leopoldo Rodriguez and Federica, his wife, at a dinner at the Circolo della Caccia – the Hunt Club – in Rome some years before. If you are lucky enough to be invited, you'll find the premises of the Circolo in the Palazzo Borghese. They are of a magnificence that White's, the Garrick, Brooks's and Boodle's cannot even begin to dream of. The occasion had been organised by my brother Johnny, who lives in Rome, and whose London club had reciprocal arrangements with the Circolo.

We took drinks before dinner in a room lined with silk. Its ceiling was at least 15 metres above us, heavy with mouldings of insignia of the Borghese family bolstered by papal crossed keys. We were waited on by flunkeys in bum-freezer jackets, velvet knee breeches, white stockings and gloves. The room we passed through on our way to the dining room had a marquetry floor that had the same disorienting artfulness of an Escher drawing. The dining room itself had the same burnished grandeur as the salon in which we had taken our drinks. And, to add the final surreal detail, every time the door swung open to let the stream of liveried flunkeys bear yet another dish to the table, it seemed there was always a cardinal in scarlet robes sweeping along the passage beyond, surrounded by a covey of black-robed priestly attendants.

During dinner I sat opposite Leopoldo. He was a handsome, compact man, with a fine, curly pepper-and-salt beard and fine, curly pepper-and-salt hair. Put him in a velvet and gold doublet and hose with a ruff around his neck, and he would not have looked out of place in a Velázquez portrait of a seventeenth-century nobleman. He struck me as somewhat taciturn and wary to start with. As their name suggests, the Rodriguez family had first come to Sicily as part of the great Spanish influx in the fifteenth century, settling originally in Lipari, before coming to Messina. Leopoldo's father had acquired the patent for hydrofoil boats, and had become rich building and running the *aliscaffi* – hydrofoil ferries – that ran between Sicily and the Italian mainland and the Aeolian islands. In spite of my best efforts and best Italian, he continued to regard me carefully through heavy-lidded eyes, responding to my blundering attempts at conversation with dutiful good manners, but not really engaging.

But then we got on to the subject of food, and all barriers dissolved. Our exchanges became increasingly animated. I felt a true sense of kinship when he described how a particular Sicilian dish – *involtini di pesce spada* – could only be made with a particular part of the swordfish, and that this particular part – my memory is blurred as to exactly which part it was – had to be cut in a particular manner or the dish would not be worth eating. That level of passion and exactitude in matters of food seemed to me to be absolutely splendid.

His mother, he went on, ran the cooking side of the family house in Messina. She was, it seemed, a stickler for tradition, and relied on an old cook to keep things as they should be. Yes, I would be welcome to come and watch the old woman at work. When? Next week? Sadly, I couldn't take Leopoldo up on his offer of next week, full of enthusiasm though I was. The party broke up at around midnight with affection being sworn on all sides, and with an invitation for a light lunch *a casa Rodriguez* the next day.

Lunch was as memorable as dinner the night before. We sat outside in the expansive gardens surrounding Leopoldo's handsome eighteenth-century villa a few minutes walk from the centre of Rome. We started with raw broad beans, tiny jade beads no bigger than the nail on my little finger, fresh and musky and slightly bitter at the same time. We seasoned them with shavings of *provolone stagionato*. There was a mozzarella, too, the size of a rugby ball, brilliant white, that squeaked when cut. It had been flown up from Campania that morning, and had an airy brightness on which floated a light coating of grassy olive oil. There was pasta too, spaghetti, lightly coated in a shimmering tomato sauce and fine slices of *melanzane* which were both crisp and soft at the same time. And then came Sicilian sausages and steaks grilled over wood, with a salad, and there would have been a pudding of some kind, or perhaps just fruit as Federica's concession to a Sicilian's notion of a 'light lunch'. Don't forget to come to Sicily, Leopoldo had said as I left.

Since then, every time I met him and Federica we talked about food, and I would say that I wanted to write about Sicily and he would ask when? Next week? And I would say next year and he would say, talk to me when you really are going to start and I'll see what I can do, and next year came and went and still no Sicilian adventure. And finally I had, at long last, been able to redeem my pledge.

Had I not been directed to it, I would not have known the Rodriguez house was there. It was tucked away behind a fence and a screen of shrubs and trees just off the Via Garibaldi, one of Messina's broad boulevards that run parallel to the coast. Like the rest of the city, it had been built after the terrible earthquake of 1908, in the local version of art deco. It was a wonderful town house, with the solid, four-square structure and order of nineteenth-century sensibility combined with art deco's expressive sense of fantasy and decoration which shaped the fabulous glass panels in the doors, ornate tiling surrounding the fireplaces, and the elegant, serpentine mouldings around the ceilings.

Leopoldo had changed little since I first met him. His fine, curly pepper-and-salt hair and beard seemed much the same as when we sat opposite each other in the Circolo della Caccia, although perhaps there was just a touch more salt than pepper these days. He had extraordinarily expressive brown eyes, which he flicked up and sideways in a gesture of subtle disbelief, irony, humour, comment of some kind. He exuded a restless vigour. When sitting, he jigged his left leg incessantly. He dipped in and out of the company. He was quite capable of remaining silent for periods, and then bursting into anecdote, comment or explanation, always lucid and always forceful. He had a fine sense of humour, and was a man of formidable purpose and with an absolute sense of honesty remarkable in a society not necessarily noted for it.

We were joined by Federica, a tall, elegant woman, always immaculate in her appearance and her judgement, her natural shyness initially masking her immense warmth and intelligence. Federica wasn't Sicilian. She came from Rome and I felt that she acted as a buffer between Leopoldo and much of the outside world, although whether she was guarding him from it or it from him I never quite made out.

The lunch party was completed by Leopoldo's mother, Signora Rodriguez, now in her eighties, who had lived in the house for the last 60 years and kept the place in perfect, unchanged condition. She was a redoubtable old lady, a bit like a walking bustle, with marcelled hair and tinted glasses. She walked with the aid of a stick, pursing her lips as she did so. She exhibited the needy frailties of old age, but at the same time I felt that she was a monument to vanished disciplines and graces, among which is an almost dictatorial attitude towards food.

We ate rather formally, at a table laid with the linen table-cloth, silverware, weighty glassware and flowers – careful order of traditional custom – and we were waited on by a white-gloved, white-jacketed Filipino major-domo and a maid, a striking synthesis of the twenty-first and nineteenth centuries.

For a moment it was difficult to reconcile this studied, solid, very old-fashioned order with the pullulating city outside, the Internet and all the buzzing, freewheeling appurtenances of modern life. It was almost as if I had strayed into a scene out of Giuseppe Lampedusa's *The Leopard*. Of course, that book deals with the collision between the resolute, antiquated power of the old regime and the irresistible force of the new.

To increase the feeling that lunch was a miraculous extension of the nineteenth century, we began with a dish that occurs in the great dinner scene in Lampedusa's masterpiece: a version of *pasta al forno*, a baked dish of *pasta casareccia*, explained Signora Rodriguez, with minced veal, hard-boiled eggs, tomatoes, onions, and many other bits and pieces. The secret, she said, lay in the crust.

'Everyone must have some of the crust so that they can enjoy the difference between the crunchy top and the mixture underneath,' she said, not so much by way of explanation as command. 'You bake the mixture for a while and then you must stir it, just at the right moment, and then bake it again to finish it. In this way it is evenly cooked through and develops the necessary crunchy topping.'

The second dish, *impanata di pesce spada*, was even more skilful, a dish straight out of the old baronial *monzu* tradition, when the grand families had French chefs and the skills of the French haute cuisine kitchen were put to work on Sicilian ingredients and eating passions (*monzu* is a corruption of monsieur). It was a deep pie with an extraordinary, almost biscuity crust, quite different for the chewy brittleness of the *pasta al forno*, with traces of orange rind and something else that I couldn't quite put my finger on. This provoked much discussion as to whether this was *pasta frolla*, shortcrust pastry, or not, and what the definition of *pasta frolla* actually was, or was this a variant, in which case, how did it vary and, well, the discussion became pretty animated.

The form might have been French, but the filling might be a metaphor for Sicily: intense, elaborate, rich and intoxicating. There were chunks of swordfish enveloped in an *agrodolce* mixture of tomato, capers, zucchini and onions; swordfish from the sea, capers from Pantelleria, tomatoes from the New World, sweet and sour from the Romans. It was *robusto* as Federica rightly said, so *robusto*, indeed, that I had to have a second helping.

We moved on to a classic *cassata siciliana* which came from Irrera, a café famous in Messina for its traditional pastries, ice creams, granitas and sundry other cornerstones of the Sicilian diet. Based on my English experiences, I had thought that a cassata was a layered ice cream shaped like a rounded-off top hat, embedded with bits of candied fruit. Such ignorance. The true cassata, it turned out, was a sponge cake, very conventional, shaped like the kind you might serve a vicar, albeit layered with sweetened ricotta studded with nibs of chocolate in place of jam or creamed butter, and covered with pistachio green, almond-flavoured icing decorated with bits of fruit and whirly sugar – decoration quite as ornate and rococo as the interior of any baroque cathedral. The appearance owed everything to a Spanish sense of drama and colour, but the structure was much the same as that of cakes I had been eating all my life in Britain. I felt vaguely disappointed, although it was nice to think that the artists of Irrera and those of the Women's Institute were brothers and sisters under the skin.

The sweet ricotta filling, however, was causing Signora Rodriguez much pursing of lips. The ricotta was '*troppo duro*' she thought. It wasn't 'abastanza raffinato'. And the sponge was too watery. 'It hasn't been worked enough to make it really light,' she said.

Leopoldo rolled his eyes heavenwards. We all dutifully tasted our helpings. Blow me if I could tell.

'Perhaps it isn't absolutely fresh,' suggested Federica, 'so the sponge has absorbed some of the liquid from the ricotta, which would make the sponge seem watery and take away some of the lightness of the ricotta.'

They discussed the precise texture of ricotta, and the proper relationship of ricotta to sponge, for 20 minutes or so. My contribution to the conversation was minimal, but to the consumption of cassata, considerable. But as I listened, I couldn't help feeling that there was something marvellous about the matter-of-fact passion that fuelled the discussion, about the patient consideration of each detail, about the authority and judgement. Would we debate the proper consistency and minutiae of simnel cake, let's say, or Dundee cake with the same passion? Deconstruct them with the same forensic skill? Do we weigh up the proper texture of a butter filling, to decide whether or not the butter has been properly sourced and used? I would like to hope so, because such passion, confidence and knowledge protects a food culture and keeps it alive; but I think not.

Whatever the reason, La Signora Rodriguez wasn't happy, and was going to get on to Irrera right away. They had my sympathies. She didn't strike me as a woman easily deflected from the path of true cakedom.

So we finished with prickly pears and further discussion, more languid this time, as to whether red prickly pears tasted better than white, or the other way round. The red had my vote.

What I found interesting about this was not whether the points were true or not, but that they were raised at all. It was like listening to scientists discussing the finer details of some theory of quantum mechanics. There was a seriousness about the subject, an acceptance that other people's views were worth listening to (although they might be wrong), a feeling that the quality of cake and the flavour of prickly pears were matters for serious discussion by intelligent people.

෧෧

Out of a kind of perverse nostalgia, after lunch I went to explore the quayside of Messina, which had been the scene of one of the less edifying spectacles in my life. It had come at the end of the epic journey that Tom and I made in 1973. He was going to catch a ferry back to the mainland and return to university. I was going to stay on in Sicily for a few days more. We parked the car on the quay near the ferry, which was due to depart in an hour or so, and went to have a last lunch together.

The forkful of pasta was halfway into my mouth when I suddenly had a vision of the car keys. They were still hanging on the dashboard. And the car was locked. And Tom's luggage, passport, etc. were inside. It wasn't the first time I had managed this particular cock-up – a design fault in the Ford Escort of the day, I would maintain – but we had always found a way round this problem.

I leapt up. 'Keys,' I said to my startled brother. 'In the car.' And without further explanation I bolted out of the restaurant back to where the car sat peacefully in the afternoon sunshine. And yes, there were the keys hanging from the dashboard, so tantalisingly close, so clearly unobtainable.

Sweating, I ran to the car hire office. It was lunch time. It was closed. I went back to the car. Tom had arrived by now, looking grim-faced. The car was completely sealed. Sometimes we left the boot unlocked, and a couple of times we had squeezed into the car that way, pushing down the back seat. This time I had carefully locked it to deter the skilful car thieves of Messina.

'You'll have to break a window,' Tom said.

'We can't do that,' I said.

'What else do you suggest?'

There was silence.

'I have got to catch that ferry,' he said.

'I know,' I said.

Silence.

'We'll have to break a window,' I said.

'*You'll* have to break the window,' he said. 'You locked the bloody keys inside.'

'All right. All right.'

Have you ever tried to break a car window? It's not as easy as you might think. It's OK if you have a claw hammer or a spark plug. All you need is a sharp tap with one of those. All I could find was a length of wood like a sleeper. Tentatively I tapped at the driver's-side window. Nothing gave. I banged harder. Nothing. Soon I was hammering away like a madman. Sweat poured off me. A lorry drove past. The driver gave me a pitying look. He had never seen such incompetent car thieves.

I switched my attack to the little triangular window with its own mini-frame, set into the corner of the main window, that cars used to have in those days. It was held shut but there was a catch on the inside. It seemed the weakest point to attack. If I could get that open slightly and slip my hand in and reach the door handle and …

I set to with a will. The window bent in a fraction. Tom took a turn. It bent in a fraction more. There were increasing signs of activity around the ferry along the quay. Ten minutes to departure. Our efforts became increasingly frantic. And then I noticed that the entire structure of the door was beginning to come apart. Perhaps we would never get the door open at all. By now Tom was desperate. The officers by the gangplank were looking around for late arrivals. Finally, finally, I squeezed my hand in through the smallest of gaps, and depressed the handle. The door opened. I almost fainted with relief. Tom grabbed his rucksack and bolted, scrambling up the gangplank as it was being withdrawn. He turned, smiled and waved.

There was a ferry waiting to depart from the same part of the quay it had left 33 years ago. I found the spot where we had parked the car. A wave of affection and happiness and laughter washed through me.

๑๑

Leopoldo wore the trappings of wealth lightly, if at all. In Sicily he drove a 13-year-old Nissan Micra, which may have had the advantage of not being a prime target for car thieves. That evening he took me in it to Il Padrino. 'It's not very smart,' he said, 'but I like it. I used to go there for lunch when I first started work in Messina as a young man. It was fast food, but good fast food. It hasn't changed a lot. Now they make *insalata di stoccafisso* specially for me.'

'*Ingegnere!*' bellowed *il padrino* at Leopoldo as we came through the door.

Everyone's head turned for a moment. *Il padrino* embraced Leopoldo with brusque affection. He must have been in his seventies, but he had energy like a force field. 'At last! For the *insalata di stoccafisso!*'

I understood what Leopoldo had meant when he said Il Padrino hadn't changed much. There wasn't a lot to change: an open-plan kitchen, utilitarian decoration, plastic-topped tables that leant themselves to being rapidly wiped, paper tablecloths, and a rapid turnaround of clientele of all ages and sexes who came to enjoy the food – and enjoyed it because it was their birthright.

The *insalata di stoccafisso* was made up of chunks of recon-stituted, uncooked stockfish, bits of peeled lemon, olives, slices of celery and a little *peperoncino*, dressed in just olive oil. It was an earthy dish, light and exact and punchy, the stockfish pungent, the lemon sparkling but slightly sweeter than the lemons we get in Britain, the olives with a salty tang, celery crunchy, the *peperoncino* warm and perky. The sun shone through it, with the stockfish giving it a potent waft of the cold, clear north. I remembered what Giuseppe Privitera had told me about why wind-dried stockfish was preferred to salt-cured cod. It seemed remarkable to me that this speciality of the Normans should still be turning up on the frontier with Africa. It was a testament to the enduring patterns of commerce. And some several hundred years after the Normans, the Sicilians were sending olive oil back along the same routes.

As we worked our way through the salad, Leopoldo talked about Sicily.

'I'm not optimistic about its future. Or about Italy's for that matter. The kind of contract between a government and the people that exists in the UK and other countries does not exist in Italy and particularly not in Sicily.' He poked another chunk of stockfish into his mouth.

'Here politics only seems to attract the least talented of people,' he went on. He had thought that things might get better under Berlusconi, who had a reputation as a decisive businessman but he had turned out no better that the rest, attempting to protect obviously corrupt friends and cronies.

'I had also hoped that the EU might bring about changes, too, to the structure and dynamics of Italian politics, turn Italy into a modern state in which a government functioned with a sense of responsibility towards the populace. But this hasn't happened.'

Leopoldo reminded me of something that Leonardo Sciascia had said: 'You have the feeling that ... the island has always been what it is, and that centuries of historic stratification have not changed it much for the worse.'

The *insalata* was cleared away and *il padrino* brought Leopoldo a bowl of *spezzatino*, lumps of veal braised in *salsa* with peas and potatoes. I reached over and tasted it. It had some of the heft of a British stew, but it was lighter and fresher. Where we would have used water, beer or wine to provide the liquid, the Messinese used tomatoes, which gave a thicker and fruitier glop. Still, there was plenty of polite exchange of flavours going on, which is the fundamental principle of all stews and braises.

At *il padrino's* suggestion I had more *stoccafisso, alla ghiota* this time, in yet another tomato sauce, reduced to a semi-sticky, vivid distillation of tomato, spiked with capers. Raw chopped *peperoncino* were served on the side. Although it was a pretty majestic concoction, the tomato sauce taming the powerful boiled socks flavour of the fish, to be honest at times during my odyssey I became distracted by the predominance of tomato-based sauces. I mean, a tomato sauce is a tomato sauce is a tomato sauce. I know this isn't really true, but there were moments when a succession of tomato sauces reminded me of the serial music of John Adams or Philip Glass, a succession of repeated chords, with only subtle shifts and changes between them – usually too subtle to hold my interest for long. I knew this was a failing on my part.

For Sicilians, the addition or otherwise of capers, the precise level of reduction and texture of the sauce made differences of such significance as to result in a completely different *salsa*. But I suppose this is not much different from the way the French take a stock and create a whole realm of related sauces round it. And Sicilians would probably think our obsession with gravy is pretty odd, and would struggle with why we add flour to this or mustard to that and cream to the other.

'In Messina nothing's changed for the better, only for the worse,' Leopoldo went on. 'The city bureaucrats take bribes to make bad decisions. They build car parks that nobody uses. They let magnificent buildings fall into ruin. The new tram system cost a fortune, and now you can't drive a car along some streets. What happens? Traffic becomes a nightmare. You can't get to the shops and so shopkeepers suffer too. Messina went through a revival a few years ago, but now established businesses are closing and new businesses aren't coming in to take their place.' He himself had only minor interests left in the city.

He broke off for a moment as *il padrino* brought us a dish of *involtini di calamari*, coins of tender squid stuffed with breadcrumbs pinging with lemon juice.

'Of course, we Sicilians don't help,' said Leopoldo. 'Sicilians are wonderful people, generous, decent, kind and hardworking, but they aren't pessimists. If you're a pessimist, you feel all things are going to turn out badly but you might take some kind of action as a result. Sicilians are worse than pessimists. They're

SWEET HONEY, BITTER LEMONS

fatalists and fatalism is passive. They accept whatever happens to them. There isn't the energy or will to change things.'

Perhaps Sicilians needed to escape from Sicily in order to succeed. Federica had said over lunch: 'We Italians have very supple minds. Italians have always had to adapt to very difficult circumstances. Our governments have been such failures. They haven't looked after their citizens in the same way the British government looks after its citizens. So we have had to look after ourselves. That's why Italians have done so well when they have emigrated, because they have adjusted so rapidly to the circumstances they found. They worked out what they needed to do to survive because that's what they had had to do back home in Italy. The minds of Sicilians are an exaggerated version of Italian minds.'

I finished off the *involtini di calamari*. It seemed almost absurd that passive fatalism could produce such a vigorous and dynamic food culture. Perhaps Sicilians expressed themselves through their food in a way that they couldn't through other forms of communication. It was a kind of coded lingua franca, the one radical, personal act against a world that bore down on you in every other respect.

இ௫

I've always been something of a breakfast man, and as such have believed that life holds few more serious starts to a day than a kipper and a cup of tea followed by several slices of wholemeal toast liberally plastered with butter and marmalade, or fragrant shavings of bacon with fried tomatoes or a of brace of pork bangers, bronzed and gleaming or something of the kind. That was until I became a devotee of Irrera.

Irrera on the Piazza Cairoli was the finest café I had come across in Sicily. In fact, only Scatturchio in Naples could equal it as a source of pastry pleasures in my experience. Its ice creams came closest to the intensity of flavour and delicacy of texture of my ideal, but it was the classic Messinese breakfast of *granita di caffe con brioche* that held me in its thrall. A cut-glass bowl on a short stem is filled with the coffee granita, and slathered with a generous layer of whipped cream. You break off a bit of hot, spongy brioche and poke it down through the cream to the slush below, draw it back up and pop it into your mouth. I was hooked from the very first bite. Did the magic lie in the exquisite contrasts in temperature, from warm (brioche) to tepid (cream) to icy cold (granita)? Was it the precise contrasts in texture from soft, spongy (brioche) to soft, fluffy (cream) to soft, fine cryrstal (granita)? Or was it the seductive contrasts in flavour from sweet, buttery brioche to bland cream to dark, cold, intense, bitter-sweet coffee slush? In spite of repeated research I could never quite make up my mind.

The place itself was an elegant, modern, glistening, gleaming temple of civilised indulgence. Inside it was laid out in an L shape, with the long side of the L devoted to dispensing goodies to be consumed on the premises, and the short side displaying those to be taken away, in all their teasing colour and inviting decoration. It was almost impossible to believe that Irrera had almost gone out of business a few years back.

'The family who owned it were tired, and they didn't have the energy to run it any more,' explained Leopoldo as I slurped on my divine breakfast one morning, He explained that this sent a tremor almost as severe as the earthquake of 1908 through the older families of the city, who relied on Irrera not just for its *cassata siciliana*, but also for all manner of cakes and *dolci* and, above all, for the magnificent Christmas hampers it put together for them to give their friends.

'So I spoke to a few friends, and we bought it. We found a young man with energy to run it and the *laboratorio* where they make the cakes and ice creams. It's just a few streets away.' No wonder his mother had been so concerned about the quality of the cassata. I decided I ought to take a closer look at this pillar of Sicilian pastry culture.

The Irrera bakery was in full swing by the time I got there at eight o'clock the following morning. The finishing touches of green almond icing and decoration with crystallised fruit were being put on the first batch of *cassata siciliana*. Long logs of 'strudel' were disappearing under waves of cream. The air was sweet with toasty wheat and sugar and chocolate, and pungent with coffee for the *granita di caffe*.

But first I had a glossy, golden-brown brioche hot from the oven; warm, comforting, slightly butterscotchy. The man who gave it to me was an impish, smiling figure known as the Arab. As I munched my brioche, he treated me to a lecture on the Messinese baking traditions. The products of Messina were always lighter and more refined than those of other cities, he said, and they have kept evolving.

'We're not stuck in the past like other places,' he said emphatically, and went back to painting the next batch of pale, plump, unbaked brioche with beaten egg. The touch of the brush caused the brioche to quiver slightly, like a bosom.

Further along *barchette di frutta*, little pastries the shape of the fishing boats bobbing by the harbour wall, were being care-fully filled by hand with wild strawberries; a long cake of layers of chocolate sponge and cream was being given a dark coating of glossy chocolate. Everywhere there was smoothing, squirting, decorating, fastidious placing of fruit, dusting with icing sugar going on. On the wall was a list of some of the day's production: *tartufino, grana, nasparo, testina di moro, zuppette bianche/nere, tartalette di frutta, barchette frutte, barchette crema, limoncini, st moritzini, sospirini, mimosini, buschet, babaini, bigne, caffe.* Where would all these go? Who would eat them all? It seemed almost inconceivable that a single town could dispose of these pastries.

In another of the four rooms that made up the production area, the day's ice creams and granitas were already being churned. As the ice creams at Irrera had been the best I had eaten in Sicily by a comfortable margin, I was curious to know what the secret was.

'*Perche sono di Irrera. E la nostr' tradizione,*' said the *maestro del gelato.* 'Because they come from Irrera. It's our tradition.' As if that explained everything.

There was nothing romantic about the process. Yes, they used a commercial powder base like all the *gelaterie* did these days. 'No one uses a custard of eggs and milk any more. But there are bases and bases, some good quality, some not so good. At Irrera we only use the very best. And we add full-cream milk to the base. Many places use skimmed milk or milk and water mixed.' The master of Irrera's ice creams raised his eyebrows, suggesting that the addition of such things was little better than adulteration.

Irrera made 22 different ice creams and granitas altogether, he said. The classic ice creams were chocolate, coffee, pistachio, strawberry, hazelnut, lemon and mandarin, and those never changed. Of course, they used the best quality flavouring ingredients for those, too. In fact, the coffee ice was made with real coffee, brewed from freshly ground beans. But today people wanted more than just the classics, so he made several fashionable ices too, such as Ferrero Rocher and Kinder. He didn't like them much himself, but the kids did.

'Which is your favourite?'

'*Nocciola*, hazelnut,' he said, looking very serious.

The mixtures went into the freezing machines, which in ten minutes produced perfectly textured ice creams. They were then specially blast-frozen so that the texture remained the same throughout.

I asked him about the difference between *sorbetti* and granitas. Did *sorbetti* include egg white, as I had been told?

'No. Absolutely not.' He seemed startled by the idea. The mixture was the same for both. The difference in texture depended on the size of the crystals, and that depended on how long they spend in the freezing machine. *Sorbetti* are churned for a couple of minutes longer than *granite*, and that produces a finer crystal.

By this time the cassata team – 11 men work full-time making pastries and ice creams for Irrera – were ready to start on the second batch. They would make up to 25 cassatas during their shift. I explained that I was surprised that a cassata was a cake not an ice cream shaped like a tall, rounded top hat. They were politely incredulous at my surprise.

'*Ma, quella e cassata gelato*. But that's *cassata* ice cream. Not from around here.'

'OK, what did this cassata consist of?' I asked.

'*Pan di spagna. Ricotta lavorata. Crostata di mandorle. Frutta candita*,' explained Pino, one of a team of two working on the cassatas. That sounded remarkably boring.

'OK, what's the secret of a great cassata?'

'*La ricotta*. Here at Irrera we only use *ricotta di pecora*, sheep's milk ricotta, the best. Most places use cows' milk ricotta, which has a heavier flavour and doesn't make such a fine filling when it has been worked.'

'Worked?'

'Beaten with sugar and sieved to make it light. Then it's mixed with candied pumpkin with some small dark chocolate buttons added at the end.'

I watched as Pino carved the blocks of ready-cooked *pan di spagna*, sponge, trimming off the dark crusts with surgical precision, and cutting the cake into slices about 2 centimetres thick with casual skill.

Pino and Marco, the other man in the team, took some of the sponge slices and laid them around the sides of each of the battered metal moulds, then placed a layer on the bottom, trimming the bits that didn't fit. They ladled ricotta mixture over the sponge base, scattering a handful of chocolate buttons on top, and smoothed the filling flat. The sponge offcuts were used to make a second layer of cake, with another layer of ricotta mixture on top of that. A final neat layer of sponge was placed on top and the mould was tapped to settle the mixture before it was weighed and then turned out on to the work surface. The icing was made with ground almonds turned pistachio green with dye – once it would have been green with real pistachios according to Mary Taylor Simeti, but this would be too expensive these days – and was rolled out, draped over the top and trimmed. The smooth surface was painted with a sugar and water mixture to make it glossy, and decorated with candied fruit until it was a riot of green, orange, yellow and red.

'Ah, but the *cassatte* they make in Palermo are much fancier,' said Marco, implying, I think, that they were just a touch vulgar.

∾ Impanata di pesce spada ∾

This is an imperious dish for a big occasion. Nothing quite sums up the force of Sicilian cooking for me better than this. It is theatrical, colourful, potent, thrilling and a pyrotechnic display of flavour, with each ingredient referring back to some part of the island's history.

Serves 8

Pastry: *500g 00 plain flour • 200g caster sugar • A pinch of salt • 100g* sugna *(pig fat) or lard • 50g unsalted butter • 1 orange • 5 egg yolks • White wine*

Filling: *35g capers in salt (from Pantelleria) • 50g sultanas • 350g very ripe tomatoes • 3 courgettes • Olive oil • 2 medium onions • 2 celery sticks • 2 tbsp red wine vinegar • 2 dsp sugar • 100g pitted green olives • 35g pine nuts • 1 dsp* strattu *(very concentrated tomato purée) • 1kg swordfish fillet*

Mix the flour, sugar and salt. Grate the pig fat or lard and butter into the flour. Work with your fingertips until you have a mealy texture. Grate the peel of the orange into the bowl and add the egg yolks. Dribble enough wine in to make the pastry stick together. Knead, form into a ball, wrap in cling film and chill for at least an hour.

Rinse the capers thoroughly. Soak the sultanas in tepid water. Peel, deseed and chop the tomatoes. Wash the courgettes and cut into slices 1 mm thick. Fry in a little olive oil until lightly brown. Drain on kitchen towel. Chop the onions and the celery. Fry in the same pan with a little more oil until the onion is soft. Add the vinegar and the sugar. Cook for a couple of minutes to melt the sugar Add the capers, sultanas, olives and pine nuts. Cook for a couple of minutes longer. Add the tomatoes and the *strattu*. Simmer for 15 minutes. Chop the swordfish into bite-sized chunks and add to the mixture. Simmer for 5 minutes.

Preheat the oven to 170°C/325°F/Gas 3. Butter a deep pie dish very thoroughly. Cut a quarter of the pastry off and put to one side. Roll out the rest until it is large enough to line the bottom and sides of the baking dish in a single piece with a little bit hanging over the lip of the dish. Fill with the swordfish mixture, layered with the courgettes in the middle. Roll out the other piece of pastry. Put on top of the mixture and seal the edges. Cut small slashes in the top to let out any steam. Glaze with beaten egg. Bake for about 1 hour until the crust is a golden brown.

∽ Insalata di stoccafisso ∽

My recreation of the sprightly delight of Il Padrino's original.

Serves 4
800g of stockfish • 2 celery sticks • 1 lemon • 2 dried chillies • 100g unstoned green olives • Extra virgin olive oil

Soak the stockfish for 24 hours, changing the water several times. Cut into small chunks. Slice the celery sticks. Peel the lemon and cut into small pieces without any pith. Chop the chillies finely. Cut the olives in half. Mix all the ingredients in a bowl and dress with olive oil to your taste.

∞ Calamari ripieni ∞

This is an antipasto helping.

Serves 6 people
6 medium-sized squid • 1 bunch parsley • 200 pangrattato
(dried breadcrumbs) • 100g grated caciocavallo *cheese • Salt
and pepper • Juice of 1–2 lemons • 1 orange • 2 bay leaves •
Extra virgin olive oil*

Preheat the oven to 200ºC/400ºF/Gas 6. Pull out the head and
tentacles of the squid and clean the body tube thoroughly. Chop
up the tentacles finely. Chop the parsley finely. Mix the breadcrumbs, cheese and chopped tentacles together in a bowl. Season
with salt and pepper. Add lemon juice to your taste. Push the
stuffing into the squid tubes. Don't fill them too much as the
mixture will expand while cooking. Sew up, tie up or seal up the
end of the tube with a cocktail stick to stop the stuffing popping
out. Put the stuffed tubes altogether in a large piece of aluminium
foil, along with a few slices of orange and the bay leaves. Dribble
a little olive oil over them. Fold up the foil to make a parcel, carefully sealing the join. Pop into the oven for 20 minutes. Take out
and allow to cool slightly before slicing the squid into rounds
with a very sharp knife. Serve hot, warm or cold. You can dribble
some of the cooking juices of over them if you like.

∞ Granita di caffè ∞

The coffee does need to be really strong. And don't forget the
whipped cream on top, slightly sweetened with a little icing
sugar. And then the brioche. Warm, of course.

Serves 4 people
*80g granulated sugar • 250ml strong black coffee • 1 vanilla pod
or 2 drops of vanilla essence • A pinch of powdered cinnamon •
100ml whipping cream • 2 dsp icing sugar*

Put 250ml water and the granulated sugar into a saucepan.
Heat until the sugar has dissolved and then boil for at least a
minute. Turn down the heat and add the coffee to the syrup.
Mix well. Take it off the heat. Slice the vanilla pod along its
length. Scrape out the seeds and add them (or the vanilla
essence) to the coffee syrup along with the cinnamon. Mix well
to make sure the vanilla seeds and the spice spread throughout
the coffee syrup. Allow it to cool completely. Transfer the
mixture into a plastic container and pop the container into a
freezer. Leave for 2 hours, stirring with a fork every 10–15
minutes. The granules should be fine, almost mushy by the end.

When you come to serve it, whip the cream and icing sugar
until quite stiff. Divide up the granita between 4 glasses and
plop a dollop of whipped cream on top of each.

Lunch at the Casa Cuseni, Taormina

CHAPTER FOURTEEN

A Time to Take Measure

@/@

Messina – Taormina

I decided to avoid the coastal road clotted with traffic and tatty towns and take a minor one that, according to my map, ran parallel to it, high up through the mountains. At least, that was the intention. I roared up the road that led to my chosen route, through the murky outskirts of Messina jumbled on the lower slopes of the Monti Peloritani that formed the vaulting barrier behind the town, but I wasn't entirely surprised when it petered out in the middle of nowhere. Previous experience of my inadequacies as a map-reader had taught me to expect that possibility.

I went back down to the coast and found another road leading up into the mountains to a village called Itala. If I could get to Itala, I was quite sure I would be able to follow it round Monte Scuderi and join up with that elusive road, marked on the map, that ran parallel to the coast. Full of hope I set off again. The road looked promising. It took me up into some lush, precipitous, terraced valleys and past San Pietro, a small Arab-Norman church with date palms growing outside it, peaceful and perfect. Then it was on up the switchback road, as serpentine as a Sicilian mind. This is it, I thought, to Itala and beyond. I felt buoyant and would have whistled 'It's a long way to Tipperary', only motorcycle helmets don't really lend themselves to whistling.

And, blow me there it was as marked, a road leading round the back of the mountain where it must join the one I had been looking for. And the signpost said Monte Scuderi and it pointed in the right direction, through dense woods of sweet chestnuts.

Only it didn't.

Oh, it went through the sweet chestnut woods all right, and past tinkling streams, stands of flowers, around the edges of plunging ravines cloaked with orchards and pelts of sorbus, ilex, holm oak and ash, and out on the other side, and showed me staggering views of the Straits of Messina and southern Calabria. But eventually it, too, turned into a dirt trail and eventually petered out somewhere in the trackless wastes of the mountain peaks. Chastened and irritable, I retraced my steps, and, ever so slightly downcast, reconciled myself to the churning traffic of the coastal road.

It was late afternoon by the time Monica and I climbed up the corkscrew road from Lido Spigone Mazzaro and came to Casa Cuseni above Taormina.

◎◎

I fell under the spell of Casa Cuseni as I bounced Monica over the pavement and in through the front gate, stopping just before I catapulted my hostess, Melissa Phelps, Monica and myself into a small pond strategically located just inside.

There was a tremendous sense of personality about the house and garden, of beauty, purpose and intelligence. It stood above Taormina, erect and confident, built into the side of the vertiginous hill, combining the formality of a Tuscan villa with the comforts of an English country house. The whole delightful domain had been designed and built by Robert Kitson in 1905. He had been an engineer by training, but building Casa Cuseni made him architect, surveyor, interior designer and gardener too. With an imagination untrammelled by correct schooling, he thought nothing of sticking art nouveau and Sicilian styles side by side, and called on his teacher and friend, Frank Brangwyn, to design the panelling, table, sideboard and chairs and paint a mural in the dining room.

When Kitson died in 1948 his niece, Daphne Phelps, went out to Sicily to sell the house. She fell in love with the place instead and decided to stay on and have paying guests to make ends meet; she told the story of her life in Sicily in a charming memoir, *A House in Sicily*. Daphne died peacefully in her bed at Casa Cuseni in 2005 at the age of 94; it was '*una partenza dolce*'. She bequeathed the house to her nephews and nieces who formed the Associazione Culturale Casa Cuseni as a vehicle for its maintenance, with Melissa, a cellist by profession, as the clerk of works and the latest keeper of the flame of Casa Cuseni. A kind friend had given me an introduction to her and, by the greatest good fortune, it turned out she was going to be in residence at the time I planned to pass through Taormina.

A succession of flights of steps led up through a vertiginous garden that stretched away on either side in a series of green and shady terraces. The rather fanciful formality of the garden's structure was softened by the luxuriant, tumbling, arcing, spreading nature of the shrubs and plants. The perfume of jasmine and lemon blossom hung in the air. Finally I arrived panting at a terrace in front on an expansive ground floor with a porticoed doorway. This led into a splendid, airy sitting room that dominated the centre of the house, with a study to one side of it and the famous Brangwyn dining room on the other. A substantial, if rather gloomy, kitchen lay behind the dining room. The bedrooms and bathrooms filled the floor directly above, and there were more rooms just under the roof.

The house was in a fairly dilapidated state. The plumbing was, according to Melissa, a touch dodgy and the garden was in need of a good deal of attention, but the vision was still there, the character, the balance – a curious combination of hedonistic luxury and engineering order. Casa Cuseni had been beautifully thought out, organised in a way that was very particular and very comfortable at the same time, both a public statement and a private place. Below was the town, and up to the right was Etna; a stream of lava traced the edge of its slope, beginning to glow as dusk fell, and Melissa and I sat drinking and talking on the terrace.

◎◎

Taormina's reputation for tolerating the louche behaviour of foreigners had been established in the 1880s by two German *baroni*, Otto Geleng and Wilhelm von Gloeden, when they published photographs of local shepherd boys in 'Grecian' poses. It was the kind of thing that would get you locked up these days. But it was the arrival of royalty, in those dear, dead days when royals were the arbiters of fashion, that really put

Taormina on the map as the Costa Smeralda of its time. Kaiser Wilhelm II visited in 1896 and Edward VII wintered there in 1906, paying a visit to von Gloeden's studio. One wonders what the British press would make of, say, Prince Charles deciding to visit the offices of *Asian Babes* magazine. The royal visits helped to attract a motley mix of Brits, Americans, Germans and Scandinavians, and before Taormina knew it D.H. Lawrence was scribbling about it:

> *Sunday morning,*
> *And from the Sicilian townlets skirting Etna*
> *The socialists have gathered upon us, to look at us.*

And the likes of Marlene Dietrich, Greta Garbo, Tennessee Williams and Truman Capote were soaking up the sun and cocktails there.

Oh, where were the socialists of yesteryear? It wasn't that the town had physically changed much. It still had the promiscuous mix of architectural styles and extraordinary panorama that Lawrence would have recognised, but the bevies of royalty with their entourages, the Britons, Germans and Scandinavians of Hellenistic bent, drunken writers and neurotic actresses, had given way to the new barbarian hordes who poured into the town from charabanc and cruise ship, good-humoured flotsam clogging up the streets.

When Tom and I had first come to Sicily in 1973, it was crowded, but yet to fall prey to the migratory herds from buses and cruise ships that rove from site to site like columns of migrating wildebeest.

Of course, I ought to have applauded this visible demonstration of democracy at work. What had once been the province of the rich and privileged few was now open to the world, but the truth was that I didn't want the monarchs and their entourages, or the Britons, Germans or Scandinavians of Hellenistic bent, or the drunken writers, neurotic film stars or barbarian hordes. I wanted Taormina to myself.

In my notebook I recorded the following entry: 'Garden full of cacti, dilapidated, run to seed; scent of mimosa; ponds; paths & steps, sturdy, purposeful, erratic; full of shady corners and crumbling stone seats; luxuriant geraniums, more cacti; fine, decayed tennis court; lonely unattended circular metal tables; metal chairs – so redolent of English expatriots before the last war, leisurely, disciplined, but having lost their way in some curious fashion – house the same; huge square and oddly ornate, eg brickwork & Indian drapes; rubber plant; king cobra light fittings; high ceilings; light shades like up-turned coolie hats; half candle, half light bulb wrought-iron chandelier; rooms arranged round large square central sitting room; 1930s furniture, a little passé, their comforts a little worn now; but still fat, still solid, still British – used to be an old folks home and then became a hotel in 1929/3 – visitor's book crammed with photos of fancy dress parties, names illegible, comments, newspaper clippings of weddings, Hungarian princes, Americans, British beauties, socialites, the completely unknown, antique cars, painting parties and picnics – where did they all go? – now there are 8 guests including Tom and myself – place run by Miss Betty, aided by a cheerful German lady and staff who are unfailingly polite – who is Miss Betty? Curious accent, slightly Midlandish, with 'g's missing at the end of words; efficient and businesslike and chatty & suddenly says "Must go. Got an important thin' to do" and dashes off to chat on the phone about social matters in a clearly audible voice echoing across sitting room; speaks bad Italian after how many years here? – How wrong can you get? The German turns out to be Swiss, overseeing family interests – a fitness fanatic – and the hotel turns out to be owned by an Italian and his Anglo-Dutch wife – and I now think Miss Betty comes from London or S.E. England.'

And then there was this mysterious postscript: 'man glaring fiercely at newspaper through monocle held at least a foot from his face'. The Villa San Pancrazio and its strange occupants embodied the idiosyncratic charm of Taormina then. How I wished I had been so industrious in keeping notes on the rest of the trip.

I went off to look for the Villa San Pancrazio and my past. I found the villa in the end, and rather wished I hadn't. It was very close to the funicular that ran between the town and the seaside below. The sign still adorned its roof, which was level with the road. The hotel itself was shut and utterly dilapidated. The gardens were still there, in form, anyway, and the cacti, too, and I could even make out the tennis court, but the rest was ruin. I saw some men in boiler suits coming out with masks over their faces and carrying chemical sprays of some kind. Bruised by this collision with the present, I retreated into the garden of memory.

@@

And so I came to the last great meal of my journey. The next day I had to return Monica to her rightful owners in Catania and leave for England. Before I went, however, Concetta had promised to cook me lunch. If Melissa was the keeper of Casa

Cuseni's flame, Concetta Cundari was the guardian of place. Daphne Phelps's keeper, minder, cook and general factotum for 40 years, she still kept a watchful eye on the house from her own more modest home to one side of the garden, where she lived with her husband, Peppino. I remembered the lunch I had had with the Richards at the Villa Ingham right at the start of my odyssey. Somehow it felt appropriate that the English connection should be celebrated at the end, too.

'Do you like garlic?' Concetta asked as I stood watching her at work in the kitchen. It was a large, crepuscular room, with an odd mishmash of equipment and surfaces, an ancient cooker and a marble-topped work surface. She was chopping garlic very finely to add to the French beans she had already trimmed.

'Yes,' I said.

'Some people don't like it,' she said. 'That's their loss because it's good.'

Concetta was referring to the British visitors who came when Daphne Phelps was chatelaine of Casa Cuseni. In those days garlic was regarded by some as a vile and dangerous ingredient, symptomatic of the loose morality and dodgy practices one expected from Europeans generally.

'What else are you going to make?'

'*Risotto con finocchio selvatico*, risotto with fennel – wild fennel from the garden. Do you know our fennel?'

I did, and loved its heady, exhilarating intensity.

'I add sausage meat as well. It's not a Sicilian dish, but la signora Daphne, she liked it.'

She began to make the risotto. She started by grating an onion to form the base. I asked why she grated it. Because that made the risotto *piu sottile*, more subtle, she said.

'My cooking is quite personal,' she said, working steadily. 'Not everything I make is traditional. Some dishes I learnt from my mother. But *la vecchia padrona* loved cooking and she was a very good cook herself. She didn't just want local dishes for her guests, so I experimented and made my own dishes.'

I thought of all of Sicily's other invaders and visitors over the centuries, how each had brought their own ingredients and dishes, too, and how they had been absorbed, transformed, Sicilianised. Peppino pottered in waving a bunch of *diavolino* peppers, from the garden like all the vegetables.

'And now we must fry the onions, slowly, slowly,' said Concetta, and the soft, sweet caramel of frying onions filled the kitchen. 'We add the sausage and the fennel later, and finally the rice and you cook them all together.'

Concetta was a study in methodical patience as she bent over the pot gently stirring the onions. Her forearms were shaped by iron muscle, the product of a lifetime of work, her face handsome and forceful, with a forehead like a bronzed cliff topped with white hair en brosse. There was something irreducible, rock-like about Concetta. She looked as enduring as Etna rearing up on the right of the house.

'And then you add a tiny bit of butter and Parmesan at the end,' she said. The smells of frying garlic, piquant and pungent, and the aniseed fennel and grassy parsley wove into that of the onions. '*Queste sono piccole cose. Non costano molto.* These are little things. They don't cost a lot.'

She measured out the rice by hand and added a splash of white wine.

She was born in a village in the mountains, she said, and came to Taormina looking for work. Life for the villagers had been hard then, but it was worse now, so difficult to make a living up there. The parents might hang on but their children would leave, and they were right. Who wanted to live like that now? So much of the mountain land has been abandoned already, she said.

Melissa came in and sniffed the air.

'I'm happy when I smell Concetta's cooking,' she said. 'It makes me feel that everything is going to be all right. That's the thing about food. You can smell it while it is being made and you can anticipate an outcome that you know will give you pleasure. I can't think of any other activity that can do this for you.' And with these words of wisdom she wandered out again to practise for a concert she was to give in England in a few weeks.

Concetta smiled as I translated what Melissa had said. She covered the risotto and left it.

'It's true,' she said. '*E mi fa bene*. And it does me good.' She folded her hands and rolled her thumbs round each other.

As she did so, the full romantic sweep of the solo part of Dvorak's cello concerto suddenly rolled through into the kitchen. Melissa was playing in the study on the far side of the house. There was one of those rare, perfect moments, there, in the kitchen. I could see the brilliant sunshine hot on the terrace outside, and smoking Etna beyond it. The light burst through the doorway and drained away into the cool, darker corners of the kitchen. The perfumes of jasmine and lemon blossom drifted in to blend with those of cooking. There was light and dark, past and present, silence and music. Concetta began mashing salted anchovy fillets with chunks of dried bread.

This was a dish of the poor, she explained, '*da mangiare*

con le verdure – to eat with vegetables. She chopped some of the peppers that Peppino had brought in earlier. She explained that some were right for one dish and some for another. These small, hot *peperonicini* were good for cooking with vegetables. She liked to add less fiery ones to salads of tomatoes and onions. She added the peppers to the anchovies and bread, and turned the mixture into a pan to fry it with oil. There was a sizzle as she added the *verdure*, spinach mixed with some of those slightly bitter wild chicories that Sicilians love. The fusion of smells evoked everything I loved most about Mediterranean food – a distillation of heat and olive oil and herbs and sweetness and pungency and saltiness and aromatic fruits, and people.

We sat down for lunch at a long table on the terrace under a pergola draped with vines, Melissa, Concetta, Peppino, their daughter and son-in-law and their two children. We ate the *risotto con finocchio selvatico, pasta con pesto di finocchio, pane con verdure e alici salate; fagiolini con aglio e prezzemolo; gelato e cannoli.* There was good bread and good wine, too. We talked of food, of *gelati* and *granite* in the town; of *ossi morti*, a local pastry; of butchers; and of Concetta's garlic and Peppino's garden at Lupina up the road. We discussed how the food of the poor had become the food of the rich. We talked of food in its seasons and food in its places. We talked of *sapori e odori e profumi e gusti.* We agreed that I could spend the rest of my life in Sicily and still not discover all its specialities.

The children had long disappeared and sun had begun to go down before we cleared the table. I kissed Concetta and thanked her. It was her pleasure, she said. She loved to cook. I kissed her again.

I sat on the terrace long afterwards, as dusk fell, looking up at where the orange glow of lava had moved further down the flank of Etna. Below were the lights of the town, and below them the lines of lights marking Capo Taormina and the curve of the bay of Giardini Naxos. It looked inexpressibly beautiful in the gathering darkness. I recalled the lines Enzo, the son of Frederic II, the Swabian king of Sicily, had written in the thirteenth century, which I had come across in a book in the course of my travels:

> There's a time to mount; to humble thee
> A time; a time to talk; and to hold your peace;
> A time to labour; and a time to cease;
> A time to take thy measures patiently;
> A time to watch what Time's next step may be.

Time had a peculiar quality in Sicily. It was elastic and relative, fluid and static. But it was time for me to go.

◎◎

I looked back over the last few weeks, and those I had spent earlier in the year crossing the interior slowly from Marsala to Catania. No matter where I travelled, I had met with kindness and generosity. I tried to recall a single example of meanness, a moment of fear, a disagreeable incident, and I couldn't. Oh, there had been days of loneliness, certainly, and discomfort and anxiety, but then I remembered the old man guiding me out of Marsala; the first communion feast and the lunch the next day with the Loreto family, and the gracious consideration of the grandfather; the pessimistic enthusiasm of

Pasquale Tornatore in Caltanissetta; Sergio Saverino's worldly passion in Modica; Cesarina's fervent advocacy of the cooking of Marsala; the inexhaustible meal in the olive grove below Pettineo with the Sanguedolce family; Leopoldo Rodriguez's restless intelligence and perception; and the majestic unfurling of Concetta's lunch here in Taormina. At every twist and turn, at every place I paused or stopped, there had been someone to help, to guide, to give. It all came back to me in full measure now. It was as remarkable as it was moving. Perhaps not surprisingly, somewhere along the way I had fallen deeply in love.

It was difficult to say exactly when and where. The first fascination had been kindled 33 years ago, when Sicily had come to occupy a particular place in my own internal geography. But there is a world of difference between first date and full passion, even if I wasn't quite sure what I was passionate about. What exactly was Sicily? Simply a region of Italy? A country in its own right? A state of mind?

Sicily is nothing if not paradoxical. It is an encyclopaedia of paradoxes presented to the outside world with an enigmatic theatricality. There was, there is, generosity and brutality, grace and subservience, decency and criminality; acute awareness of history, tolerance of vandalism of cities and landscape; sense of exploitation, the creation of one of the world's more exploitative corporations; subtlety and suppleness of mind, rigidity of social structures; Christian mores, Islamic manners; individual vitality, collective inertia; individual courage, collective cowardice. Was there anything that bound all these disparate elements together? To come up with a Unified Theory of Sicily is a good deal more challenging than to come up with a Unified Theory of Physics.

Politics gave no clue. Conventional, mainstream politics, which we in northern Europe assume to be the fundamental guiding force to social stability and development, plays an even smaller part in Sicilian life than it does on mainland Italy; and, heaven knows, that's small enough. In fact, aside from a few words from Leopoldo Rodriguez, I couldn't recall having a single political discussion in over two months, in spite of one of my visits coinciding with the election of the president of the Sicilian Council. Nor was there an obvious rational or evolutionary template for Sicilian society, or any sense of the direction in which it might be headed. Leonardo Sciascia observed, 'the island has always been what it is, and centuries of historic stratification have not changed it much or for the better'. Sicily was the way it had always been.

So had Goethe and Barzini been right in their views that Sicily was Italy writ large, or more crudely? Or was the island *'la fine dell'Europa'* as a young woman in a *pasticceria* in Palermo had said with an elegant spread of her hands.

Perhaps there was some truth in each these observations, but none sat easily with my own experience. To describe Sicily simply in the terms of a proto-Italy or the place where Africa and Europe meet fails to appreciate its true essence, its complexity and importance. In Sicily you can choose to look northwards to Italy and continental Europe for your orientation, or, just as easily south to northern Africa and the Maghreb. You can even look eastwards, towards Byzantium and Asia beyond.

Yes, I found much of Italy in Sicily – the suppleness of mind, regional sense of identity and loyalty, family loyalties, deep pragmatism, despair for conventional politics and passion for food. And yes, the island is the point where Europe and

Africa meet; the Moorish sense of hospitality, manners and time are as much a part of the texture of Sicilian life as the foods and cooking methods they introduced.

But it is also the point where Europe and Asia meet, where Christianity and Islam and paganism meet, where past meets present, where the modern world confronts the classical and medieval eras, where rationality interweaves with superstition. It is the place where the times, forces and cultures that have shaped the whole of Europe still erupt into the modern world. In the age of global brands, Internet communities, instant access to instant everything, Sicily presents us with our own past and shows us what our own present is made of.

That still leaves so much about the island and its people unexplained. In the end there are simply too many mysteries, contradictions and paradoxes about it. I'm not sure that Sicily is susceptible to the conventional analysis that the Age of Enlightenment, the traditions of empirical science and the sequential logic of academia have made the pillar of our rational existence. Perhaps it is a place that needs to be felt, not explained.

Perhaps not surprisingly, the Sicilians I met had a profound sense of their history. In terms of everyday life and expectation it weighed down on them, encouraging a kind of spiritual inertia from which, it seemed to me, they escaped by using food as the medium for their escape, as an expression of their identity and as a solace. If ever there was a country whose history was written in its food, it was Sicily, in the methods of cooking, ingredients, finished dishes, even in agricultural techniques. This gave an extraordinary richness to the texture as well as the range of Sicilian food. History was woven through the fabric of the Sicilian kitchen. Food was – is – the history of the island. Some dishes owe their origins to the Greeks, some to the Moors, to Rome and to Byzantium. You could spy out the Spanish love of embellishment and theatrical gesture and the French insistence on structure and technique, and even trace shades of England and Germany.

In keeping with their history, their food had many bewildering, intriguing levels, was full of sharp contrasts: *agrodolce*; *leggero-robusto*; simple at one moment, bewilderingly complex at the next. It had layers of flavours, effect was piled on effect. It had invention that gave life to the most boring of foodstuffs, and the capacity to find infinite variety in a single ingredient. In absolute contrast to the fatalism and passivity Sicilians themselves proclaimed, it was brilliant, bold, even brash on occasion, the confident statement of people who knew exactly who they were, and were proud of it.

True, superficially there wasn't quite the same sense of regional variety you find in Italy, where every region, valley, town and village has its own range of dishes with their own very particular names, based on local produce that follows the seasons. In Sicily *caponata* was ubiquitous, *sarde a beccafico* were as common as starlings, *farsumagru, involtini* and any number of other stuffed cuts of meat and fish were regular visitors to the plate no matter where I happened to be. There was grilled pork and grilled sausage and grilled veal here and here and here, and where there weren't grilled meats, there was grilled fish, fresh from the sea. There were *cannoli* and *mostaccioli* and *cassata* smiling seductively at me in display cabinets from Messina to Catania, and from Catania all the way round the coast back to Catania again.

There were *granite* and *sorbetti* and *gelati* and seven seas of tomato sauces.

But this apparent uniformity was misleading. In reality no two versions of the same dish were alike. They might have a name in common, and possibly, although not invariably, ingredients, but the way the ingredients were put together, and the consequent effect, was completely individual. And the differences weren't simply regional or local, but personal. The quality and primacy of local ingredients were recognised, understood, exploited and celebrated with open minds and sure techniques. Sicilian cooking had always moved with the times, drawing inspiration from whoever happened to be in control, and it continued to do so.

Yet, the same pressures were building on Sicilian food culture as those elsewhere in Europe. Although the island had been part of so many other nations' portfolio of colonies down the centuries, perhaps even because of this, Sicily has always been a place apart, a special case, somewhere that didn't conform to the comfortable norms of more conventional societies. Now the homogenising forces of a global culture were beginning to stalk the towns, and the economics of global food production were having an impact on the land. Sicilians had been escaping from the harsh realities of a harsh land for centuries. As Concetta had said, who wants to live that life any more? Now there were fewer and fewer reasons to stay on the land. And as the world of the *contadini* eroded, with it would go much of Sicily's treasure house of vegetables, fruits, cheeses, ingredients, and the knowledge of how to grow or produce them.

Prophecy is always a dodgy business, and in view of what I had found, been given, eaten, this may seem a pessimistic view.

It may be several decades before it becomes evident. I would hope, never.

It was certainly true that I could go on travelling round the island for ever, and never exhaust its beauties, curiosities, uglinesses, layers, contradictions; never fully penetrate its mysteries or unravel its paradoxes, fully reconcile the sweetness of its honey and the bitterness of its lemons. For me, Sicily was not unlike one of its own divine pastries, the *millefoglie*, made up of dozens, possibly hundreds of different layers: layers of history, culture, urban and rural patterns, politics, crime, society. Each layer seemingly existed and operated independently of the other, but was, in fact, connected by tiny, almost imperceptible, flakes of communication, shared interests, shared values, attitudes and activities, history. Between each layer were squidgy fillings, some soft, sweetish and emollient, like *crème pastissiere*, sweetened with honey and studded with bitter shards of lemon. When I bit into the *millefoglie*, crunched my teeth down through the layers of pastry and fillings, they mashed together, filling my mouth with an intoxicating mix of friable delicacy and softness and sweetness and perfume and bitterness. It was that extraordinary range of different sensations with which I had fallen in love.

As Nanni Cucchiara had said, 'All the foreigners who come to govern Sicily end up becoming Sicilian – Greeks, Romans, Arabs, French, Germans, Spanish. Even you English. There is something about this island.'

About the Author

Matthew Fort has worked on the food pages of the *Guardian* for more than ten years. He also writes for the *Observer, Esquire, Country Living, Decanter* and *Waitrose Food Illustrated.* He appears as a judge on BBC2's *Great British Menu* and is one of the presenters of UKTV Food's *Market Kitchen.* He won Glenfiddich Food Writer of the Year in 1992, and both Glenfiddich Restaurant Writer of the Year and The Restaurateurs' Association Food Writer of the Year in 1993. One of Matthew's greatest passions is Italy, which he visits every year. *Sweet Honey, Bitter Lemons* is his fifth book.